Llanfair Waterdine

and

Lloyney

by

The people who live there

Llanfair Waterdine

and

Lloyney

by

The people who live there

First published July 2000 by the people of Llanfair Waterdine and Lloyney.

Frontispiece: Joseph goes to church.

Animal sketches by Phillipa Boast.

Plant drawings by Mary Simmons.

ISBN 1 903360 01 3

Set in Bembo and Gill Sans and printed in England by Orphans Press Ltd, Hereford Road, Leominster, Herefordshire.

Funded by the National Lottery through the Help the Aged Fund's Millennium Awards.

Millennium Awards

Contents

Part One - Llanfair Waterdine

Part Two - Lloyney

Part Three

Part Four

Part Five

Part Six

Acknowledgements

In 1988 Jocelyn Williams and Brenda Davies published "A Parish Remembered" a history of Llanfair Waterdine and Lloyney as they remembered it. John Harper produced his "History of Llanfair Waterdine and St. Mary's Church" shortly afterwards. These two publications tell us a great deal about the history of our community.

Our book takes a different view but we hope it builds on what has gone before. It is "a snapshot" of life in Llanfair Waterdine and Lloyney through the eyes of the people who live here at the end of the 20th Century.

The River Teme divides us, Llanfair Waterdine is in England and Lloyney in Wales but to all intents and purposes we are one community. We have used the memories of older people to tell us about the past but there is also a great deal of the present in our book. We of course hope that our children will learn a little about their personal histories from it.

Anne Singleton asked Joan Hobby, Mary Morgan and Jocelyn Williams to join her in producing this book in 1998 after a chat at a coffee evening. After some discussion it was agreed that Anne should apply for funds to the National Lottery via "The Help The Aged Millennium Fund". We were lucky to be given a grant which will almost cover the printing costs of this book.

We have had tremendous support from many people. Our special gratitude is due to John Harper who gave us permission to use and even to precis his book. We also used exerpts and photographs from "A Parish Remembered" and we are grateful for these. Janet Lewis had taken hundreds of photographs and we have used a great many of these. Mary Townshend with wonderful patience has read and corrected everything at least three times. Ruth Davies has supported our efforts in many ways and it was she who suggested we put the census and archive material in the Everest Hall for three days so that local people could "look up" their family histories or the histories of their houses. When over eighty people spent many hours in the hall we had an indication of how much interest there was in our project. Gordon Singleton has provided technical and moral support throughout the project and many other people have helped in many different ways.

Well over an hundred of you have written something about your homes, your lives or your interests or concerns. Thank you all.

We hope you enjoy the results of your efforts. There will of course be mistakes, omissions or even perhaps "embarrassing bits" we hope you'll forgive us for those and that our efforts will help cement the great feeling of community which exists in Llanfair Waterdine and Lloyney at the end of the 20th Century and the beginning of the 21st.

Joan Hobby, Mary Morgan, Anne Singleton, Jocelyn Williams.

Part One

Llanfair Waterdine

Llanfair Waterdine

Belmount

Belmount was until recently a small cottage with low ceilings and two bedrooms. It is believed to be a shepherd's cottage and may be over 300 years old. It has 19 acres of land. Dick Price who later moved to Lloyney lived there from the age of 4. He sold the property to Barry and Lindsay Baker in 1988. There was at that time no road to the property. Barry and Lindsay built a road and with the help of Victor Adams and his digger made a flat open farmyard. Barry and Lindsay sold the cottage to John and Polly Riddle who have doubled its size. They have a young son Billy.

Belmount 1999

Black Hall

Black Hall is a very old house. It was a cruck house, and has been altered and added to over the years. The house was listed in 1985, along with two of the farm buildings. It has some fine timber work inside, and some interesting details outside, including a little timber face, carved on the west side of the house.

Timber face carving at Black Hall

The first people, within living memory, to own and farm Black Hall, were Mr. and Mrs. Noel Price, who had no children. Noel was the brother of Maurice Price of Garbett. Isy Hughes and Ron Morris both worked at Black Hall for a while. Isy lived in the house, and Ron lived in the corner house Lloyney at the time.

Noel used to rent some grasskeep at Pembridge, and his ewes had to be walked all the way there, as there were no lorries in those days. He bought some little speckled faced ewes in Newtown one day, and they too had to be walked all the way home. Apparently they lay down for the whole of the next day because their feet were sore.

He kept a flock of Clun ewes and was always very particular about their wool. As soon as they were shorn it would be taken on the wheel cart up to the granary, above the goose house, on the East side of the house to be stored. Before the War wool was packed with great care, with some of the better fleeces at the seam end of the wool sheets. It joined the wool from the Graig, and was taken to Knucklas station to be loaded in to the goods wagons for Shrewsbury, then by horse-drawn dray to the wool repository and unloaded in stalls, with the labels and the seam ends facing the gangway. Buyers would come from Bradford, and other large towns, and inspect the wool, which would only be opened at the seam end. Having assessed the wool they would assemble in the auction room and bid for what they wanted. In later years the Wool Board took over.

Llandinshop

When Noel Price retired he moved to Myrtle Cottage in the village and just kept Llan-y-Vidi. Alfred Davies from the Goetre followed Noel Price to Black Hall. He had three sons and several daughters, one of whom married Fred Hughes, Isy's brother. The Davies family farmed Black Hall throughout the War and into the 1960s. After the Davies family left, Victor Adams farmed Black Hall from the Vedw, where he and his wife Joan were living. His brother, Trevor lived at Black Hall with his family. Fred Beavan bought Black Hall farm from Victor in 1970. He put in a new water system to serve Black Hall, Llandinshop and the Graig. In 1986 his older son, Andrew got married, and moved into Llandinshop while Black Hall was renovated. The house was in a very dilapidated state and the wattle and daub wall on the West side had to be replaced. Much of the plaster was removed, and some partitions were taken out, making it much lighter inside. Although it was modernised and a central heating system put in the more interesting features still remain.

Black Hall

Blaen-y-dre

Blaen-y-dre was a family farm until the early 1970s. It was then bought by Mr. Chris Thomas from Bryndreanog outside the Parish and the house was empty for some years. Mike and Lyn Thomas and their three children moved into the house in the early 1990s and Mike has brought the fabric of the house into good repair.

In the 1841 census Blaen-y-dre appears to have been quite a large farm. William Hughes aged 40, his wife Mary aged 35

Blaen-y-dre 1999

and their seven children lived there along with three workers, Hannah Francis, John Evans and William Clee aged 15. By 1861 two families ran the farm one of which was headed by John Gwilt aged 59 with his wife Martha and their six children. He had come from Clun. Thirty years later Martha, his widow was still there with her single daughter and two sons.

Brackenway, Nether Skyborry

Bracken Way was built in 1959/60 for the Williams' family Monaughty Poeth by Deacon Builders, Kington. It was first occupied by Jim (the son) his wife Jocelyn and their three children Sally, Simon and Kate. In the autumn of 1982 father and son exchanged homes. Mr. Lawton Williams retired to Brackenway (where he lived until his death in 1997) together with his daughter Miss Glenys Williams. Jim and his family moved to Monaughty Poeth taking with them the pet labrador Tina, two cats, one of them a Birmingham street cat rescued by one of Kate's nursing friends and Sally's small pony Romany. Romany is still alive today and ridden by Sally's six years old daughter Lucy at their home, Shadwell Hall, Clun. Brackenway, slightly elevated commands a panoramic view of the Teme valley, surrounded by the picturesque hills of Radnorshire and Shropshire. With a southerly aspect it is a sunny and warm spot and often the first violets and primroses can be found in the hedgerows and adders are attracted to the warm shelter of the undergrowth. The village of Knucklas can be seen in the distance and one can just discern the wonderful thirteen arched viaduct over which travels the one or two coach diesel train on its daily scenic route between Shrewsbury and Swansea.

Brackenway

The view from Brackenway with the River Teme in flood

The house itself nestles into the foot of Panpwnton hill, it has three bedrooms, a bathroom, a large lounge and a big kitchen. There is a lawn at the back and flower beds at the side.

The poets words:-
"If there's peace to found in this world
A heart that is humble might hope for it here"
could well be an apt and fitting description for this pretty, secluded house.

Broad Oak

Broad Oak

Broad Oak was built in 1960 by Trevor and Rupert Edwards the sons of Mr. F. Edwards Builder. Mr. and Mrs. George Astbury had bought the building plot from my uncles Mr. Bill and Jack Evans.

Mr. Astbury died in 1979 and my husband Bert Hobby and I bought the house in 1980. We had previously lived at Melin-y-Grogue Farm for 36 years. Few alterations have been made to the house. The lounge and dining rooms have been made into one large room and we put in double glazing throughout. Joan Hobby.

58

Mr Hobby 17/12/53

40 Cigs	7. 2
Swan	4
19. 1 lb Butter	3. 4
2 lbs Margo	1 6
1 lb 2oz Cheese	2 5
4 lb Sugar	2 8
½ lb Tea	2. 6
Candles	3. 10½
Tomato Sauce	1 6
Large Rinso	11
1 lb Soap	11
1¼ lb Cake @ 2/4	2. 11
	£1-10-0½
	5-7½
	£1-15-8
	3 7
	1-19-3

Paid M Sawyer 21/12/53

A grocery order for Joan Hobby 1953

Bryn Bedw

Jack Stephens who was born in Beguildy moved to Bryn Bedw in about 1940 with his brother and sister. The family who had lived there moved up to the Hurgin. Jack and Edith, nee King from Newbridge on Wye were married at Llanfair church in 1945, probably the first wedding to take place after the War, Jack retired from active farming in 1982. The farm was then let as grazing. He died in 1992. Edith continued to live in the house although badly crippled by arthritis. She took a great interest in village affairs and continued to let the grazing each year.

Bryn Bedw is not an old house, probably being built about 150 years ago. It has a range of traditional buildings which are in their original condition. There are cow ties for about 40 cattle, a hay loft and calf pens.

Edith had intended to write about her life at Bryn Bedw but because of her untimely death she didn't do so. Comments made at her funeral by the Rev. Eileen Lloyd sum her up well and tell us a little about life at Bryn Bedw.

"...Edith was born just outside Llandrindod at Newbridge on Wye. She grew up in a large family when times were not easy. No doubt home life was fairly strict with so many youngsters, and with jobs for everyone. Schooling finished at the age of 14 and Edith went to work in a restaurant. When the War broke out she became a land girl and came to Llanfair to work at The Green. Life was not all work, of course, and Edith would socialise with the local young people and could be found dancing along with the best of them. She loved the countryside and she fell for Jack Stephens. They married in 1945 in Llanfair church and then went across the road to The Red Lion for the reception. In those times there was little money for wedding fripperies and land girls were special in that there was a pool of wedding dresses, once worn by the famous, which could be borrowed for the day. So when Edith got married, she wore Googie Withers's wedding dress - a great thrill for her given her passion for clothes. Farming doesn't normally lend itself to haute couture, but Edith was an inveterate shopper who would come back from a day out with a new outfit which she would wear whenever an occasion arose - and if the occasion didn't arise she just hung it up unworn. Along with the clothes, would go the make-up and right up to her last days, Edith was never seen without her eye shadow and pencilled brows and her lipstick. She loved the countryside and she and Jack really cared for their animals - they had some of the best Hereford cattle around. Farmers wives of Edith's generation kept a good larder and she was no exception - her food parcels back home were well received - especially the home churned butter and the faggots. Edith was a lady who spoke her mind - and some of the words she used were not suitable for children or those of a delicate disposition. She was a terrible gossip and skilled in the art of character assassination, yet she was not essentially a hard woman - it was that sheer grit and determination, that outrageous manner, that kept her going over the latter years when she suffered so much from arthritis.

Bryn Bedw 1998, sold by auction in April 1999

Each one of you who is here today will have your own particular memories of Edith Stephens. Some will be of the bigger events - family affairs or community happenings. Some memories will be more personal - maybe you had a tot of whisky with her after bidding for the grass keep; perhaps you remember her bouncing down the lanes in her old Riley. Maybe you sampled her cooking or you are a fellow smoker. Some of you will recall that she and Jack would never work on Sunday and yet everything got done. Some memories maybe known to you alone - a nickname, a certain look in the eye, a particular conversation...." 22 December 1998.

Brynheulog

We bought the site from Victor and Joan Adams in 1971 and started building a bungalow that year. We moved in in 1976. At first it was a four bedroomed bungalow but in 1994 we extended it into a seven bedroomed house. In 1996 Dilys started to do Bed and Breakfast and we now let four rooms with en-suite facilities. We advertise on the Internet and meet people from all over the world. Many of our visitors come from Australia, New Zealand and America.

Brynheulog

We are very lucky to have the Red Lion across the road because we can send all our guests there for their evening meal.

I work as a site manager in the construction industry and we have four sons, Shane who is 26, Liam 24, Geraint 22 and Eirian who is 15. The three older ones went to Bournemouth University and Shane and Geraint work in accountancy at Chase Manhattan Merchant Bank in Bournemouth. Liam is in computer software engineering for Kaye JL French at Presteigne. Eirian attends John Beddoes High School in Presteigne. Dilys came from the nearby village of Lloyney and I am originally from Trefeglwys. We enjoy living in Llanfair very much and find it a peaceful area and we find the people very friendly.

Iorwerth Waters.

Brynorgan

Brynorgan nestles on the side of Brynorgan Hill with Offas's Dyke path running by the front door. Originally it was a small holding with a typical small stone cottage built around the mid-l8th century. The 1845 census shows Brynorgan was a holding of 92 acres, 2 rods and 8 poles, and the amount of rent appropriated on the land was £4.0s.2d., the occupant was Thomas Venables, and the owner the Earl of Powis.

In 1871 William Lloyd lived at Brynorgan, and in 1881 John Davies was the occupant, although Brynorgan now belonged to Selley Hall, where John Davies was the waggoner.

In 1968 when Mrs. Lloyd and her family moved, Llewelyn Morgan (of Selley Hall) sold Brynorgan cottage to Mr. & Mrs. Wright, who improved and modernised it over a number of years, installing electricity, telephone and water, and also stoning a roadway. Phil Green purchased the property from the Wrights in 1978, and he and his family have enjoyed Brynorgan for the last 21 years.

The following is a most interesting and informative extract from a diary by the late Judy Green:-

"Friday, 15th July 1996

An afternoon to remember and record. Don and Muriel Lewis of *29 Ffrydd Terrace* visited us. Muriel lived in Brynorgan around 1930. She was the eldest child living in the house (age 13/14)- one had already left home and she lived with seven brothers and sisters, her parents and at one time a Granny. Her father, a Mr. Jones, worked as a cow man at Selley Hall Farm, then owned by the Bright family. The Jones family came from a farm at Stowe and prior to that worked in the mills in Rochdale. Mr. Bright worked the farm on a pony - and also owned a pony and trap. As Muriel talked it became apparent that the difference in country life around 1930 compared to the 1980's is far greater than a similar time gap in a town. The cottage had no electricity, no bathroom - the toilet was a hut out on the dyke - the water was fetched in from a spring (our spring I think). She remembers clearly that if the cows had been drinking from it you waited for the water to settle before you brought in the supply for the cottage! The physical differences in the cottage were as follows:- sitting room - no back window and an iron black leaded grate and rough stone floor, dining room - brown crock sink under window, large stove in corner where the cupboard now is, clothes boiler in corner by shelf, she thinks an earth floor, kitchen - was a kind of large cupboard/pantry, no windows, and the slab for salting the pig was where the sink now is, stairs - exactly the same.

Brynorgan in 1968

Bedroom 1 - the same except for new windows over garage, and it had no door.
Bedroom 2 - the same except for new window looking down valley.

Bathroom - was the 3rd bedroom - no window. No landing window. The pig sty was where the downstairs cloaks is. The large lean-to shed was where the garage is. There was land attached where the father cultivated vegetables. Our 'right-of-way' existed only as a small lane - they approached the cottage up what is now Offa's Dyke path, and in at a gate where we park the car. She remembers a small front garden and the back bank being much nearer the house.

She then described her life - she was *very* vivid about the room that is now the dining room - their kitchen. The large stove in the corner with all the food always being cooked - they were sent out to gather gorse and bracken from the hill to help the fire - the mother made everything: bread, sausages from the pig, etc., etc., and in the other corner the clothes boiler always alight and boiling away. The youngest child was born at Brynorgan. All the children used to walk to Llanfair school (Everest Hall now), and children from Selley Hall, Little Selley, Garbett and Garbett Villa would all meet up at the cross roads and walk together. One of her brothers had rheumatic fever, so they used to take it in turns to give him piggy backs all the way. In winter they walked back in the dark. They used to play in the stream, and as they didn't own bathing costumes or spare clothes, it was Muriel's job to sew up old vests between the legs and make garments to play in the river in. They ate an enormous amount of rabbit – particularly at harvest time when the petrified rabbits used to end up in the centre of the field being harvested, and then all the children would kill them. When a pig was killed it hung for two or three days covered in a white sheet from the dining room beam (main beam near the stairs). She actually found the large hole the hook was in! As children they were terrified by this white apparition, and used to scurry up the stairs! The sheet, of course, was meant to stop them being frightened by the dead pig!! After the pig had hung for a few days it was then jointed up, some joints given to neighbours, some salted, and some eaten fresh, and then the intestines used to make sausage skins, etc., etc. Muriel's first job was at Skyborry Farm where she cooked for Colonel Cummins (Jim Cummins father)

Brynorgan in 1999

They walked to church, and church-going was the main social event - where they met 'the boys' who all sat at the back! She met Don whilst she was posting a letter for the Cummins, and he lived at Heyope. He used to come and 'court' her at Brynorgan - walking of course!

The Green family at Brynorgan

Muriel's family moved to Worcester - Mr. Jones had been cow man to the Brights and he moved on. She couldn't be separated from Don, so returned to the area and married him. When we asked Muriel if they ever got snowed in she just said "No there weren't any cars around"! The implication being that it's the cars that get snowed in - not people!"

Coach House - The Somershey

The History of The Coach House - Jane Nickerson.

It is difficult to write with any accuracy the history of The Coach House as there is no direct reference to it as a house. There is no mention of it in the records of Nether Skyborry in the census return since 1841. It can be seen on a map for 1830 showing the estate, then named, Lower Ysguborian - Welsh for Skyborry and meaning two barns. It also appears on the tithe map of 1843 as a shed. In the sale details of Nether Skyborry 1920 a Coach House is mentioned. Photographs taken in 1969 show a substantial building in a bad state of repair. Miss Muriel Jones bought the estate of Nether Skyborry in 1969 and the following year commissioned a local builder, Bert Trillo to convert and restore the Coach House. Once finished John and Christine Harper moved in (sister of Miss Jones) and stayed until 1991. John Harper made the weather vane of the small boy and the crows (local legend described in "A Parish Remembered," the barn mentioned still stands at the bottom of the drive). They also tamed the garden, removing the bracken and building stone walls at the back of the house. A local estate agent bought the house from them and 18 months later sold it to John Stewart Anderson and Richard Church - an actor and his agent. It was they who renamed the house The Somershey. It had always been known as the Coach House or The Old Coach House. The studio became a small theatre and one man performances were given for the next two years until 1994 when we bought the house.

The Nether Skyborry estate remained intact until 1987 when Miss Jones sold the big house and boundaries were then drawn up between it and the Coach House. Two Victorian gravestones which we found in the courtyard in undergrowth commemorate pet dogs.

Water to the house comes from a spring at the top of the hill. The stream is the overflow from the tank which also supplies Nether Skyborry, Lower Skyborry and Weir Cottage. It costs the princely sum of £1 a year payable to Jim Williams of Monaughty Poeth on whose land the spring rises. The water is so clear and pure that when friends come from London they always take a few bottles home.

The garden was described as an "ornithologists delight" when we bought the house. The bird boxes are inspected every year for pied flycatchers etc which are ringed. Buzzards circle constantly overhead and owls are busy at night - a barn owl has nested in the garden. In the courtyard we have seen great spotted woodpeckers, nuthatches, goldfinches, jays, tree creepers and wrens.

Pied flycatcher

Personal History of the Coach House.

My husband, mother and I had been searching for months in this beautiful county for a house which suited all our needs. Curiosity made us make an appointment to view the Coach House, it wasn't big enough with only two bedrooms and one bathroom but the green tunnel of a drive twisting away from us and hiding the house was irresistible. One glorious summer morning we drove up and knew instantly we had found our home. The view across the valley, the trees rising up behind the house to Offa's Dyke and the stream were overwhelming - we would just have to make the house fit our needs.

Coach House - The Somershey, 1969 before renovation

Three months later we took possession and started work. The garage was converted from a breeze block space into a dining room and the existing dining room became my mothers bed-sitting room. The large room, originally a hayloft and then studio and theatre became a self contained flat and my husband built bookcases on every available wall space. The door came off the elderly electric cooker when I opened it, so a new Rayburn was installed and also central heating throughout the house. We widened the perilously steep and narrow drive and the muddy area outside the front door became a paved and terraced courtyard. It was perfect.

It took three and a half years and almost immediately my husband became ill and died. Eleven months later my mother followed him. We had expected to stay for many years but in spite of the sadness it is a happy and beautiful house and I hope future owners will love it as much as we did.

Coach House - The Somershey, 1998

Coed-y-Hendre

Coed-y-Hendre

Coed-y-Hendre is one of the oldest, if not the oldest dwelling in Llanfair parish. It was a timber framed house of cruck construction probably first built in the 14th and 15th centuries with alterations and additions from the 16th up to the 19th century. The farm buildings are also extremely old, some of them also dating from the 15th century.

The house and buildings are part of what was a small settlement, there being an old house at Redgate which is now farm buildings. Coed-y-Hendre Mill was probably built later to provide services for both houses and for others which have since disappeared around the Runnis, Hidmore, Llanwooley and the Cwm.

Many of the beams and timbers at Coed-y-Hendre are original and the black and white structure is quite rare in this area. The staircase is 16th or 17th century and is certainly the only remaining one of that age in this part of the parish.

Tyn-y-Coed

Geoffrey and Ruby Thomas have lived at Coed-y-Hendre all their married lives and have a son James and a daughter Sandra.

In 1881 the house was occupied by a Griffiths family who had come from Beguildy. They had two small sons and six farm workers, four of whom were indoor workers. There were several empty properties in Llanfair by 1891 including Melin-y-Grogue, The Wain and Tregodvah. Coed-y-Hendre is not mentioned in the 1891 census although it appears in every other one since 1841. As the house is large there were always several indoor servants and in 1841 there were two aged 12 and 13 who called themselves manservants. One was called William Clee a name still found locally. There were at that time 12 people living at Coed-y Hendre.

Ruby and Geoff Thomas have always had a keen interest in gardening and so has their son James. He has planted many trees on the farm and as time goes on many of these will become landmarks in the parish.

Coed-yr-Hendre Mill

Coed-yr-Hendre Mill is owned by Bob and Marilyn McIntyre and their three children Donald, an engineer, Ann, a language student and Andrew a planning student. They have a dog called Jay. Bob points out that they have not taken much active part in the local community yet as all their time is devoted to renovating the Mill. He writes:- We intend to rectify this as the property nears completion. We are in the strange position of seeing familiar faces particularly those who drive by the Mill regularly; but apart from the Thomas', the Bevan's and Colin Morgan we have very little knowledge of names.

Until last year we lived in two caravans while the property progressed. We recently got rid of the last caravan and it was with mixed feelings that we watched our mobile home slowly disappear down the lane for local recycling.

It would be nice to think that the whole project, including the Mill workings might be complete by the new *mill*ennium, but lack of resources - funds and time - may preclude this. At the very least it should look complete on the outside.

We purchased the old Water Mill from Mr. and Mrs. Geoff Thomas and James in January 1991. The legal interpretation of documents dating back to 1742 had slowed down negotiations. The original building comprised a barn, a loose box, hayloft, millers cottage, store and millworkings on three floors. At the time of purchase the road side wall had caved in and the temporary roof had collapsed

Coed-y-Hendre Mill 1980

Coed-y-Hendre Mill 1999

bringing two internal floors down on to the ground floor. It is our intention eventually to reinstate the mill machinery completely and dependant on the water supply, to get the mill working occasionally. We are excavating the old mill pond and assessing possible sources of water to impound, to power the proposed new waterwheel. During refurbishment we obtained permission to build a garage in similar style to the mill. We are currently attempting to obtain permission for outbuildings for storage and recreation and renovating the pond shed.

Crwn Cottage - Caravan.

The Bright family lived at Crwn Cottage before moving to Lower Tregodfa in about 1906. The remains of the Cottage are still on Lower Tregodfa land and Ben Swancott, who is Giles' younger brother has had a caravan on the site for many years. He was born at Tregodfa and attended school at Llanfair. He was then employed by the Local Authority. Now retired Ben keeps a well stocked garden of his own and helps several other people with theirs.

View towards Crwn from Lloyney

Cwm Farm

According to the Census of 1891 The Cwm, then known as Cwm Shirk was lived in by William and Edwina Gough a couple in their thirties and farmworkers Margaret Lewis and John Baylis. They were followed by the Deakins, the Prices and the Richards and then Alan Humphries from 1956 to 1958.

Doug and Freda Powell moved to the Cwm in 1958 with their three daughters, Shirley, Edith and Olwen who were all born at Great Cantel Farm the previous family home. David was born at the Cwm in 1961. Shirley, the eldest, left home in 1967 to work as a nanny. In 1969 she went to London to work in Bourne & Hollingworth, a large department store. She later married Steve and they have one son, Andrew who is now 23. They all live in Shrewsbury.

Edith worked in the Chemist's in Knighton on leaving school, then moved to Shrewsbury where she met her husband. They have a son Gareth, now 18 and in 1981 they emigrated to Australia. They had another son called Ryan who is now 14. Edith worked as a child minder in Australia and they returned to live in Knighton in 1988.

About 1982, David Johnson and Doug Powell

Olwen married a local farmer from Llanbadarn Fynydd they have three children, Shane aged 24, Michelle aged 22 and Elaine 17. They still farm at Llanbadarn.

David left school at 16 to work on the farm with Doug and Freda. After his father's death in 1985 he and his mother continued to farm The Cwm with the help of a workman. David went to Australia in 1982 to stay with his sister and sample life "down under". Always a keen rugby supporter David went to a rugby International at Cardiff Arms Park in 1986. While there he met an old school friend - Mandy! Romance blossomed and they married in 1988 and lived at The Cwm with Freda. Mandy works at Llandrindod and Knighton Hospitals as a midwife and nurse. Freda moved to Knighton in 1989 leaving David and Mandy at The Cwm. David and Mandy have three children Jodie aged 9, Thomas 7 and Emily 5. They all attend school at Beguildy and travel by bus along the main road. They should attend Newcastle school but there seems to be an imaginary line through the parish from the Anchor to Springhill: people either travel towards Newcastle and Clun on the one side or to Llanfair and Beguildy on the other.

Charlie Hughes the mole catcher has a field named after him at the Cwm

The children enjoy living in the country but would welcome more local activities. A Youth Club has started recently which has generated lots of enthusiasm from all the local children. The population of younger people is quite low. There seems to be a shortage of people aged between 16 and 22 because of a lack of employment in the area. Farming is under great stress, farms are fewer and many farmers are selling up. Village life also seems to be dying with the closure of the local Post Office and Shop. The only places to meet locally these days are the Public House, the Church or the Village Hall. The area is a very friendly one in which to live and if one needs help at any time it is always available from someone. The Powell family do not see themselves moving away from the area and cannot imagine living anywhere else. The children do not have clear ideas about what they want to do, they just say they want to stay at home with Mum and Dad for ever!

Cwm Farm

On the farm are the remains of a dwelling known as Upper Redwood which stands in a field called "Charlie Hughes". Charlie Hughes lived at Upper Redwood and had a son called Dick - this son remembered walking to school at Llanfair on the morning in 1902 when the copper beech tree was being planted outside the Church.

Cwm Brain

Cwm Brain

In 1946 Horace and Amy Johnson and their two children David aged 7 and Anne 8, moved to Cwm Brain from Worcestershire. After the death of his father David decided to emigrate to a farm in Manitoba, Canada. Amy planned to go with him. Sadly she died on the day they intended to travel. David emigrated alone and has been very happy with that decision.

Anne left Cwm Brain to work as a teacher and returned to Llanfair with her husband Gordon to retire, at Lower Bryn Bedw. They have two sons Adam and Matthew.

Before 1946 the Bywater family lived at Cwm Brain and prior to them the Hughes family. Relatives of the latter still live in the Parish. Cwm Brain is not an old house, having been built about 150 years ago. There is some evidence of a previous dwelling on the site. Mains Electricity was not laid on until the early 1980's and dairy cows were milked by hand until the late 1970's. Water was laid on to the cowsheds in the early 1950's before it was piped into the house. The holding was about 165 acres but land was sold to Llanfair Hall, Bryndraenog and Lower Tregodfa in 1988. An old stone hearth has recently been found behind a modern fireplace in a living room.

Cwm Cole

John and Joy Hunt

Lord Hunt of Llanfair Waterdine died in early November 1998. He and his family had had connections with Llanfair for many years and he recently wrote about his life here.

Llanfair Waterdine Memories of our life in the Parish 1945 to 1998.- John Hunt.

For nearly ten years after the end of the War in 1945, our first home since our marriage in 1936 was Weir Cottage in Lower Skyborry. A few years earlier (1942) I had brought my Battalion, of which I was second in command, to Stanage Park, from which I organised training exercises on Beguildy Beacon and the wider high country on the Welsh side of the Teme Valley. Thanks to the kindness of Jack and Louise Watkins of Heartsease Farm, Joy and our two children were able to join me during that training period, and we soon fell for the charm of that area of the border and its welcoming people. When the Watkins' accepted my family as evacuees from the menace of German V2 bombs over our rented house in a London suburb, we both knew that this was the country where we wanted to live. A postcard from Louise when I happened to be on three weeks' leave from Greece decided us to hurry down to view a house which had come on the market just outside Knighton. We put our bikes on the train from London and went to have a look. It was a case of love at first sight! We were so excited that we bought Weir Cottage "on the spot" and cycled all the way to Snowdonia and back to celebrate the event. Perhaps it was an unrealistic decision for my military postings after the War made it impossible for me to settle there; I had to commute from London at weekends, using our only car and the limited supply of petrol coupons to visit the family whenever possible. Joy soon endeared herself to our neighbours up and down the Parish; she took a leading part in organising social activities. The Llanfair Follies in the Village Hall, running Sunday School classes, masterminding the "floats" to represent the Parish at the annual Knighton Shows. She lent a hand to our neighbours, the

Llanfair Wakes - The Hunt family, Jenny, Joy, John and Prue

Beavan and Matthews families at the Graig and Skyborry Green at harvest time; she became very much part of Parish life. Her achievements were all the more remarkable because all the journeys were undertaken by cycle, in all weathers and sometimes late in the evenings.

The bond between ourselves and the Parish became even closer following the first ascent of Everest. We shall never forget the welcome home we received when we returned from Kathmandu in June 1953. For a while I was able to enjoy a sense of belonging and I wrote my book "The Ascent of Everest" in our annex at Weir Cottage, in the peace and quiet I badly needed at that time.

Between times, we explored the countryside far and wide, pursuing our passion for the higher hills by cycling to Cader Idris, The Elan Valley and elsewhere; more prosaically, we cycled to and from Bishop's Castle to fetch our ration cards. Our two children (more were to follow) cycled daily on their way to school at Brampton Bryan. Life was very good. This idyllic period was short lived, for I was soon to be posted overseas again after a spell at the Army Staff College, where Joy and the children joined me. We needed to keep the family together; so after some unsatisfactory leases we took the hard decision to sell Weir Cottage. We mourned the loss of our first and only home. We missed the daily run of the train, powered by two steam locomotives fore and aft - and occasionally, a third engine in the middle huffing and puffing it's noisy way towards Heyope! Despite the inconvenience of lack of electricity (for "The Electric" had not been extended up the valley and we had to subsist on a messy generator and oil lamps) we were content to live in the ambience of an earlier age. Most of all we missed our close friends and neighbours Wilf and Ellie Gough who were at Panpwnton Farm down the road and Wilf brought a supply of milk on his tractor; Wilf had established a reputation as a Dance Band Leader in Knighton and was in great demand in the wider neighbourhood. Mr. and Mrs. Bright with their numerous and talented family lived opposite Panpwnton with their "picture postcard" garden. Mrs. Lloyd cycled from her cottage beneath Cwm Sarnum Hill to tidy up the house, while Vin Davies came up from his house near the station to help in the garden. Our immediate neighbours were Grace Barnard and Mr. and Mrs. King. Grace, a relative of the historic Harvey family of Brampton Bryan, enjoyed the most superb view along the Teme Valley to Heyope and beyond. Mr. King helped me to house and rear a piglet I had bought at Upper Pits Farm beyond Stanage. We grew very fond of 'Alexander' and it was perhaps just as well that I was again posted overseas before the time came to dispose of him.

Some years passed before an opportunity came to return to a new home in the Parish. In 1966 Harold Wilson invited me to sit as a Life Peer in Parliament and Joy and I decided to ask if we might link my title with the Parish. Fred Beavan, then the Council Chairman expressed the delight of his colleagues and we began to look for a new home (albeit a 'second' one) where we felt we belonged. Joy was abroad at that time helping with our daughter Sue's young family in Chile, but I began looking around. I looked at a group of derelict cottages collectively known as Cwm Cole (or 'Cold' according to the Ordnance Survey). The prospect was discouraging; it seemed that it might be possible to restore two semi-detached cottages at the lower end of the group. At that time, Joy and I were shortly to embark on an overland journey to Nepal. We entrusted the redesign and refurbishing to the architect Mr. Moore and the builder Bert Trillo. We were unable to be around when this work was started; by and large, I reckon they made a good job of it. From the plans, dated June 1972 it seems we cannot have taken possession before the latter part of that year.

Cwm Cole 1940

Our neighbours were Tom Evans, who owned the group of cottages and sold "Cwm Cole" to us. Tom continued to occupy a wing of the remaining cottages until he decided to sell these to Andrew and Janet Lewis. Ted Owen had a small farm at The Bwlch and soon endeared himself to Joy and all our family. Ted had enjoyed a Grammar School education and took a keen interest in the world beyond our little valley. He loved children and animals. It was a common sight to see Ted lumbering down the lane with his dog and three of four ginger kittens in his pockets. Above all, he was devoted to his horse, which was his maid of all work, dragging a cart or various decrepit items of farm machinery, held together with binder twine. When our grand children were around, Ted and the horse always had time for them. To visit Ted at the "Bwlch" was always a pleasure despite the mess in his kitchen with the ashes from the stove raked out on to the floor. There was no gainsaying his offer of a whisky in a very musky tumbler! I used to watch Ted toiling up the steep lane and wonder how the end would come; we could not foresee the tragic fire which destroyed him and his farmhouse one night. Our only other neighbour was Dick Price who owned Belmount and ran a few sheep on the hillside above. We had known Dick's brother Jack when we lived at Weir Cottage. He was a rabbit catcher at The Graig in the years before myxomatosis, and the poulterer's shop in Knighton was well stocked with all manner of game. Our old friends in the village and neighbouring farms were still there to welcome us; for many of them had been, in their youth, involved in her social activities while Joy was at Weir Cottage.

We have no knowledge of earlier occupation at Cwm Cole; we understood that the ruin had not been lived in for many years. A family from the Midlands once came to peer over the gate and I will always regret not having questioned them about their claim to have lived there, and what kind of occupation they enjoyed.

Cwm Cole 1999

I would like to return to the affinity - the privileged sense of belonging to the community in Llanfair. I sometimes wonder if this may be traced to a more distant past. When looking Southwards from Beguildy Beacon towards the Black Mountains and Brecon Beacons; or Northwards from Llanfair Hill, tracing the course of Offa's Dyke across the Clun Valley, on it's long journey North to the estuary of the River Dee, I have felt aware of the turbulent history

Welcome home from Everest June 1953

of this Border country. I think of my heroes, Llewellyn ap Gwnffyd and Owain Glyndwr, seeking to defend their country from the English Border barons - the Mortimers and their Norman masters. I have wondered whether, in some way, the character of the kindly people which we so greatly value is not a product of a blend of cultures, in the aftermath of those Medieval Wars. But I have strayed too far from the subject of Cwm Cole and must resist peering into an even more distant prehistoric past which I sense when standing on the remains of Bronze Age settlements. I have to remind myself that our little valley was covered by dense forests in those days when the inhabitants of Cwm Cole were wild boar and deer.

8th September 1998

After the successful conquest of Everest Llanfairwaterdine was in the public eye for a short time. **The Birmingham Post**. Monday 6th July 1953.

Best day of all for Colonel Hunt.
Everest Leader Has Homely Welcome From Shropshire Villagers.
Llanfair Waterdine Sunday

"Oh, this is a good day", Mrs. John Hunt said here this afternoon. And so it was, her husband, Colonel John Hunt, leader of the British Expedition, came home today to this tiny Shropshire village lying on the borders of Wales. Waiting to greet him were nearly 400 villagers with rose petals, a victor's garland of laurels and the spontaneous warmth of their friendship.

And that friendship made this the best greeting that Colonel Hunt has yet had. "This is the supreme moment of the whole of the Everest story" he told me. "We have been feted ever since arriving back in Nepal and all the way through India back to London. But this is the best of the whole lot. I wish I had the whole team with me to share in this moment. It surpasses all my expectations. It is the most genuine welcome from one's own people".

Showers of Rose Petals

Colonel Hunt who was accompanied by his wife, arrived in the village from London in his blue saloon car right on time. As the car turned from Knighton back across the border of Radnorshire into Shropshire and up the long lane that leads to his home Weir Cottage, the villagers waited on the borderline between Wales and England. They asked Colonel Hunt to step into an amber and blue governess cart over which the vicar, the Rev. John Williams and Mr. Penry Evans chairman of the Parish Council held a "Welcome Home" banner. A laurel wreath was placed on Colonel Hunt's shoulders, wild rose petals were scattered on him and then he was shaking everyones hands and laughing, "Hello Fred - nice to see you, Bill." "Yes I'm glad to be home" he said.

Everest pioneer Lord Hunt dies

By Charles Holland

THE Queen last night led tributes to Lord Hunt, the leader of the first successful assault on Mount Everest, who has died aged 88.

After leading the pioneering 1953 expedition, he became the first director of the Duke of Edinburgh Award Scheme. The Queen and Prince Philip spoke of their sadness at his death.

Lord Hunt: inspiration

A statement from Buckingham Palace said: "The conquest of Everest was an early landmark of the Queen's reign and Lord Hunt brought the same spirit of adventure and leadership to many other areas of national life."

The explorer Sir Ranulph Fiennes said the life peer's achievements had inspired him. "He was a very, very great man; one of the great mountain-climbers."

His planning allowed Sir Edmund Hillary and Sherpa Tenzing Norgay to reach the summit.

Lord Hunt, a brigadier with a distinguished Army career who later became the first chairman of the Parole Board, died peacefully at home in Henley, Oxfordshire, on Saturday night following a short illness.

Obituary: Page 23

Obituary Telegraph November 8 1998

Three cheers were called for and the singing of "For He's a Jolly Good Fellow" sent the birds scattering over the hills. Then 40 men and women caught hold of two ropes 30 feet long and prepared to pull Colonel Hunt up the hill to his home. Beside him sat his daughters, Prudence aged 6 clutching a bouquet given to her by 6 years old Tony Gough who had also given flowers to Mrs. Hunt and Jennifer aged 5 the youngest daughter.

Gift of Fruit Cake

"Just a minute" Colonel Hunt called, "Where's Jenny". Mrs. Hunt leaned out of the car. "Jenny's not coming with you" she said. "She's too overcome". And so the trap moved up the hill between the flags and triumphal archways with a small Union Flag fluttering from the ice pick which Colonel Hunt held aloft. At the cottage, a white gabled building looking out over the quiet hills and valleys of the border country with the upper Teme flowing just beyond the garden, there was more excitement. A cake was waiting for Colonel Hunt - a fifteen pound fruit cake made by the village women folk and iced by the vicar himself. On top the icing was built up to resemble three Himalayan peaks a most imposing representation. "Cut it" someone suggested. "No not now" Mrs. Hunt said. "To tell you the truth I think we are both a little sick with excitement and pleasure". "Will you eat it tomorrow? asked someone else. "I don't know, we might keep it 'till Christmas" Mrs. Hunt laughed.

Dance on Village Green

The lawn outside the cottage was packed with people. Colonel Hunt, who admitted to being a little tired, was still shaking hands, still greeting old friends - for all the world a villager in his grey flannels and sports coat returning home, except for the laurel wreath, the fourth Indian Divisional tie which his old Brigade had had presented to him by the West Bengal Congress Committee. What of the future? "A few days rest" he said "and then I must start writing a book on Everest which I hope to complete within six weeks". Tomorrow the villagers are having a bonfire, fireworks and dance on the village green, and later in the week Colonel Hunt returns to London for a tour through the City. But tonight he and his wife walked in the garden,"Just to see if the birds have eaten all the peas".

John and Joy's grandaughter Camilla has recently married and lives locally at Knucklas. She has a young son called Harry. She recalls happy visits to Cwm Cole and talks about "Ted The Bwlch" as he was known locally with great affection. Lord Hunts Obituary in The Daily Telegraph of 9th November 1998 indicates that he led a very full life and gave tremendous service to British society. In Llanfair Waterdine John was a 'local' and Joy still is. We named our village hall Everest Hall to commemorate the conquest of Everest and we felt great collective pride when John decided on being elevated to the Peerage to become 'Lord Hunt of Llanfair Waterdine'.

Cwm Cole

Cwm Cole sometimes appears on maps as Cwm Cold or Cwm Cawl. We bought it in August 1986 from Tom Jones Llanfair Hall as Cwm Cole Cottage. The Hunt's house next door is Cwm Cole too. Since an address is really for the postman we also became Cwm Cole.

Being incomers (and even after twelve years this seems to be the case) it may be worth mentioning why we are here. Incidentally soon after our arrival Harold Gwilt told us that there had to be two generations dead in the churchyard before one was considered a local. I do not like the idea that someone has more weight if they have a family tree stretching back centuries. We can't help the geography of our birth and surely, if we choose where we live, we take an interest, care about the place, invest in it and like it.

After leaving college Andrew and I spent 7 years travelling in South America and the Far East and working in Japan and later Java. While in Indonesia we decided we would like to buy a house back in England and started saving. After going to the British Council Library and poring

Janet Lewis with Puzzle

over maps and geography books we found a corridor a few miles wide stretching from just south of Shrewsbury to just north of Hereford. The same library provided a list of local Estate Agents and a black and white photo of enfolding hills entitled the "Welsh Borderlands". My parents down in Kent began to search. We wanted it to be very rural, probably needing doing-up and with Bed and Breakfast potential for income, therefore near a long distance footpath. We had no idea that they were looking at properties on our behalf as by this time we had left Indonesia and were in India. Our first glimpse of Cwm Cole was a snapshot of a fairly tumbled down house on the edge of a muddy road. The letter with it said they had started proceedings to buy it and if we liked it we could go ahead when we got back to the UK. We met this news with some horror. What were they buying? We showed the photo to our Tibetan landlord who was horrified that we might be parting with good money for a ruin, especially as the town we were in had just suffered an earthquake and was full of similar looking buildings.

On arrival back in Britain we came straight to Llanfair. We certainly liked the scenery and it was near Offa's Dyke footpath. We loved what seemed to be the long winding lane from the village with the thick oak woods on the one side and the hills on the other. Wonderful. There was also a stream through the garden and the classic English pub in the village, even roses round the door.

We got married and all the presents were beautifully wrapped hammers, saws, chisels etc. most of which later fell down the cavity walls for future house dismantlers to find. We spent all the following year knocking down walls and re-building full time, seven days a week and living in a tiny 12 foot caravan on the site. Of course the first winter was the worst we have ever had here. The gas froze and we ran out of food. We decided to walk to Knighton, so donning rucksacks and waterproofs we waded off through deep snowdrifts, not realising that it would have been much easier to walk across the fields. For the first few months we had no car so all our shopping was carried by bike, because of the weight and bulk potatoes and beer soon gave way to rice and gin. For most of this first year the highlight of our week was a trip to the Red Lion for a pint or two and a sit in a proper armchair. We also collected The Sunday Times. We chose this newspaper because it was the thickest and provided us with a good week's "flush" for the organic toilet. This type of toilet didn't smell even in the heat of summer and was better that a chemical one because we could also fertilise the garden.

Halfway through the first year I began to get fat yet I was doing a lot of hard physical exercise. It turned out that I was four months pregnant. Horror stricken midwives and a good summer spurred us on with the building. Any visitors had to join in with the work and seemed to enjoy it as for them it was a novelty rather that a daily routine. Apart from these occasional visitors we did everything ourselves apart from JCB digging (done by Iorwerth) and the plastering. Andrew had to put the roof up single handed as by then I was so fat I couldn't even hold the ends of bits of wood.

We had to dismantle most of the house before we could build it again. It still has the same floor plan except for the kitchen/bathrooms which join what was two separate buildings into one. Two out of four of the chimneys and bread ovens are still intact with the original ironmongery.

One lady we spoke to who had lived in the end cottage at one time said that when it rained she used to weep because water seeped through the walls at back of the house flowed across the floor and out through the front. The water supply is a well that serves all the cottages and the

Richard Jordan

Hunt's. Each cottage had its own toilet - one back-to-back one still being there in 1986 with two holes, big and small for cosy and sociable ablutions. This bucket and chuck system has produced a fertile garden. We found part of a perfect stone floor about three feet below the toilet, perhaps the remains of an older house. We also found an old school photograph of Llanfair school children with Miss Priddy later Mrs. Bufton. I went along to see her to ask if she could identify anyone. Her face lit up when she saw the picture: she remembered the colour of the dress she wore and even where she bought it. She told a few tales about school... hobnailed leather boots drying on the heaters which of course shrunk and she said she hadn't realised how awful this was as they were the only footwear the children had. We also found a small wood offcut carved with the words "Richard Jordan very good joiner and carpenter Mellinagrouge Shropshire 1887". This inspired us to leave a time capsule ourselves in the wall we were building which is now part of the kitchen, the only totally new bit. The one thing we did change was the route of the track to Belmount. This used to run on the Bwlch side of the house. We had it moved to the other side. Despite being a matter of yards the process took over a year and a public enquiry.

We built the house with Bed and breakfast in mind and this was part of our income for a number of years. Travelling became essential to earn a living as we are not farmers. Like many people we have kept chickens and ducks over the years which have provided a constant food supply for foxes and badgers. We have also always kept two goats. Our most recent one Jack Jack was reared by hand as her mother died. Jack Jack was raised in the kitchen and as she got bigger she often left droppings on the floor, of course a B&B guest came down with bare feet, luckily he felt it was all part of the rural experience. We have had Puzzle the cat ever since we came here. We think he must have been one of the kittens Ted the Bwlch used to carry around with him as it was tame from the beginning. We choose to live here because of the beautiful landscape, the space and freedom to roam and explore, especially for the children, the small community and the lack of commercialism, materialism and greed which we think is so evident in urban areas and in the South. There are sadly too few places like this left in the British Isles, especially ones that haven't been overtaken by the ravages of tourism. We are luckier than most in that we have been able to put where we live as a priority above income. Most people have to go where the work is. However we now pay a heavy price to stay here as Andrew has to work abroad. It is a common dilemma for many

Cwm Cole before renovation

Cwm Cole 1999

incomers who are not connected with the land or local services that they have to go away for income. In the end we think it's worth it. The census indicates that there were several dwellings at Cwm Cole over the years. As poorer people were driven back into the hills by the Enclosure Acts they built small cottages and settled in flexible groups using bits of one ruined house to build another. We have followed this pattern and our house walls probably consist of stones from many generations of previous cottages.

Janet Lewis

Cwm Collo

Hazel, John and Trevor Gwilt live at Cwm Collo. Their mother Elizabeth was born there and was the daughter of Richard Swancott and his wife Louise. Richard later bought Lower Tregodfa. Percy Gwilt, Elizabeth's husband was born at The Green. The Gwilt family have lived in Llanfair since at least 1860 and probably before that. John Gwilt lived at Blaen-y-Dre in 1861 having moved from Clun. Cwm Collo house and buildings had many alterations and repairs done in 1905 and 1906 after a serious fire. We are lucky to have the work books of the carpenter Robert Davies who did the building work. Louise Swancott died in 1905. She is said to have had a heart attack when the fire occurred in the farm buildings. She feared that two of her young children were playing in the barn and had been trapped. One of those children was Elizabeth who was aged about six at the time.

Hazel Gwilt (right)

The farm building built by Robert Davies in 1906

Mrs. Elizabeth Gwilt lived to the age of 91 and later owned Hawthorn Cottage in the village. Her grandparents were Jonathan and Ann Swancott who also lived at Cwm Collo. They had eleven children. Sadly as can be seen from the excerpt from churchyard records ten of them died while quite young. Richard, Mrs. Gwilt's father was probably the only one to marry and have children of his own.

Trevor now farms Cwm Collo (which he rents from Llanfair Hall) and the Bwlch which he bought in 1985, while Hazel keeps house for him and his brother John. John works at Llanfair Hall. Their brother Harold was for many years the local postman and with his wife Ann ran the village Post Office and shop. He also worked as a builder and did a great deal of work on local properties, the Church and Everest Hall. The Post Office closed on his death. His sons Anthony and Robert are builders and carpenters and Robert lives at Rose Villa once the Post Office. Their sister Pauline is married to a local farmer and teaches at Knighton Primary School.

1905

Mr. Swancotts Cwmcwlo

July 19	Hang Gate	R. Davies	½ day		
Dec 5	At new stable	R. Davies	½ day	W. Bowen	½ day
Dec 6	At new stable	R. Davies	1 day	W. Bowen	1 day
7	Ditto	R. Davies	1 day	W. Bowen	1 day
8	Ditto	R. Davies	1 day	W. Bowen	1 day
9	Ditto	R. Davies	1 day	W. Bowen	1 day
11	Ditto	R. Davies	1 day	W. Bowen	1 day
12	Ditto	R. Davies	1 day	W. Bowen	1 day
14	Ditto	R. Davies	1 day	W. Bowen	1 day
15	Ditto	R. Davies	1 day	W. Bowen	1 day
16	Ditto	R. Davies	1 day	W. Bowen	1 day
18	Ditto	R. Davies	1 day	W. Bowen	1 day
19	Ditto	R. Davies	1 day	W. Bowen	1 day
20	Ditto	R. Davies	1 day	W. Bowen	1 day
21	Ditto	R. Davies	1 day	W. Bowen	1 day
22	Ditto	R. Davies	1 day	W. Bowen	1 day
23	Ditto	R. Davies	1 day	W. Bowen	1 day
26	Ditto	R. Davies	1 day	W. Bowen	1 day
27	Ditto	R. Davies	1 day	W. Bowen	1 day
28	Ditto	R. Davies	1 day	W. Bowen	½ day
29	Ditto	R. Davies	1 day		
30	Repair roof of shed & Parlour & make & hang two doors at Cwmmawr.	R Davies	1 day		
					£6-9-0

1906

Mr. Swancott Cwmcwlo

Feb 5	Put up collar shelf & slab side of stall in cart stable	R. Davies	1 day		
May 11	New building	R. Davies	1 day	Bowen	1 day
12	Ditto	R. Davies	1 day	Bowen	1 day
14	Ditto	R. Davies	1 day	Bowen	1 day
15	Ditto	R. Davies	1 day	Bowen	1 day
16	Ditto	R. Davies	1 day	Bowen	1 day
18	Ditto	R. Davies	1 day	Bowen	1 day
19	Ditto	R. Davies	1 day	Bowen	1 day
21	Ditto	R. Davies	1 day	Bowen	1 day
22	Ditto	R. Davies	1 day	Bowen	1 day
23	Ditto	R. Davies	½ day	Bowen	½ day
24	Ditto	R. Davies	1 day	Bowen	1 day
25	Ditto	R. Davies	1 day	Bowen	1 day
28	Ditto	R. Davies	1 day	Bowen	1 day
29	Ditto	R. Davies	1 day	Bowen	1 day

30	Ditto	R. Davies	½ day	Bowen	½ day
31	Ditto	R. Davies	1 day	Bowen	1 day
June 2	Ditto	R. Davies	1 day	Bowen	1 day
4	Ditto	R. Davies	1 day	Bowen	1 day
5	Ditto	R. Davies	1 day	Bowen	1 day
6	Ditto	R. Davies	1 day	Bowen	1 day
7	Ditto	R. Davies	1 day	Bowen	1 day
8	Ditto	R. Davies	1 day	Bowen	1 day
9	Ditto	R. Davies	1 day	Bowen	1 day
13	Ditto	R. Davies	1 day	Bowen	1 day
15	Ditto	R. Davies	1 day	Bowen	1 day
16	Ditto	R. Davies	1 day	Bowen	1 day
18	Ditto	R. Davies	1 day	Bowen	1 day
19	Ditto	R. Davies	1 day	Bowen	1 day
20	Ditto	R. Davies	1 day	Bowen	1 day
21	Ditto	R. Davies	1 day	Bowen	1 day
22	Ditto	R. Davies	1 day	Bowen	1 day
23	Ditto	R. Davies	1 day	Bowen	1 day
25	Ditto	R. Davies	1 day	Bowen	1 day
27	Ditto	R. Davies	1 day	Bowen	1 day
28	Ditto	R. Davies	1 day	Bowen	1 day
29	Ditto troughing	R. Davies	1 day	Bowen	1 day
30	Ditto "	R. Davies	1 day	Bowen	1 day

£	s	d
11	5	0

Stone tomb.

South side. In memory of ANN, MARTHA, EMMA and JANE daughters of Jonathan and Ann SWANCOTT

Ann died June 6th 1863 aged 20 years Martha died Aug 27th 1865 aged 20 years Emma died Dec 3rd 1861 aged 13 years Jane died Sep 24th 1863 aged 13 years.

Them also which sleep in Jesus will God bring with Him. North side. In memory of WILLIAM, AARON, JONATHAN and MOSES sons of Jonathan and Ann SWANCOTT

William died 31st Nov 1866 aged 26 years Aaron died Nov 26th 1871 aged 30 years Jonathan died March 25th 1864 aged 17 years Moses died Oct 9th 1861 aged 9 years

For here we have no continuing city but see one to come. JONATHAN SWANCOTT died Dec 22nd 1903 aged 82 years. In memory of ANN wife of Jonathan SWANCOTT of Cwmcwllo in this parish who died October 21st 1865 aged 47 years. West side. Also of MARY SWANCOTT who died 22nd April 1875 aged 13 years

East side. In memory of JOHN SWANCOTT who died July 27th 1876 aged 20 years.

Cwm Collo 1999

Cwm Sanaham

There were three dwellings on the present day farm.

1) A small workman's cottage.
2) A larger dwelling with a barn and cow shed constructed in one length.
3) The present day farmhouse.

They all stand on the old bridle path which runs past Brynnorgan, towards the road to Clun.

The farmhouse has been built in three separate sections, in the shape of the letter 'T'.

The earliest mention found of any of them is the 1841 census return, and the 1849 tithe map, showing Mr. John Davies of Oswestry owned the property, along with Selley Hall, and the Bwlch Farm (in Clun Parish). All three farms have iron railings on parts of their land, which are believed to have been put up in the late 1880's presumably by the landlord.

Mr. Davies used to stay at Cwm Sanaham when he was in Llanfair-Waterdine. Although he owned property in Montgomeryshire, and around Oswestry, where he was a town councillor, and Mayor of Oswestry, Llanfair seems to have been a favourite home of his, as he and his wife are buried at Llanfair. He seems to have taken an active interest in the affairs of Llanfair parish. He actively opposed the building of a new church, supporting the group of parishioners who wanted to repair the old one. His name also appears as a trustee etc. on several documents in the county archive. Shortly after Mr. Edwards of London purchased the Skyborry Estate, Mr. Davies and Mr. Edwards applied to enclose the open hill ground on both properties. The enclosure act was passed in 1854. Both Mr. Davies and Mr. Edwards would ride to Newtown to purchase cattle which would then be walked home by drovers.

The census return of 1861 shows:

John Davies	Landed Proprietor
Ann	Wife
Ann	Daughter
William	Son
Elizabeth Hamer	Visitor
Richard Meath	Servant
Eleanor Jones	Maidservant
John Kinsey	Jockey

Cwm Sanaham (Cwm Sannum)

Cottage 17 acres

Richard Price	
Elizabeth	Wife

Cottage With Buildings 82 acres

William Harris	Farmer
Anne	Wife
Frederick Smith	Carter
John Ratcliffe	Farm Servant
Mary Meacham	Servant

At sometime in Mr. Davies' ownership bricks were made in one of the fields at Cwm Sanaham.

John Davies owned and trained racehorses at Cwm Sanaham where there used to be a stable block complete with a groom's living quarters. In 1869 and 1870 his horse, 'The Colonel', bred by Mr. Hamer of Bicton (Clun) won the Grand National at Aintree, the horse was ridden both to and from the racecourse. In 1870 bonfires were lit on Cwm Sanaham hill and the horse was taken into Llanfair Church to celebrate the victory, many locals would have made money on the race.

Mr. David Wilding and his family moved to Cwm Sanaham in the 1870's (he and his family appear on the 1871 census return at the Wain Farm, Llanfair Waterdine)

In September 1916 he held a farm sale at Cwm Sanaham.

120 ewes	£5.50 -£2.50
57 ewe lambs	£2.50 - £1.25
41 wether lambs	£2.15 -£1.30
14 wethers	£3.40
10 rams	£5.77-£3.15
10 ram lambs	£4.46 - £1.70

Cwm Sanaham

3 cows	£18-£16
their calves	£11 -£10
7 heifers & calves	£24.50 - £19.25
5 heifers in calf	£17 -£15
5 bullocks	£14 -£11.25
3 heifers	£11.75 -£10.12
1 bull	£29.50
1 mare	£44.10
1 gelding	£46.40

Mr. Wilding' s family, his wife Jane, and their three daughters are all buried in Llanfair, he was the last of his immediate family to die in 1917.

His grand-daughter's husband William Matthews bought the livestock at the sale, and took over the farm tenancy. William and his wife Olive lived at Cwm Sanaham after their marriage in 1912 and their three children were born here, they went to Llanfair school, and would have walked, sometimes following the road and at others taking various footpaths. William Matthews travelled the area on horseback pursuing his other trade as a castrater of farm livestock. His children all farmed locally, David Matthews at Skyborry Green, Mary married Isaac Bevan from Bowdler Farm, Knighton. John remained at home, taking over the farm tenancy in 1939. The landlord was then a Mr. P. A. Watson of Avon Lodge in the county of Armagh. The rent was £144 per year, payable in equal half yearly payments, this is exactly the same as had been paid by his father in 1925. An extra £20 per acre would be charged for any meadow or pasture land ploughed without prior permission. All trees, minerals, quarries etc. belonged to the landlord and were not to be used without permission. All game, rabbits and fish were the landlord's. No manure, forage or crops were to be sold off the farm, and all grain crops to be grown in rotation, and the land laid back to clover and grass before the end of the tenancy.

A hay 'gambo' or sledge used locally until the 1950's

John Matthews purchased the farm from Miss Watson of Armagh in 1950. Cwm Sanaham is now farmed by John, Ann and Richard Matthews.

Hay making. The Matthews family working together before the introduction of tractors

Before 1940 all the farm work would have been carried out by horses or by hand. Swedes and turnips would have been hoed by hand, and weeds pulled out of corn crops. Ploughing and hay making were done with horse drawn equipment, the corn would be cut with a binder, stooked by hand, then lugged on a wagon to a stack in either the yard or field to be thrashed later in the year with a thrashing box. There would have been two workmen 'living in' plus the family labour. Livestock would have been fed on mainly home-grown produce, while any household scraps and skimmed milk from butter making would feed the pigs. Except for the horses, trap pony and a few cows none of the livestock would have been housed for the winter. The poultry belonged to the farmer's wife who would sell eggs and butter at the weekly market in Knighton. Chickens, turkeys and geese would be ready for the Christmas markets, either in their feathers or dressed. For many farm wives this would be their housekeeping money. The work in the farmhouse would have been very different from today, oil lamps and candles for light, a wireless with batteries that had to be taken to Knighton and re-charged weekly. The cooking would have been done on a solid fuel range which had an oven and small water boiler either side of an open fire. Not even a cup of tea in the morning until the grate had been black leaded, and the fire lighted. Bread was made once a week in a separate bread oven. Washing would have all been done by hand, using a 'copper' for hot water, a mangle to remove most of the water, and a 'flat' iron heated on the range for ironing. Besides feeding the family there were the farm workers living in to provide meals for. During the second world war Mrs. Matthews also had three evacuee boys from Liverpool to care for.

Cwm Sanaham House in the 1940's

At the turn of this century life both on the farm and in the house has changed!

Most of the work is done by machinery, the farm has five tractors, and many more implements, all of which are much larger than the horse drawn equivalent. Hay bales can vary from 20 Kgs small bales to 500 Kgs round bales or 1 tonne large square bales. Either of the latter can be wrapped for silage. Less corn and root crops are grown, but a lot more manure is spread

Modern day Dwm Sanaham

as most of the livestock is wintered inside. Livestock numbers are greater.

550 ewes & ewe lambs

46 - 50 cows and in calf heifers

The only thing which remains the same is one bull, but not a Hereford as it would have been for the previous hundred years, it is now a Limousin. No horses are kept for working.

Richard Matthews is an agricultural contractor, as with changes in farming methods many jobs that were previously done by the farm's own labour are now let out to contractors, such as shearing, hay or silage harvest and combining grain.

Electricity has changed the household work, washing by machine, easy cooking, hot water 24 hours a day, baths, showers etc. television, radio, videos and computers. In 1980 a self contained flat was created from what appeared to be the oldest part of the house, which in former times had been used as bedrooms for the farm workers who lived in. There are no pigs kept now, and the poultry are only to provide eggs etc. for the family.

Ann Matthews

John Matthews as a boy

Fairfield

Fairfield was built on a field once belonging to Jack and Bill Evans from The Vedw. This was bought by Doctor M. Hilderbrand. The plans for the house were drawn up by Harper and Sperring Architects from Cradley Heath, the builders were Edwards & Sons of Knighton. The property was completed in 1961.

Roy and I moved into Fairfield in March 1993. After a visit to friends in Knucklas we were so impressed by the beauty and quietness of the valley after the hustle and bustle of the South Coast that we decided it was the place to spend our retirement.

Fairfield

After a long search we were given details of Fairfield and we decided it was the place for us. The grounds have approximately twenty different species of tree, some quite rare, and we liked the unusual design of the house itself.

We have made a few improvements, enlarging the kitchen, installing a new fireplace, shower rooms etc. The garden has taken a lot of hard work but is very worthwhile. The local people have been very friendly and welcomed us into their midst.

Pat Middleton

Garbett Hall

Maurice and Edith Price bought Garbett Hall in 1920. Maurice, one of five children, was born at Cefn Vron and Edith, (nee Griffiths), one of thirteen children, was born at Bwlch Llananno. They had six children themselves and moved from Cwm Mawr to Garbett Old House, which is believed to have been built in 1560.

Mr & Mrs Price who bought Garbett Hall in 1920

The house had a wash house with two copper boilers with fires underneath them: one was used for boiling clothes and the other when a pig was killed. Joining the wash house was a back kitchen with a range and baking oven, which was used to bake the bread once a week. There was a large hook lodged in a beam to hang the pig. This room was also used to feather the geese and turkeys. Down a passage was the dairy, where the milk was stored in leds (vats). This was then used to make butter. Also in this room was a salting stone on which to cure the bacon. Down in the cellar were barrels of cider and rhubarb wine. In the living room there were flag stones on the floor, and there was an open black range, which was used to hang pots over the fire, with a hook to hang the kettle on. Underneath the fire place was a concealed ash pit, which was emptied once a week. Baths were taken in this room, in a tin bath in front of the open fire. There was another room, the front room, which was not used very much. An oak staircase led up to four bedrooms and another removable staircase led on up again into the attic.

On the farm they used to keep sheep, cattle, horses, hens, ducks, geese and turkeys. Rabbits were caught using ferret nets and a spade and the money earned from selling these was used for buying groceries. In the '30s sheep and cattle were a poor price, but the farmers were much better off after the late '40s with subsidies paid by the Government. The sheep were taken to Knighton market from most farms in the area. They came over the hills from Newcastle-on-Clun, past Garbett Hall, with four miles still to walk before reaching Knighton.

Garbett Hall

The children from Garbett Hall went to school at Llanfair Waterdine. They walked over the fields which were mostly covered with bracken, and the hedges were fairly open. Not many fields were ploughed and seeded - the years of subsidies and tractors had not yet come. On their journey to school the workmen in the fields used to give them a drink of cider from their kostrell (a small wooden barrel). There were rabbits everywhere, and the Hereford cattle that they passed had long horns. Close to Llanfair, the farmer with the best sheep would be pouring corn into troughs for them. While they were eating he would have a pipe of tobacco and then turn the troughs back over again. If you wanted a pig killed, he was the man to do it. He carried a gun to shoot rabbits, and his apron under his arm. He had a brother who was lovingly known as Uncle Bill, who used to give Easter Eggs to most of the children of Llanfair. He was also the Church Clerk and used to blow the organ - a great chap.

Onoff Tortoriello in his uniform

There were good neighbours at Garbett, and the children from a neighbouring farm, just up the road, used to walk to school together. Although they have now moved away, they still keep in touch. Down the road was another farm where, in the early 1940s, a young man came to work on the farm (not by choice). He came from a peasant farm among the mountains in Sicily to the hills of Shropshire. He came with several others who went to work on other farms. They worked for food and a few shillings, whatever the farmer thought fit to give them. He was not able to speak English, but was soon taught a few words by the local men and maid servants. He used to go to Knucklas in the evenings to meet up with friends from Italy, and to mix with the "senoritas". He later met a local girl. They married and had four children and eight grandchildren. Most of his friends returned to Italy, but a few stayed in England to farm at Lingen, Presteigne etc. The family is still at Garbett Hall, trading as Price Bros. Their son Keith with Dana and their two sons Sean and Mark now live at and farm Garbett Hall. It is about 268 acres and carries about 850 sheep and 25 cattle. The house was restored in the 1980's. Keith wins many prizes at Knighton Christmas Fatstock market. In 1964 The New House was built and Onoff and Cecilia Tortoriello now live there.

The New House

Garbett Villa

We bought Garbett Villa when I still had about 7 years to do in the Birmingham Police Force "for my pension". It had been put up for auction in Knighton with a reserve of £1300, but that price was not reached and we bought it for £1050. As it stood it was a stone built, slated roof cottage, "2 up and 2 down". A man named Jones who had previously lived in the house and had been a carpenter had built a wooden extension on the North side of the house and had cut a doorway through to it. It consisted of a garage, kitchen and bathroom. There was a bath in the bathroom but it wasn't plumbed in so although the Rayburn gave hot water we had to put a piece of hosepipe on the hot tap of the washbasin and lead it into the bath. The water came from a spring which ran into an underground tank and from there it was pumped, by hand, into a tank in the loft. The non-return valve on the pump was broken so we had to prime the pump every time we used it. The windows in the house were all very small, with iron frames and small panes of glass and outside the front door there was a wooden porch reminiscent of Buckingham Palace. The guardsman was NOT supplied! Attached to the gable end of the house was an outbuilding, for want of a better word. It was built of stone, brick, slate, asbestos, wood, and in one place, plasterboard. It housed the water pump and the coal, (and rubbish).

"The man from the Council" came to have a look at the house and declared that, as it stood, it was not fit for habitation. However, he offered us a £1000 improvement grant if we were prepared to have everything put right!!. We were.

Garbett Villa in 1960

Today it has been re-roofed, felted and insulated, a damp membrane inserted, double glazed and centrally heated. We have replaced the sentry box with a stone porch and added a double glazed sun room. The electric water pump automatically fills the tank in the loft and we are at the moment in the process of having a rectifier fitted which will correct the fact that our water, although pure, is slightly acid. The septic tank was completely replaced and gives no trouble at all. The wooden extension was demolished and rebuilt in stone block to give a bathroom with shower and toilet and a kitchen which is fully fitted. The "outbuilding" was demolished and rebuilt, also in stone block and provides a workshop with room for my beekeeping equipment and also a two stall loose box where for some years we kept two goats. We were very fond of them and only gave them up to a good home when the strain of milking twice a day 365 days a year became too much. They were very tame and quiet and we used to take them for walks along with the dogs and cat, much to our neighbours amusement. The garden soil is very good and our good neighbours are always ready to supply manure so we grow vegetables, a lot of soft fruit, and the greenhouse supplies pot plants, tomatoes and black grapes.

Garbett Villa in 1999

Both Joan and I have a country background and we have run the whole gamut of country pursuits. We have kept poultry and laying ducks, but in spite of a gun and dogs the foxes beat us and we had to give them up. We have also bred table rabbits, which have got to be the most delicious meat there is. We have made wine from wild fruit and berries and we now make some from our own grapes. With the help of our Italian neighbour and good friend, Onnif, at Garbett Hall I am now in the process of extending this to have an outdoor vineyard.

As we are only about 100 yards from the Offas Dyke Path, some years ago we installed a picnic table on the paved area in front of the house and put two small signs on the path indicating that we were prepared to supply tea, coffee, cakes, etc. This has been a success in that we can truthfully say "we don't make much money but we meet some very nice people". We have literally had people from all over the world here. Large numbers of Dutch walkers, but also Australians, Canadians and Americans. We once had a letter from New York from a lady who said that now she was back in New York she thought longingly of us living here. I think part of the success has been Joan's Welsh cakes, which we serve warmed up in the "Micro". One man who came here said he had been told about these Welsh cakes by a man he met in Boston, U.S.A.!. There is another side to this enterprise, we have two collecting boxes on the table, one for the C of E Childrens Society and the other for Guide Dogs for the Blind. Almost everyone who comes here contributes (some people leave a "tip" and we put that in as well) and we have collected large sums for both charities. Last year we were given a presentation photo of a guide dog for being the top collectors in the area. People are very kind.

When you read about the trouble and strife all over the world it makes one very thankful that we live in a place like this. We have never heard as much as a cross word in the 22 years we have lived here, and we certainly never intend leaving.

Personnel

Joan Beatrice Thomas.

Born in Birmingham 1922. After school worked in offices, typing, shorthand and book keeping. After the war started in 1939 there was a call for women to take over men's jobs and she went as a conductress on the Midland Red buses which ran to various parts of the Midlands. Her home was bombed during the war and she went to live with a married sister in another part of the City. At the end of 1943 she moved down to Upton on Severn and lived with a family who had also been bombed out by the same bomb and had moved down to a cottage. Here she worked for the American Army base at Ashchurch, near Tewkesbury, firstly in the office and later as canteen manageress. After 1946 she and her husband lived on farms in the area until 1950 when he joined the Birmingham City Police. They lived in Birmingham until 1976 when they moved down to Garbett Villa. She is very keen on cooking and was a founder member of Knighton W.I. Market and regularly enters cookery classes at the local shows, with considerable success. At the age of 76 she is presently engaged in learning to speak French with the help of a course on the computer.

Sidney John Thomas.

Born in Shelfield, near Walsall in 1920. Later moved to Lichfield, Staffs., and then to Birmingham where he got a scholarship to a commercial school and studied economics, shorthand and typing and German. When he was 17 he met Joan and joined the Territorial Army. Coming from a Railway family he went to work for them and when he was mobilised for the war went to a Railway Unit of Royal Engineers at Derby and then to France. After returning in 1940 he went into Combined Operations and went on the landings in North Africa and then Normandy. He was in Germany when the war ended and was retained in Hamburg for several months using his German to sort out returning German prisoners of war and their families. After being demobilised he worked for 3 or 4 years on farms and then joined the Birmingham Police. After a period on the beat he became a Traffic Patrol Car driver and because of the fact that he had a firearms instructors rating was put in the Explosives and Firearms Dept. For the last 5 years of his service he was engaged mainly in dealing with I.R.A. terrorist acts including the Birmingham Pub Bombs, but managed to survive long enough to retire. After moving to Knighton he worked for about 5 years for Ranks at their fuel depot at Bucknell. Is now a keen bee-keeper, in fact Joan says he is a bee bore, only she spells it B Bore!

Joan and Sid.

Have three children. A son who went to King Edwards Grammar School and thence to Sandhurst and was an Army Officer for about 26 years. He speaks 4 languages and is a computer expert. Our eldest daughter is a hairdresser and the younger daughter took an H.N.D. in Catering . She also at the age of 15, had a brain tumour and was only saved by the expertise of the Doctors in Birmingham and the use of Cobalt Ray treatment. They have 5 children between them, all very good kids, none of them "problem children" two have degrees and one is a company accountant. We also, now, have a great grand daughter born about 3 years ago but mentally going on 15. We married when I came back from North Africa at Christmas 1942 so have now been married nearly 56 years and as far as I am concerned "it ain't been a day too long".

Sid Thomas

Goodwin Cottage

Goodwin Cottage has been owned by relatives of Mr. and Mrs. Davies who lived there until their deaths in 1954 and 1960. Many branches of the family have lived there since. There have been other houses on the site before the present one. In 1891 Jeremiah Baylis, a labourer aged 66, his wife Elizabeth also aged 66 and their 10 years old grandson Charles lived in the cottage. In the 1861 census the first mention of Goodwin or "Gooding" cottage and the "Spite House" shows that two Baylis families lived in the cottages. The men appear to have been father and son. Jeremiah aged 69, a labourer and his wife Ann 60, lived at Gooding Cottage and Jeremiah, also a labourer, aged 39 with his wife Elizabeth, also 39 and their children Jane 12, Mary 5, and Elizabeth 2 lived in the Spite House. The Spite House is said to have got it's name because when it was being built the walls used to "fall down" while the builder was away. Local people believed that either somebody didn't want the house built, or the house itself was spiteful!

Goodwin Cottage in early spring

Graig Cottage

Oscar Serck, who built Graig Cottage and Lower Graig, left Russia with his family in about 1917. They arrived in this country sometime later having journeyed here via Scandinavia. He owned a company manufacturing car radiators in Birmingham called Serck Radiators. In about 1938 he bought an acre of land bordering the River Teme from the Beavans at the Graig and built a house for himself and a smaller one in the grounds, which is now Graig Cottage, where his sister Vera used to stay. He was apparently a large and loud man of an inventive turn of mind who always spoke with a strong accent. He employed several local people to build his properties. At first he used the house as a country retreat and he would bring his friends to shoot and fish etc. Gradually it became his main residence. His daughter, Mrs. Stafford, inherited the properties, put in mains water and sold Graig Cottage (known to some locals as the Doll's House because of its quaint appearance) with a small area of land to Ian and Ann Perry in 1980. Ian was a potter,

Graig Cottage before renovation

Ann a junior school teacher and they had two children. They bought an extension to their land down to the river. They advertised the property in the Guardian Newspaper, offering it for sale in order of it's attractions, the river, the garage (built as a pottery) and the house. We bought it in 1983. Before moving-in in 1984 we spent school holidays putting in a septic tank and drainage and thinning out the fir trees which proved to be a good way of getting rid of moles. In 1983 Graig Cottage (Waterdine Pottery as it was then) was a tiny house with one room downstairs with a bath behind the chimney and two rooms upstairs and a lean-to wooden kitchen. I remember happily sleeping on mattresses on the floor, watching the river flow past and using the 'Elsan' outside in a shed, Andrew's ginger beer exploding and hitting the ceiling and then filling our dinner plates and David stamping on the wet ground to attract worms for fishing bait. We had a goat, chickens and ducks on the river and tried to grow vegetables.

Graig Cottage after renovation

The roof of the house was corrugated asbestos and the walls were one brick thick strengthened by brick pillars which amazed the building Inspector because of their strength and dryness. Many conifers and birches on the site must have reminded Mr. Serck of his Russian childhood. Over the next three years we built on a large kitchen, bedroom and bathroom and re-roofed the house. We improved the garage to live in whilst the house had no roof. In about 1991 we built on to the South side of the house a ground floor living area for elderly relatives and extended the bedroom above. When we moved to Llanfair from Yorkshire in 1984 we were a family of four: John Boast a retired Metallurgist/Steel Salesman from Sheffield. Philippa Boast Art Teacher, Painter originally from Hereford. Andrew aged 12 and David aged 10. Two older daughters, Helena and Melanie were at Universities and only home in the holidays. On our retirement we had plans to renovate or build our own house. We moved here to be nearer to my Mother in Hereford and to give us all the benefit of the countryside and more space and to some extent to escape the roughness and materialism we experienced near Leeds. In many ways the boys

The Boast family

An Otter

benefited from a gentler approach to life but they gravitated to the Navy and Hereford as they grew up, in search of more life and excitement. Some of the things we have enjoyed here which were different from urban life were the mixed social gatherings with all ages together and village fairs where children could take part instead of just watching the experts. We loved the lack of footpath signs and restrictions on walking. We found Llanfair a most welcoming and friendly place. The interest people take in each other in a sparsely populated area can be helpful and reassuring though the anonymity of town life can have benefits too. There were very few children in the parish when we came but happily numbers are increasing now. Even in the short time we have been here there have been changes. We regret the loss of the village shop/Post Office and wish there was more public transport.

From the point of view of wildlife Llanfair is a wonderful place to live. The badger population has increased hugely due to their protection by Law and there are setts and signs everywhere. We often see polecats and there are otter signs down by the river, especially in the snow, when one can see where they have slid and run and rolled in and out of the water. We hear foxes and tawny owls at night. There are kingfishers, dippers and goosanders on the river. The fish population has declined seriously recently. We have seen the occasional red kite and buzzards are very common. I think the hare population has decreased recently and the rabbits come and go due to myxomatosis. I counted 386 pipistrelle bats coming out of our roofspace this summer.

Philippa Boast

1 and 2 Graig Wood Cottages

Graig Wood Cottage (No 1.)

Graig Wood Cottage is a semi-detached house built approximately 40 years ago as a farm labourers dwelling and belongs to the Graig Farm.

The building stands adjacent to the lane running through Graig Wood and in May is surrounded by a mass of bluebells .The wood is home to a large variety of wild animals and birds. The lane passes through to the Graig and then on to the Offa's Dyke Path. Walkers coming off the path call by to chat to Mr. & Mrs. Pearson on their way past and all marvel at the unspoilt beauty of the area.

Mr. and Mrs. Pearson moved to Graig Wood in 1984 after retiring from the industrial area of the Black Country. Their son William joined them in 1994 and occupies himself by doing gardening and other tasks for people in the Parish.

3 Graig Wood Cottages

Hawthorn Cottage

Hawthorn Cottage is situated in the village and was built in 1790. The first school classes held in Llanfair were in a small schoolroom in the cottage. The Bowen family moved-in in 1891 and their son and daughter Mary and Alfred lived there until their deaths in 1964 and 1965. Mary was an expert needlewoman and dressmaker and later when school lunches were provided at Llanfair school she took responsibility for serving the meals and washing up. The meals were delivered on a daily basis from Knighton where they were cooked. Her brother Fred was the postman for many years and rode his bicycle around the parish every day whatever the weather.

Church Day about 1910 with Hawthorn Cottage

Hawthorn Cottage and the Old Tithe Barn

On their deaths Elizabeth Gwilt from Cwm Collo bought the cottage and it is now owned by her daughter Hazel. In 1993 the interior of Hawthorn Cottage was used as a film set for the film "Second Best" which starred William Hurt. Many local people appeared in the cast and for the six months the cottage was occupied by the film crew a great deal of excitement was generated locally.

Dresses made by Mary Bowen - she didn't use a pattern!

Hawthorn Cottage 1999

Hazeldene

The first house in Llanfair Parish, as you travel from Knighton.

It was our very happy home from 1938 — 1977 and is still owned and lived in by a member of our family. Our father, Hubert Bright, was born in Llanfair Parish at 'Llanwoolly' in the late 1800's. He attended Llanfair School with his seven brothers and sisters and Mr. Matkin was Headmaster at that time. On leaving School he went to the Army and served through the 1914-1918 War. On his return to civilian life he met and married our mother, Alice Owen, who was born at Letton nr. Brampton Bryan. They proceeded to have seven children, all of whom are alive today.

In 1938 our parents moved with us from Knucklas Road, Knighton and bought Hazeldene — which our father always said was on the sunnyside. He was a carpenter/joiner by trade and also a wonderful gardener, growing vegetables and fruit to supply us all the year round — which was no small feat with a large family —we also kept a pig and always had chickens and, luckily, all through the second World War were never short of food. Mother was a wonderful provider also, who hardly ever went from home.

We have several memories which we think may be of interest.

We remember Mr. Tom Price around 1940, who then farmed at Upper Panpwnton, who had the misfortune to fall from a load of hay and break his neck.

Around 1942 another old man, known as Tommy 'Treacle' Price, lived in a caravan at the bottom of Panpwnton Hill. Unfortunately his caravan caught fire during the night and all that was left the next morning were the metal rims from the wheels. (His faithful dog perished with him).

Hazeldene, a view of the garden

Further up Panpwnton Hill was another little hut (which is still there today) and in there lived an old gentleman, Mr. Tom Griffiths. He spent many hours standing at the stile, which looks down towards the river Teme and no-one passed that way without a long chat. He was related in some way to Mrs. Gough, who with her husband Tom and her son and daughter in law, Wilf and Elsie, farmed at Panpwnton. Wilf had quite a varied life being a farmer by day — with a herd of milking cows. He had a daily local milk round delivering milk from door to door. On Saturday mornings he would do the weekly collection of refuse from all the houses in Kinsley Road with his horse and cart and a couple of days each week he would again take his horse and cart and go to Knighton Station and offload coal from the railway trucks and take it to the local Gas Works in Station Road — where the gas was produced for the whole of Knighton. At night he would transform and after a quick wash and brush up he would be driving off again with his dance band, known as 'The Wilf Gough Band' or 'The Scarlet Troubadours' if it was a posh affair. He was a wonderful musician and his band was well known over a wide area.

In 1953, what an achievement!! Mount Everest was conquered and the leader of the expedition was none other than Sir John Hunt, of Weir Cottage. What a memorable day when the news came through. On his return great celebrations took place and Sir John was met at the parish boundary and pulled to his home on a governess cart. Everyone in the vicinity was very proud and pleased to join in the celebrations.

The Bright family.

Herb Cottage

According to the census (1851) Skyborry Green (the place of the barns?) was quite a large thriving community. The area included four dwellings and a wheelwrights shop. The cottages comprised Skyborry Green farmhouse which was actually two houses, Oak Cottage where Stan Davies lives and Herb Cottage which I believe to be the oldest. It would be interesting to sort out the names and discover who lived where. Most of the men were involved in farming; some were carters, wheelwrights and stonemasons and the women housewives servants and some dressmakers. After a fasinating chat with Jos Williams I discovered that her great grandfather was a stonemason called Griffiths— a name that constantly recurs between 1851—1891. She said he may have been involved in the building of Knucklas viaduct and I suppose it's just possible that the family may have been employed on the estate earlier in the century. Another name that often crops up is Francis. They were mainly wheelwrights and doubtless worked in the shop where Ray Matthews now has his contracting yard. By 1881 Arthur Francis was employing men so he probably owned the business.

The whole of the Skyborry estate was in the hands of absentee landlords. The deeds of Herb Cottage which only go back to 1913 reveal that the Edwards family from Middlesex were in possession then and had probably bought it some years before that. There is a plaque in Llanfair church to the memory of Alfred Edwards who died of a fever in South Africa in 1903 aged 31. A.E. Bechley Crundall (a name to conjure with) was the next landlord but I cannot trace any definite dates. William and Fanny Price of Top Row Lloyney acquired the estate around 1946 and it was almost immediately offered at auction in July 47. The Cummins family were of course living in the main house and had been there since 1936 They bought the farmhouse and about twelve acres of land but most of the rest, including Herb Cottage, was unsold.

Regarding the tenants of Herb Cottage the earliest I can trace is a family called Cookson and can find out nothing about them. They are remembered by John Matthews of Cwm Sannum and Di Evans of Kinsley Rd. John who walked to Llanair school with his brother David tells me they were there in the mid 1920s. A little later the name Gough is remembered by Di who recalls going to a firework party at Herb Cottage. The next occupants were the Stephens family. Owen helped in the garden at Skyborry Farm and his wife, Millie in the house. Hazel Lewis (who now lives in Knighton,) their daughter moved to Herb Cottage as a baby. Her parents probably moved there in 1933/4 and they had left by 1938. This was when Miss Jones became a tenant, with her old and very arthritic mother. Miss Jones herself was also to become disabled but she is well remembered as a very pleasant person who took an active part in the community. She was involved in the local youth club at Llanfair and produced plays for the amateur dramatic society. During the war she collected foxgloves, which grew then in even greater profusion than now. The digatalis was needed for medicine. Her elder1y mother died at Herb Cottage and Miss Jones purchased the property in 1950. This is the first time Herb Cottage went into private ownership. She sold

Herb Cottage 1991

in 1957 to a Mr. and Mrs. Foster from Cheshire. Miss Jones died in a home in Church Stretton. The Fosters lived at Herb Cottage for 20 years. They built the garage and probably put in the bay window as the old window frame was discovered in the garden by Michael Shoesmith the subsequent owner. He and his wife Jill bought Herb Cottage in 1978 and made some extensive repairs. Steve and I came in September 1988 and in the following year obtained planning permission for an extension. We purchased a piece of land from the Matthews and extended the cottage to include a largish lounge and bedroom above. We also built on at the back to make a bigger kitchen with bathroom above also, putting a new window to the West and blocking the door leading to the garden. We installed a Rayburn in the chimney space, sadly losing the old bread oven. However, we were delighted with the results of our rather big 'spend' and considered the appearance of the cottage much improved with the porch now central and the whole more balanced. In 91 we replaced the crumbling front porch with an exact replica. We also errected a greenhouse and a new shed at the rear of the garden.

In many ways coming to the valley reminded us of when we first moved to the Isle of Wight in 53 — the same quiet unspoiled countryside, friendly people and farming very much family based. We felt immediately happily at home here. As a besotted bird watcher I was delighted to have a close aquaintance with nuthatches! They didn't like flying across the Solent so we never saw them on the Island.

To sum up I consider myself very lucky to live here and wish that Steve had been able to enjoy a longer retirement in a place we both loved.

Brenda Ross.

Escalating house prices Herb Cottage was on offer in '78 at £15,750 and in '88 at £80.000.

Hidmore

Hidmore was sold by Fred Thomas in 1981. It is now occupied by Robert Thomas aged 29, his wife Annette 27 and their three young sons Ieuan aged 5, Gethyn aged 3 and Huw aged 1.

When Fred Thomas farmed Hidmore he kept Hereford cattle and Clun sheep. It is said locally, that the first Clun sheep were actually bred at Hidmore. The present house was built in the 1960's. The previous stone house fell into disrepair and was knocked down. Before Robert and Annette moved there the house was used as a holiday cottage. It is now a sheep and beef farm and the children already show signs of being interested in animal husbandry there being five cats three dogs and two pet rabbits called Bisto and Daisy.

Ieuan, Gethyn and Huw

Hidmore

Hill House

Gene Davies lives at Hill House alone but his mother Violet Bufton who lives in Clun tries to visit every day. He was born in the wooden bungalow across the road from Hill House. He farms land belonging to both dwellings which amounts to about 140 acres. Hill House was built in the 1880's and appears in the census of 1891 when William Harding aged 41 a labourer and Ann Wilding his housekeeper aged 36, a widow lived there. If other houses existed on the site one could have been called Hill Top. This appears on the census of 1861 when a Gough family lived there. Any other building was probably called Stoneypound - a name which related to a patch of land on which two or three houses were built.

Hill House

Stoneypound bungalow was built in the 1920's by Gene's grandfather. There was certainly a house there before. The flag floors and the remains of a stone wall were found when the barns were being built.

Gene has discovered that his great uncle, George Cadwallader lived at what is now Lower Bryn Bedw and kept his horses on Stoneypound land. He has a field near Offa's Dyke which has always been known as George's Field. George was a haulier who was given a watch for his 21st birthday in 1903. When he was not working he hung it on a nail in the chimney breast at Lower Bryn Bedw. It has been owned by several people but is now back on the original nail in the fireplace.

Hurgin

Within local memory there have been two holdings called Hurgin. According to the census 1841 to 1891 there were often three or four. The Hurgin near Blaen-y-dre burned down in the early 1950's and has not been rebuilt since. It was, at that time occupied by two men with the surnames Smith and Pritchard. They earned a living through general dealing and rabbit catching. The Hurgin which is occupied at present by Barry and Kate Hicken and their son Dean is situated on the hillside above the Lower Wain. According to the census of 1891 John Breeze aged 42 lived at the Hurgin with his wife Mary aged 30 and their children George 13, William 10, Susan 7 and Ellen a baby. John Breeze is the first person in Llanfair to state his occupation as Mechanic in the census of 1891. The Breeze family remained in Llanfair for many years and relatives still live locally and in Aberystwyth. A Mr. John Breeze owned a threshing box which was used locally up until the 1940's. He was probably the son of George or William.

John Breeze with his threashing box at Wernygeufron

Hurgin 1999

In about 1940 the Barnett family went to live at the Hurgin having been at Bryn Bedw until then. The house and land were later owned by Mr. Hughie Gardner who sold the house to a young city couple in the 1960's. They quickly sold it again and it changed hands several times until Barry and his family arrived. The land is still farmed by David Gardner who lives near the Anchor.

The House is said to be haunted and local people tell dramatic stories about a murder at the turn of the century. It is said that doors fly open and that dogs dislike going into the house and tend to whine and bark to get out. The present occupiers Barry and Kate have had no ghost problems and Barry writes:- We bought the property from a couple from Surrey who owned it for less than a year. They had bought it from Mrs. Sanso, a Canadian lady, who had lived there for several years. The Hurgin appears to have been a meeting house as it is situated where four public footpaths converge. Kate and I have lived here for six years with our son Dean who has Down's syndrome.

Kate and I met and got married while we were Zoo keepers at Dudley Zoo. I now run a Landscape and Building Construction business and Kate looks after the Pet's Corner at Weston Park in the Midlands, Lord Bradford's Estate. We breed German Shepherd dogs which are trained for Police work and for Civilian Working Trials.

Lady Croft. Empty in 1999.

Lane House, Skyborry

The present owners are Robert H. E. Bailey (Bob) and Diana J. Bailey (Di) husband and wife. We are both in our mid fifties. We bought the house in July 1996 from Christopher and Lesley Pimm Jones.

Bob works as a farms manager on a 1800+ acre arable and dairy farm in Bedfordshire.

We are currently renovating the cottage which will be our home when we retire. As newcomers to the area we are very happy to find the village has a thriving community. Many families have been in the village for several generations. It is very much a livestock farming area with beef and sheep. We have been made to feel very welcome and have made a lot of new friends and acquaintances. It is a three hour car journey of 150 miles from our home in Bedfordshire.

When we bought the cottage it had been empty for about seven months. The garden, which contained quite a few ornamental shrubs, was waist high in weeds, especially chicory and tall coarse grasses.

The cottage was built from local stone. The walls were made in two parts and infilled with stone and rubble. The east facing gable end wall was badly bowed and had large cracks running down one side. We were advised by a local civil engineer that the wall would need taking down and rebuilding or a complicated system of pinning could be carried out to secure it for an indefinite period of time. We opted to have the wall dismantled and rebuilt. Planning consent was obtained and the work was carried out in September 1996. The wall was rebuilt in concrete blocks because it was to be roughcast rendered on the outside and painted.

Lane House

The cottage consisted of a living room with a Rayburn range, and a large hall with a very narrow staircase. The landing served as a bedroom but provided very little privacy for the user! There was a larger bedroom over the living room.

Access from the hall through a narrow doorway leads to a single skinned lean-to living room with a bathroom leading off. This was very cold and damp.

The previous owners had an extension built on the west end of the cottage consisting of an integral garage with stone steps leading to a large room above. This extension was only a shell when we bought the cottage. It was built by a well known local builder, Mr. Robert Gwilt of Llanfairwaterdine. There was no connecting doorway between the existing cottage and the garage. Robert Gwilt made a doorway through in 1997.

All our free time since buying The Lane House has been taken up by renovation work.

On the Enclosure Map of 1853 the House and garden was No. 1350a. It consisted of 1 r. 8 p. (1214 M_2) and was owned by the Earl of Powis. The annual rent was £4. 3. Od. (£4.15) per annum and the tenant was Mr. Edward Price. Also shown adjoining the south border of the garden was a small area of land No. 1350 and marked "nursery". It was shown as farmed by Monaughty Poeth in the Schedule. This piece of land is no longer identified on current maps and its past existence cannot be detected by walking in the field where it once was.

Edward Price (aged 45 yrs) and Jane Price (45 yrs), John Price (l2yrs) and Mary Watkins (23yrs) were occupiers of the cottage at the 1841 Census. Edward and Jane Price were still occupying the cottage at the 1851 Census. At this time their daughters Margaret, and Mary Griffiths were also on the Census. By 1861 Edward Price, Vaughn Amis and Mary Griffiths were shown on the Census but *not* Jane Price.

In 1881 George and Emma(wife) Maund, Cathrine, Sarah and Edith were the occupiers. George Maund was classed as an agricultural labourer. Unfortunately, I have no record of the ownership of the cottage during these years but assume it still belonged to the Earl of Powis.

In the 1891 Census, Entry No. 34, the occupiers were Aaron James, agricultural labourer, his wife Charlotte, and Charles, Ada and Cecil.

The period between 1892 - 1975 has not been researched.

In May 1975 the owners, C.E. & C.H. Barnhurst, sold to B. & C. Gregory. Mr. & Mrs. Gregory owned the cottage for just over ten years and then they sold it to Christopher and Lesley Pimm Jones who had two children, Ben and Amber.

In February 1998 Bob and I and our three adult sons demolished the lean-to living room and bathroom. We built an en suite shower/toilet in the room above the garage. During the summer of 1998 Robert Gwilt built a new lean-to to house a new kitchen and bathroom. It was built to enable the cottage roof to be continued straight over the lean-to without a visible join. Bob and I have carried out the majority of the internal renovation ourselves. We have replumbed and re-wired the cottage.

There are the remains of some building foundations near the south west corner of the garden fence. We are told by a neighbour that this was the site of a pigsty. It was common for villagers to keep pigs and cure their meat before and during the 1939/45 war and even a few years after the war.

There is a large shed in the south west corner of the garden which was used as a studio by a previous occupier and which we now use as a garden shed/workshop.

There is a well in the garden approximately two metres from the door in the east end of the lean-to extension. Some years prior to 1986 water was pumped daily from this well into water tanks against the back of the cottage. This water was used for drinking, washing and for the W.C. There was no bathroom at this time and the W.C. was entered by an outside door and stood at the east end of the south facing back wall. The cottage also has a right of way to collect water from the well in the field on the opposite side of the road. Presumably this would have been used if the house well ever ran dry.

Mr. & Mrs. Pimm Jones had a borehole made in the garden during their ownership and this now provides all the water for the cottage. It is pumped automatically by electricity into a water tank in the loft and is controlled by a floatswitch. When the water in the tank drops to a certain level the electricity is switched on and water is pumped until the tank is full again.

Christopher and Lesley Pimm Jones installed the Rayburn cooking range in the living room which was also used to heat radiators and water. They also blocked up the front doorway, which faced north, and put a window in the top section. We have removed the Rayburn and installed an oilfired boiler (kerosene) in the garage to heat the radiators and water. We have opened up the fireplace in the living room and have a grate to burn wood logs. We like an open fire to look at and we have a radiator for additional warmth.

We have stripped the paint from the stone walls in the living room and kitchen by "sand" blasting. We are leaving the walls as natural stone.

The cottage has cesspool drainage and new drains were laid in 1998.

Little Graig

I live at The Little Graig with my daughters Jessica who is 12 and Michelle who is 10. We have two dogs and two guinea pigs. We rent the house from the Beavan family. It was the home of Mary Beavan who was Fred's sister and it had been empty for a short time when we moved in. There are so many wonderful reasons for living here, it's too difficult to put them down in order so I shall just say what I have to say in any order. The first thing that I love is the countryside. No matter what the weather it is always breathtaking. I can walk up to The Dyke and on a cold day the wind feels as though it can actually cut you, it is so exhilarating or one can go further down and be sheltered and take a walk in the lanes or in the Graigwoods and smells and sounds are utterly different from the Dyke. There are many old-fashioned wild plants and I feel it is a privilege to see birds and animals which I have never seen close up before in their natural environment.

Then there is the river, we are so lucky here, we can hear it and see it from the house. I can easily become transfixed just looking at it. On some days it is sparkling in the sun and very gentle, on wet days it is rushing and swirling and brown where the bottom has been disturbed. The children love it. They swim in it on sunny days, spend hours exploring, and come back really excited and happy. They take the dogs to swim. The young dog jumps in and splashes everyone around him. The old dog paddles carefully, sniffing each stone before he ventures further in. Our neighbours, Philippa and John Boast lend the girls their canoe sometimes and they have an adventure shrieking and giggling and trying to stay upright.

A Heron in the Teme

Then there are the people. Everyone here has made us so welcome even though we are 'from off'. It really does feel like home to us because everyone has been so kind. I love the good oldfashioned values that were instilled in me when I was young, and for my girls to see this all around them and experience it, to become part of it is so important. Politeness, respect, thoughtfulness and the things that sometimes get lost in modern society are so strong here in everyone. The age gap between generations doesn't seem to matter. I feel I can go either to friends of my own age or to older friends and I would be sure of help if I needed it.

The church is important of course, it has always been part of our lives wherever we have lived. St. Marys has a friendly family feel to it. There are no grand choirs, just the congregation trying our hardest to sing in tune which I can't manage but I am glad to say some people can. The church is lovely and peaceful and full of spiritual goodness.

Little Graig

The village hall is quite a hive of activity. Six of us parents have recently started a Youth Club there for which we have had fantastic support from everyone in Llanfair. We entertain twenty to thirty children each week with various activities including pool, bar skittles, table tennis, juggling, soft hockey, disco, tee-shirt painting etc. We always end the evening using the village hall library. The connection with John Hunt is significant to the Youth Club. I didn't have the opportunity of meeting him but Andrew Beavan told us in his opening speech when we started the youth club that John would have loved it and supported it wholeheartedly. It was quite a poignant moment as at John's memorial service a collection had been made for the youth Club.

We have many meetings in connection with the youth club usually at least once a month, which brings me nicely to The Red Lion. It is a cosy and good meeting place whether we drink beer or tomato juice we always have a pleasant evening.

To sum up my view of Llanfair Waterdine in a nutshell. It is the feeling I get about living here that's important. It's wonderful.

Kate Martin

Little Selley

Little Selley is a farm situated at the head of a valley of a tributary of the River Teme. In the 19th and early 20th century the farm was known as Cwm - y - Grant, this name possibly deriving from the Welsh for "Cwm" meaning Valley, "y" - of the, and possibly "garnant" -small brook, which may have been shortened over time to "grant", giving the "Valley of the small brooks", which is an apt description of the situation of Little Selley. The name Little Selley is possibly derived from a legal document from the late 1800's which describes the property as "Cwm-y-grant on the little Selley road".

Originally a farm in its own right Little Selley has been merged in more recent years since the second world war with land that surrounded a cottage then known as New House, now, Garbett Villa, and is now combined with the adjoining Selley Hall.

The house itself is of mainly stone built construction with the date of building being unknown. The house is estimated as being at least 400 years old and was built with cow sheds at either end under the same roof to provide warmth for the house in the winter from the housed cattle. One of the end cow sheds was converted in the 1950's into the dining room and bedroom above. The other end cow shed is now the garage. The ceilings in the house are very low, with many being well under seven foot, (2.1 metres), in height. The walls of the house are over 2 feet (0.6 metres) thick in many places with a very large fireplace and chimney at the centre of the house. An extension to the back of the house was added in the 1950's with a grant under the then farm improvement scheme. A pigsty is also attached to one end of the house, a pig being reared in the sty for consumption in the house until the 1970's. If the pig became ill, one of the cures would be to collect a gallon of beer, mainly slops, from the pub and feed it to the pig, who would promptly go to sleep for around 24 hours and would wake feeling somewhat better, supposedly!.

Little Selley

Records show the farm being sold in 1854 and then in the early years of the 20th century the owner of Little Selley lived in Hereford and owned further property in and around Hereford including warehouses in Maylord Street. The house and farm was then the subject of a dispute between the descendants, granddaughters of a previous owner, and someone who had lent money against the farm to some of the grandaughter's husbands to set up in business. The lender then claimed the farm upon the failure of whatever business the money was lent to and after the death of the original owners' two daughters when the property should have passed to the four grandchildren. This led to a dispute between the two grandchildren who were still alive and also with the lender as to the legality of the lender's claim and the distribution of any monies from the property. The property was eventually let in 1911 to a John Jarman and then to George Watkins.

The property was eventually acquired by George Watkins. During the 1939 - 45 war years the Watkins family, which was a fairly large family, were living at Little Selley and two or three of the sisters from the family would cycle the four and a half miles into Knighton to work at the aircraft factory, situated where Knighton Primary School is now. Many relatives of the Watkins family still live in the local area today. The Watkins sold the farm to the current owner, Mr. Llewelyn Morgan, in 1970. David and Llynda Morgan with their children Kate and Bethan have lived at Little Selley for the last 15 years.

Little Selly

Little Selly

Little Selly was built on the edge of Wain Common between 1841 and 1851. The 17 acres of land were probably enclosed from the common. The property belonged to the Lewis family from 1851 until at least 1891. More recently Mr. and Mrs. Harold Smith and their son David rented it from Norman Ellis for several years. Norman lived at Little Selly as a child with his parents and ten brothers and sisters. The house and another small one nearby were part of a collection of cottages built around the common but, because it had 17 acres of land it was a more solid building than some of the others. The house is probably still the original one although several more modern farm buildings have been added over the years.

Llanfair Hall

The original farmhouse at Llanfair Hall was situated where the big cattle shed now stands. In 1829 the new house was built in its present location, a stone above the central upstairs window commemorates its completion. As described in the sale details of 1919, "The excellent farmhouse, suitable for a Gentleman's Residence, is built of stone and slate and contains:- Entrance Hall, Large Dining Room, Drawing Room, Breakfast Room, Kitchen with range, Scullery with sink and bake oven, Dairy, Wash House with two coppers, good cellar. Approached by the principal staircase are six bedrooms with landing. There is a secondary staircase to two men's rooms. Earth Closet in garden". Apart from several additional mod cons, and changes of room usage, this has altered very little in the past 80 years.

The 1841 census records Thomas and Elizabeth Tudge farming at Llanfair Hall, along with their 10 children and 6 servants. By 1851 Thomas Tudge had died and his son Edward was farming 300 acres. In 1857 Edward died aged 31 and Llanfair Hall was taken over by his brother Thomas, still employing 6 people and one boy. Thomas died in 1865 at the age of 42 and his brother Charles is given as head of household in 1871, together with his mother Elizabeth who by then was aged 74. Charles died in 1872 and Elizabeth in 1878, and by 1881 John Beavan and his wife Mary Ann who had three children were the tenants at Llanfair Hall. In 1891 they were still here, together with another farmer, John Edwards from Cwmdeuddwr and his son and daughter and three workers. It was at this time that the Land Commissioners issued a conveyance to enclose the far hill (Llanfair Hill) adding a further 216 acres to the size of the farm.

In 1904 Thomas Stephen Jones, Tom's grandfather took over the tenancy. Born in 1863 at Castle Cwtta, Llandinam, his father Evan Jones had farmed latterly at Llanwyddelan near Llanfair Caerinion. T. S. Jones had previously farmed 240 acres at the Oakley Estate, Lydham and rented ground from the Earl of Powys at Hopesay. In his younger days he had joined the Mongomeryshire Yeomanry and served as a recruit with Sir Watkin Williams Wynn. A fine horseman, he became prominent in military tournaments and won numerous silver trophies in competitions open to the whole British Army. Having attained the rank of squadron Sergeant Major he was offered a commission, but decided his real vocation was farming.

On September the 6th 1919 the Millington Educational Foundation, or Millington Trust, sold the Llanfair Waterdine Estate. T. S. Jones bought Llanfair Hall comprising then about 668 acres. Thomas Jones' children were Louisa, Tom Evans' mother, who died in childbirth; Beatrice, who later lived at Cwm Collo; Evelyn, who married a Pugh from Albrighton; Gladys, who married a Shanks of Albrighton, and (Evan) George born in 1896, who inherited the farm upon the death of his father in 1950.

The wedding of Louisa and Tom

In 1951 George Jones married his long time sweetheart Kathleen Mary Brown. In 1952 Christine was born, and Thomas S. F. followed in 1954. Christine married Edward James and now lives at Holford Farm, Craven Arms, with her three children Rachel, Geoffrey and Elizabeth. In 1975 George Jones died aged 78, in 1985 Kathleen died aged 74.

In 1988 Tom was engaged to Christine Magowan, and in 1993 they were married. Today, Tom and I are the sole occupiers of Llanfair Hall, with occasional live-in lambing students; and Tom's cousin, Tom Evans, who lives in a caravan beside the house, having lived in the village all his life, previously at Cwm Collo and Cwm Cole. The valuations in 1942 for Llanfair Hall, give a good insight into the changes that have taken place over the past 50 years. In 1942 there were 10 cart horses, 20 hill ponies and three riding horses. There were 18 milking cows, 63 fattening cattle, and one stock bull; 578 breeding ewes, 12 rams and four store pigs. Approximately 52 acres of oats, barley and potatoes were grown, and thirty five acres of swedes and mangolds. There were 200 gallons of cider in the cellar in six casks! The farm possessed a 1932 Morris Saloon, along with eight carts and waggons; it did not have any tractors or other motor vehicles.

Today, although the acreage has increased substantially (approx 1200 acres) proportionately there is a far greater increase in the number of breeding ewes to about 2500, and suckler cows to about 350, the numbers of which were limited only recently by the introduction of quota schemes and an agreement with the Clun ESA. There are still 8 breeding mares running wild on the hill, but the other horses have been superceded by tractors, land rovers and a farm bike. The milking cows have been replaced by suckler cows, the pigs have gone and oats, barley, potatoes and mangolds are no longer grown.

Up until the 1960's Tom's father, George, kept Kerry Hill sheep walking 1200 two year olds to Knighton to be sold over two days, annually. After that Suffolk and Hampshire rams were introduced, and the farm started producing fat lambs. In 1975 the first Charolais bull was purchased, previously Hereford and white Shorthorn bulls were used. In those days cattle were not fattened until they were three to four years old, unlike the thirty month limit imposed since the BSE crisis. Tom's father and grandfather were big livestock dealers; hundreds of ewes would be purchased at the Kerry sales, and walked back, stopping overnight at the Anchor. Cattle and sheep were all walked to Knighton to be loaded on to rail trucks and sent elsewhere in the country. The yards around the house at Llanfair Hall, contained several old buildings, probably older than the house (described in detail in the 1919 auction particulars). Although no longer functional (they require mucking out by hand) they are of historical interest and aesthetically

Llanfair Hall

appealing, and are currently protected under the ESA. The weight of snow in the winter of 1947 caused the roofs to collapse and they are now roofed with corrugated iron. Tom's father had the cattle shed at Nant-y-Twydy (Tuthy) erected in 1962, the sheep shed there followed in 1992. The big cattle shed at the house was put up in 1973, and in 1980 the cattle unit at Cwm Mawr was erected, following the abandonment of the dwelling there several years before.

After the second World War, in an effort to increase food production, it was decided to improve many of the hills, from heather and bracken, into grassland. George Jones wrote to the then, Ministry of Food, and asked if while he was ploughing the Far Hill (Llanfair Hill) he could have a grant to "level that mound". The Ministry replied that if he had levelled it they would probably have paid him a grant, but now he had brought it to their attention, they had noticed it was actually Offa's Dyke. And so, the Dyke still stands. The rest of Llanfair Hill was ploughed and 216 acres of rape was fiddled by hand by George, Tom Evans and Charlie Pritchard. The Radnorshire Company reported that this was the largest patch of rape ever sown in the area at that time. The past 12 years, while I have been at Llanfair Hall it has seen few changes. There are still three full time men employed; John Gwilt, John (Stan) Poole and John Francis, together with extra help for lambing, shearing, silaging etc. There has been a small pheasant shoot here in the Autumn for nearly 20 years; and the past 12 years has seen three joint meets of the Teme Valley and United Pack hunts. All this is likely to change in the new millennium, as is the way we farm; livestock numbers may be dramatically altered by the effects of Agenda 2000. The most significant difference lately has been the huge increase in paperwork and record keeping imposed by Brussels and MAFF in the wake of the BSE scare. Associated with this crisis has been a fall in livestock prices due to a lack of demand for beef and an increase in the supply of lamb... However, as the original TS Jones said "Llanfair Hall will always be farmed, while there are horses on Llanfair Hill".

Christine Jones.

Llantroft

Derrik and Shelagh Jenkyns live at Llantroft. They write:-

We have discovered that Llantroft was built between 1790 and 1820. It was, until we bought it in 1975, always run as a smallholding. Soon after we came the land around us changed hands and is now farmed from a distance. This does mean that, although the only domestic animal on site is a silver tabby called Finchley, we are surrounded by sheep and cattle

Llantroft

and lambs in their season. The wild life is wonderful. We share our home with spiders, woodmice, swallows, and owls. Beyond the house are buzzards, foxes, badgers and rabbits all of whom entertain and amuse us daily, completely compensating for our lack of television and a road to come and go on. The mud is a curse we share with those who lived here in the past. We bless the Royal Mail who nobly deliver our letters come rain or shine.

We have made alterations to the living space of our home. We enlarged it in 1976 and made a kitchen and upper bedroom and again in the 80's to provide a study and a lovely chapel/library. My husband retired in 1996 and we moved to Llantroft. We love it very much and struggle to make a garden and to grow vegetables and fruit which we can enjoy.

Llanwooley - an empty house

Llanwooley

Thomas Clee left Llanwooley to his daughters Gertrude and Annie Clee in 1925. Annie married Joseph Griffiths in 1933 and died in 1936. Her sister Gertrude, then living in Hereford sold the property and New House in 1949. Llanwooley was a smallholding of about 12 acres. The land was farmed by Percy Gwilt who lived with his family at New House. John, Bill and Sarah Price rented Llanwooley House. John and Bill worked as farm workers and casual labourers until their old age and Sarah kept house. As there was no water supply she walked down to Redwood Cottage each day to a well. As she got older this task took several hours. There was no electricity and the house was heated by open fires in the living room and kitchen. Wood was collected on every possible occasion. The barn was connected on to the house and there was an opening directly from the bedroom into the upper part of the barn. The animals provided some warmth in winter. Layers of newspaper about 2 centimetres thick were stuck on to the inside of the stone walls to conserve some heat.

In 1949 the land and house were sold to Horace and Amy Johnson from Cwmbrain. The house was used as a holiday cottage for a few years and then to house animals. Anne Singleton nee Johnson sold Llanwooley to Roger and Jane Thomas in 1988 since when it has been almost entirely rebuilt and extended a great deal.

Roger writes:- Llanwooley was empty and derelict when we bought it in 1988. It had been unoccupied for many years, apart from the occasional courting couple escaping the rain. I have no certain knowledge of the history of the original house and holding: it has no pew of its own in St Mary's and would have afforded a very scant living to its tenants. Long ago there may have been a forge in what is now our kitchen - for shoeing the cattle driven along the ridge from the Anchor, Kerry and beyond. The new house is built for the most part upon it's own new footings and so its story is also for the most part new and not yet told. These are only the first few chapters of the great labour of building the house and of the great and growing joy of living in it with my wife, watching our children growing up and growing out into the encircling landscape. Because the house is planted upon a

Ludo born April 14th 1999.

Llanwooley 1999

hill we live only half our lives within the bounds of Llanfair Waterdine, for the other half our parish is the broad sky, drenched with light and bright in the wind's eye. Very soon another child is to be born into this house. I have never seen, or ever heard, nor yet can I imagine a finer place to be born into than this.

Roger and Jane and their family have continued the pattern of building a new house partly on existing foundations and using existing stone from the previous house and buildings. There are signs of several older houses on the site before the present dwelling.

Lower Bryn Bedw (Waun or Wain Common)

According to the census there have been many cottages around Wain Common. At some times between 1841 and 1891 there were up to six at any one time. Lower Bryn Bedw was owned by a Davies family from 1841 up to the beginning of this century. In 1853 the Tithe valuation indicates that George Davies owned the cottage and he stated he was a farmer of 3 acres. The three small fields still exist with their hedges intact although they are now part of Bryn Bedw Farm.

Lower Bryn Bedw winter 2000

By 1891 George Davies was 76 years old and his wife was 68. He was by then a molecatcher. Judging by the number of moles in the fields and garden he was probably kept quite busy. The stream seems to attract them. In 1861 the cottage may have been called the Dingle, or it is possible that the family moved to another cottage of that name on the Common for a time. By 1903 a nephew of George Davies had moved into the cottage for a while. His name was George Cadwallader. He kept horses at Stonypound where other relatives lived and earned his living hauling stone for road repairs and collecting goods from Knucklas Railway Station for local people for a fee. He also did ploughing and general farmwork. He was given a watch from Kays of Newtown for his 21st birthday in 1903. When he was not working he hung it on a nail in the chimney breast. It hangs there still! .

Lower Bryn Bedw was owned by Jack and Edith Stephens from Bryn Bedw farm from the 1940's until about 1970 when it was sold to Gordon and Anne Singleton. The cottage had fallen into a state of disrepair but part of it, especially the chimney breast with it's bread oven was still intact. The cottage had consisted of one room joined on to a cowstall above which, for warmth, was a bedroom. Gordon set to work to renovate the cottage to make a two up two down holiday

Silver laced Wyandottes, Gordon and Skip 'Summer'.

home where the family spent every spare moment for the next twenty years, travelling from Newport in South Wales where they worked. On retirement Gordon and Anne moved in permanently and spent several months building an extension consisting of an enlarged living room, an extra bedroom, a garage and storage space. The cottage is centrally heated by a Gas Rayburn and water is obtained from a private spring, and there is septic tank drainage. Over the years Jack Stephens and Hughie Gardner agreed to sell a couple of acres of land part of which is some of the original three acres once owned by George Davies. Gordon and Anne's sons, Adam who lives in Newport and Matthew who lives in Bristol spent their holidays and weekends at the cottage all their lives and still continue to do so. They love the natural surroundings, the peace and the quiet and both enjoy observing wildlife and taking long walks and mountain bike rides in the area. Gordon and Anne intend to stay at Lower Bryn Bedw as they firmly believe that finding such a place is a once in a lifetime experience. They hope that Adam and Matthew, now in their early thirties will also remain attached to the area.

The oak beam over the fireplace was replaced in 1995, it came from the Bear Hotel in Newtown built in the 17th century and before that was a ships timber.

Lower Duffryn

In 1841 Richard Hammer aged 42 and his wife Mary aged 37 lived at Lower Duffryn with their six children. By 1851 there were eight children and Richard had died. In the early 1930's a Miss Hammer owned the farm and rented it out. She lived in Llandrindod Wells. In 1936 Edward (Ted) Charnock and his wife Margaret rented the farm from Miss Hammer. They had one child Thelma then aged 3. Ann Davies now married to Thelma's son David Davies writes: Lower Duffryn Farm lies between two parishes, Llanfair Waterdine and Bettws. The boundary runs through the sitting room. A cupboard built into the wall marks this. It is said that many years ago parishioners would walk the boundaries and "beat the bounds" (beat sticks together). The farm is 138 acres. There is a large farmhouse with four bedrooms, two sitting rooms and a dining room, which was once the room where the pig was butchered and salted for family use. There is also a big family kitchen with a utility room and a pantry. The family who have lived at Lower Duffryn for the past three years are David and Ann Davies with their three children Joanna 15, Vicky 13 and Joshua 9.

Lower Duffryn 1948

Lower Duffryn 1999

David took over the farm from his father when he retired at the age of 65. He now lives with his wife Thelma in the second house on the farm, Maes-y-Garn which is in Newcastle parish so the farm is in three parishes.

When we moved in extensive work was carried out, new floors, windows, doors, stairs, ceilings, electrics and insulation. While this work was being carried out we found a large ingle nook fireplace two metres wide and one and a half metres high. Stuffed into the side wall by the fireplace we found an old dog whistle and a letter dated 1855 addressed to "My Dearest Mother". We think the Hammer family lived here then. There was horse hair built into the walls and there were many runs made by rats and squirrels. A second fireplace has a beautiful bread oven built at the side of it. It is said that Lower Duffryn was a Public House at the beginning of the 19th century.

John and Thelma Davies bought the farm from Miss Hammer in 1965: before that Thelma's father had rented the farm from Miss Hammer. When he died in 1965 they decided to buy it. Ted Charnock had been a carpenter in Coventry but an injury at work forced him to find another occupation. He decided to farm and rented Lower Duffryn. Thelma was three at the time and although at first he had no stock, within a few months he had managed to buy three working horses, sixty sheep and six cows. Later a full time workman lived in, the access to his room was by ladder leading out of the kitchen. The family used the main stairs. There was no indoor toilet or bathroom, and the house is probably at least two hundred years old.

We keep sheep and beef cattle and have a horse and a few chickens. Our younger daughter Vicky is a talented swimmer and runner and as we are a good distance from suitable tracks and swimming pools we have to travel to Ludlow or Shrewsbury almost daily. Our daughters attend school in Bishop's Castle and travel by bus each day.

Joshua attends Clun village school where there are about 100 children and 4 teachers.

Lower Duffryn Cottage

Lower Duffryn Cottage is situated almost within sight of Newcastle village beside the Newcastle to Anchor road. The boundary between Llanfair Waterdine and Newcastle runs a few yards from the back door. The house was built in about 1840 in a sheltered spot below a steep rock face. John and Brenda Cross have lived there for about ten years. John has to travel quite long distances to work but they both look forward to retirement in the cottage. They have a productive garden and two well loved cats and a dog, and more unusually these days, two tortoises. Brenda is involved in the local social life, enjoys the countryside and feels that she and her husband have been welcomed into the community.

Lower Duffryn Cottage

Lower Graig

5th November 1923

The Paget family, Francis, Katherine and Mary sold field No. 1524 to Mr. Francis Ernest Beavan of 'The Graig' Llanfair Waterdine.

19th August 1939

Mr. Francis E. Beavan sold the, then still just a field, to Mr. Oscar William Serck, a Russian architect and the Co. founder of Serck Radiators of Birmingham.

There seems to be no record of the date the barn was built or indeed if permission was needed to build it.

The beginning of The Lower Graig as we know it today

8th July 1946

7 years on, permission was granted by the Rural District of Clun for a dwelling house to be erected on the land.

26th March 1947

Only 8 months later Mr. Serek informed the Council that he had completed the cellar and asked permission to carry on with the building.

The cellar is believed to have been built to store apples from the orchard before they were transported to market in the Midlands.

The bottom half was brick

The cellar compartments, eight altogether, were recently used to keep goats not apples.

The joining of the house to barn

Progress of Lower Graig

The garden area was fenced off and the bottom half of the barn looked more like a house.

The veranda or conservatory began to take shape.

5th July 1947

Ministry of works gave a licence for the installation of the bath and lavatory accommodation in the building.

16th September 1947

Mr Serck asked the Radnorshire District Council for a licence to purchase a bath.

19th September 1947

Just three days later the Radnorshire District Council said,
"No priority could be given in this case"

Permission must have been granted at a later date, as there is still a giant cast iron bath in place.

The water for this large luxury bath must have been pumped up from the river Teme. The well from which the water was pumped is still present today. The well was discovered with an electric motor by the side, which was to pump the water up to two storage tanks on the second floor of the barn, the highest part of the whole construction, probably to gravity feed the house with water.

25th November 1970

Mr. Oscar William Serck died.

30th June 1971

Records of a 'Deed Of Assent' transfer the property of house, barn and land to Mrs. Irene Stafford, Mr. Serck's daughter and beneficiary.

1st March 1975

At last, mains water to 'Lower Graig'. 'Deeds of Easement' were granted by the owners of the land which was needed to lay the pipes, Mr. and Mrs. R.J. Matthews and, Mr. E.J.E. Davies and Mr. C.B. Williams. The water pipes were to be laid over land at Lloyney House Farm to bring water to 'Lower Graig'.

The property remained unoccupied, until January 1983 when Mrs. Stafford sold it to the present occupiers Mrs. Maureen & Mr. Granville Bates, who moved in with their two sons Iain and Simon and daughter Lisa.

The first major job for the Bates family, after getting a log burner installed for heating, was to convert the barn into living quarters, as the boys were sleeping on the ground floor in the barn, with no heating and only three tiny windows. Converting the barn, gave them three extra bedrooms, a kitchen, a utility room and a larder.

Lower Graig fully lived in

Another major job was the garden, completely overgrown with brambles and nettles, it was to be transformed into a vegetable plot.

The house and land became a real family home with sheep, hens & chickens, also ducks, rabbits, goats even a pony and last but not least, geese which are still around today.

The children eventually left to pursue their own lives and Mr. & Mrs. Bates took steps to make the grounds, including vegetable plot, into a beautiful garden.

Present day Lower Graig

Lower Skyborry.

In 1924 Henry Adams sold the plot of land on which Lower Skyborry is built to Theodosia Pursaill from Northampton for £50. Her brother Frank Weale built the house for her while the Adams family continued to live next door and farm the adjoining land in a small way. The house was built in 1926/7 and Don Richards who now lives in Knighton remembers visiting his Aunt Theodosia.

Lower Skyborry 1981

In 1931 the property was sold for £550 and by 1936 it had been renamed The Elms. It was resold in 1936 for £800. In 1940 the house, garage and just over 4 acres of land leading down to the River Teme was sold to Miss Grace Barnard of Weir Cottage. In 1940 Miss Barnard also bought the house next door. She renamed the house Lower Skyborry taking the name from the house next door which she called Lower Skyborry Cottage. She probably did this as the cottage was let to tenants. Miss Barnard remained in the house until her death in 1980 and her brother Canon George Barnard lived there for a year after that. In 1981 Doctor and Mrs. Richard Townshend bought the house at auction for £46,000 while Skyborry Cottage was retained by Miss Barnard's Estate until 1985.

Grace Barnard

The Townshends did major internal restructuring over a period of 12 months and finally took up residence in August 1982. They spent much time landscaping the garden and from 1984 it was open to the public each year in aid of charity. Richard was a keen ornithologist and he erected 50 nesting boxes in the riverside field and in woodland belonging to Nether Skyborry

Mary Townshend

Lower Skyborry Cottage 1985

Lower Skyborry Cottage.

At the end of the last century the land at Lower Skyborry was owned by Thomas Edward Jones who died on 21st April 1899. He left the land to his wife Elizabeth until she died and then to his children Mary Lillian, Thomas Edward, Charlotte and Clara. Elizabeth died in 1907. In 1920 the land was sold to Henry Adams of Garbett Hall. Henry Adams probably built Lower Skyborry Cottage between 1920 and 1924 and then lived in it. He sold the plot next door, Lower Skyborry to Mrs. T. Pursaill in 1924. The property was sold to Miss G. M. Barnard in 1940. Rights to a water supply from a spring on the hill were agreed with Mr. Williams from Monaughty in 1954. Miss Barnard lived in Lower Skyborry and rented out Lower Skyborry Cottage to Mr. and Mrs. Harry King. Mr. King was well known as a local electrician. Mr. and Mrs. Silsby later took over the tenancy. The last tenants were Mr. and Mrs. Cliff Walker, they paid a small rent and helped Miss Barnard in her house and garden. When Miss Barnard died she provided for them in her will and Lower Skyborry Cottage was not sold until they were ready to move. After she died Mr. and Mrs. Walker cared for her brother Canon Barnard who had returned from Africa to live with her. When the Walkers left, the property was sold to us (Graham and Anne Mary Davies). We moved in in 1985 with our sons Adam and Dani and Roger the dog. Jane Edith Davies was born on 21st April 1986. We had an extension built to accommodate our growing family. The foundations were dug out by hand by Graham sometimes working until late at night by floodlight.

Dani, Adam and Janey

The agricultural road which was built up to Panpwnton Hill before we moved here has enabled us to get up to the Dyke to enjoy the views, good access to Kinsley Wood and a place to go kite flying on our family walks. However the year after we moved in it proved to be less of an advantage. Silaging was taking place up near the Dyke. While the tractor was driving down the brakes failed and the tractor and trailer rolled down the hill demolishing a gate, a tree and a telegraph pole and landing in our orchard. Luckily the driver was unhurt, although rather stunned.

Graham died in an accident at work on the 17th July 1987 at the age of 34. We have continued to live here with the support and love of our neighbours Richard and Mary. Roger the dog lived to the age of 15 and more recently we have acquired two cats Towser and Mogli.

Lower Panpwnton

Lower Panpwnton

The house is a Grade II listed yeoman's house, built we believe, in the late 17th century perhaps from 1680 - 90. It was possibly built on the frame of an older house. We believe that at one time it was two houses with a passage between them and although this was only about 60 years ago there is no trace of that now. Alterations made in the 1960's and the early 1980's have destroyed much of the east end of the house. We rediscovered and restored an inglenook fire place in the central room. We - June Tabor and Mark Emerson - came here in April 1991. Prior to that the owners were Brian and Dinah Reason who owned it for about 4 years and before that Reginald and Bettina Smith were the owners. They bought the house from John Williams at Panpwnton who had bought it from the Gough family when it ceased to be a working farm. Any land and buildings that did belong to Lower Panpwnton while it was a working farm were sold off at the time of the sale.

We live on the extreme edge of Llanfair parish, almost in Knighton. We are professional musicians, and our work takes us all over the British Isles to Europe and to North America. Our time at home is largely spent, when we are not doing administration, the burden of the self employed, in practising. We enjoy gardening, cooking and eating, and sharing the company of our animals: Bosco and Suni the Abyssinian cats, and Brando, Sharif and De Niro the standard Dachshunds.

Lower Redgate

Mrs. Barbara Merrett lives at Lower Redgate she writes: We moved into Lower Redgate during the 1980's. Previously it had been owned by Ivor Thomas and had been built by his father in 1916. While it was being built his father had lived in the adjoining cruckhouse reputed to be about 500 years old, but now a ruin. Originally the house was surrounded by about 46 acres of land but when the house was sold the land became the property of Mr and Mrs Thomas of Coed-y-Hendre. We still have about an acre to the front of the house. We kept a small flock of Jacob sheep, and then bought a further field of about an acre down the lane which had previously belonged to Upper Redgate.

Lower Redgate

Lower Tregodfa

Lower Tregodfa is probably about 250 years old and there seem to have been other dwellings on the site. We have found out more about previous owners, especially the Swancott family, than about the house itself.

Richard Swancott bought lower Tregodfa in 1908. At the time the Swancott family were living at Cwm Collo. Tregodfa was purchased from Mr. Griffiths of Melin-y-Grogue. Until the first World War Mrs. Bright, a widow and her children stayed in the house and the Swancott family farmed the land while living at Cwm Collo. Mrs. Bright had ten children. Members of this family later moved to Knighton and at least two people who are relatives still live in the area.

The Swancott family moved into the house in 1920 and have remained there ever since. Giles was born at Tregodfa. He had nine brothers and sisters, several of whom still live locally. He married Margaret nee Lloyd from the Green Farm and they have two children Marion a nurse who is married to John Pugh from the Spoad, Newcastle-on-Clun and has two daughters Elaine and Juliet, and Barry who rides out racehorses and helps his parents on the farm.

Lower Tregodfa

According to the census a Swancott family arrived in Llanfair in about 1851. They lived at Thegodfah - Tregodfa. At that time William, a farm labourer from Llanbadarn aged 26, with his wife Mary also aged 26 from Norton and their one year old son James who had been born in Presteigne lived there. Also in 1851 Jonathan Swancott a farmer aged 40 his wife Ann aged 32 and their children, William 10, Aaron 9, Ann 7, Martha 6, Jonathan 4, Emma 2 and Jane 10 months had moved into Cwm Collo. He came from Llanbadarn but she was from Llanfair. Their first child had been born in Knighton. By 1861 Jonathan and Ann also had Moses 9, Elizabeth 7, John 5, Richard 3 and Mary 10 months. Aaron had become a carter, Ann a dairy maid and Jonathan Junior a shepherd. By 1871 Jonathan was a widower and a farmer of 200 acres. Aaron by then aged 30 and Elizabeth 17 were working on the farm and both were still single. John, Richard and Mary were still at school. John was 15 by this time so this was quite unusual. By 1881 Jonathan aged 71 still farmed 188 acres along with his son Richard and several farmworkers. By 1891 Jonathan was 82 years old and Richard had married Louise from Heyope aged 31 they had a son also Richard aged 10 months. It would have been he or his father who bought Lower Tregodfa in 1908.

Lower Wain

Bill Parry lived at the Lower Wain for most of his life. Sylvia, his sister married Albert Lloyd from the Upper Wain where she still lives. Bill moved to a bungalow in Knighton in the 1980's and the farm was sold. Doctors Bob and Carolyn Wilkins bought the house and the 85 acres of land. They write: We are both graduates of Birmingham University Medical School. My parents retired from Birmingham to Knill near Presteigne where we were married in 1965. We have always loved the area so when we were able to buy a weekend home we chose Lower Wain Farm. One of its attractions is, that being in the ESA its natural beauty can be preserved. We have restored one stable/barn and are in the process of restoring the other.

We worked the farm for about 5 years with the help of Mr. Harold Smith of Little Selly. We kept 100 ewes and 14 cattle. Sadly, since Harold's death we have been unable to continue to keep animals and we now let the land as grass keep. We come up from London whenever possible to visit my parents Doctors Humphreys and my sister Nicola Humphreys (Editor of the Broadsheep Magazine). Our three children who are now in their 20's love to spend weekends in Shropshire. We have a grandchild who also enjoys it especially at lambing time.

Lower Wain

Melin-y-Grogue Farmhouse

Age and History. When we bought the farmhouse in 1997, we were led to believe by the previous owner that the house was built in the mid 18th century. After a visit to the Shrewsbury Records Office we could find no record of when it was built. The building does not appear on a map of the late 18th century, nor on Robert Baugh's map of 1808. The first map reference to it we could find was 1886, although, unfortunately, several maps were missing from the Record Office.

It would seem that the house was built between 1808 and 1830 as written evidence states that by this date it was in the ownership of the Millington Educational Foundation, a charity founded by the Shrewsbury draper, James Millington. It thus became part of the Llanvair Estate which comprised some 1880 acres. At this time Melin-y-Grogue Farm was 163 acres.

In 1920 the farm was purchased from the Millington Foundation by Percy Bevan, who had been resident as tenant since 1913. It was sold to Bert Hobby and his wife Joan in 1945 and they lived there until 1980. Between 1980 and 1987, whilst in the ownership of Trevor Price, the farmland was sold, leaving only 4 acres belonging to the farmhouse. In 1997 the farm buildings were split up, the house being sold and the outbuildings being retained by Mrs. Mary Simmons.

Our first overriding impressions of living in the parish were of the dramatic and largely unspoiled beauty of the countryside and the comparatively peaceful atmosphere. Being able to hear the landscape as well as see it was an unexpected bonus. It is a joy to ride or walk along the intricate network of lanes and not be passed by too many motor vehicles.

Melin-y-Grogue Farmhouse

On a slightly negative note it is sad to see this most beautiful landscape often marred by the presence of modern dwellings in neither a vernacular style, nor constructed of local natural materials. This, however, is not just peculiar to Llanfair Waterdine. Returning to the positive attributes of the parish; in spite of more "incomers" than we imagined, there is a sense of community spirit, with various activities designed to bring parishioners together. Above all, Llanfair Waterdine has an individual identity sadly lacking in so much of Great Britain in the late 20th century.

Rosemary M. C. Crum
Carol Akellian

Mellin-y-Grogue Mill

Mellin y Grogue is a small hamlet about half a mile from the village of Llanfairwaterdine As the larger estates and farms have been sold and become divided up Mellin y Grogue now consists of five dwellings. ' The Mill' a house and attached corn mill, was rebuilt in stone in 1857 after a fire had destroyed the old wooden mill. The mill at one time was used by the monks who stored their grain locally at Skyborry ~ and brought it to the mill to be ground into flour.

The name Mellin y Grogue has the religious connection of meaning 'The Mill of the Cross'.

We the present owners came here in 1993 and have found that female occupants with the name MARY have lived here since early 1900.

Early 1900 to 1946	Mary Clee
1952 to 1993	Mary Gough
1993 to present day	Mary Bufton

We have seven acres of pasture land on which we graze sheep, part is used by a neighbour and we have our own seven sheep - six are in retirement and one we reared on the bottle and is more of a pet.

We have two dogs 'spollies' cross between a collie and a spaniel: their names are Ben and Sam, they are brothers and were born in March 1991. Three hens after many years still supply us with our daily intake. The river Teme runs the entire length of our property.

We have one acre approx in Wales and the rest in England.

Prior to 1920 the property was owned by the Trustees of the Millington Educational Foundation who rented it and twelve acres to Mr. Alfred Clee. According to the deeds dated 10th August 1920 the Mill was in the parishes of Llanfairwaterdine and Beguildy in the Counties of Salop and Radnor. On that date Mr. Alfred Clee became the new owner: he was the miller and a smallholder. He died on the 2nd January 1941 and ownership passed to his wife Mary. She died on the 26th April 1946 and her executors passed ownership to Mr. Robert Winton Shuter on the 9th November 1946.

19th November 1952 the Mill was purchased by Mr. Thomas Gough and his wife Mary.

The present owners purchased the Mill from Mr. & Mrs. Gough on the 5th November 1993.

Sometime between 1951 and 1952 six acres were disposed of.

During 1989 further acreage was purchased to bring it up to the seven acres approx it is today.

The mill pond was filled in by the local council in circa 1950 due to the health risk of stagnant water because the mill was no longer being used. The original mill pond wall and cobbled bottom is still here. The original mill pond sluice pipe which runs into the stone cobbled race which we have uncovered runs from the mill down the fields to the river. The weir created in the river to divert water to the mill at Lloyney can still be seen.

The mill pond was fed by Crocken Brook which also runs on the righthand side of our property into the Teme.

A footpath from the mill to the lane and to the track down and over the river enabled easy access from both the Shropshire side and Radnor side for horses and carts etc to use the mill.

The stables, cow sheds and granary are still original in every aspect. We have the bell which was used in the mill to alert the miller when the corn bags were full and also the stencil for marking the word Mellin y Grogue on the sack bags. The grinding stones we found in different parts of the property are now in a pile in our garden. We aim to leave everything as it is as much as possible. We have fenced both the riverside and the copse which marks the other boundary to conserve the wildlife and flowers etc. We have seen many of both return especially in the last two years - green and spotted woodpeckers, redstart, jay, bullfinch, goldfinch and many others including the heron which has been here for many years which we have on video hunting and gorging moles. 'Yuk'. The wild flowers of different species are very slowly appearing but that is nature i.e during the last three years the bluebells have spread from a mere handful to cover the floor of the copse. There are trout in the river albeit small and we suspect an otter (what a joy if it is) and polecat and stoat. We have the 'For Sale' estate agents sign not sure if it was 1946 or 1952. Also the original deeds from 1920.

Mellin-y-Grogue Mill

It is impossible in this day and age to obtain a living from seven acres; how they did it years ago is a mystery. We are fortunate that we have our own business in Herefordshire in the motorcycle industry and other farming interests in Worcestershire. It does entail travelling and occasional accommodation but on return it is well worth it, although all the administration and management is handled from here at the mill.

We feel very privilaged, lucky and humble to have found such an idylic place to live and with trust in God it will continue.

Present Occupiers/Owners:
Mrs. Mary Elizabeth Bufton. Age: 56
Mr. Michael Alan Bufton Age: 63
Mr. Frank David Blundell Age: 56

Monaughty Poeth

Monaughty Poeth has a history which dates back as far as the 12th Century. Monaughty (Mynachty in Welsh) means Monastery Grange, a grange being a group of buildings e.g. granary, barns, stalls and pens for livestock, maybe a mill and living quarters for labourers. Here food was produced for the more learned monks, which in this case were the monks at Abbey Cwmhir.

Monaughty Poeth. Farm buildings 1908 before a fire destroyed them

According to David H. Williams, historian, Monaughty Poeth was given to Abbey Cwmhir in approximately 1199 by William Fitzalan. The Fitzalan's were a powerful Clun family in the Welsh Marches, related to the Duke of Norfolk.

Poeth in Welsh means warm, but in place names often means burnt which suggests that Monaughty Poeth has suffered many disastrous fires, and this no doubt accounts for the typical Victorian brick house of today. The stone chimney breast is all that remains of the original building, there is also a little wattle and daub up the back stairs from a later date.

The Roberts family in the kitchen 1908

When the Roberts' family moved out in October 1937 the Williams family moved in. Mr. Lawton and Mrs. Rene Williams, with their four children Glenys, Jim, Margaret and Betty and over the 60 plus years many changes have occurred. In their early years the ploughing, reaping, sowing etc. was done by cart horses. There was always a waggoner, cowman and shepherd most of the men living in. The farm house kitchen was a hive of activity, with a living-in maid to help. Bread and cakes were baked in the bread oven, butter churned, eggs put ready for the collecting van and Monday was always washday with a fire lit under the two big black furnaces in the back kitchen. One or two pigs were killed on the farm each year by our local butcher known as "Parry the pig killer," who would cycle around from farm to farm, and these were salted on a stone slab in the dairy. The slab had a groove running around the edge for the brine to drain away. When the bacon and hams were ready, salted, in approximately six weeks they were hung from the kitchen ceiling. Cold, fat bacon was the usual farmhouse breakfast. Cider was also made on the farm.

The kitchen is hardly recognisable today. The large open fire has been replaced by an oil fired Rayburn Aga cooker, there are built in kitchen units and the remains of the bread oven has become a small china display.

In 1943 another son was born, John who brought much happiness, but sadly after a short illness he died of leukaemia in February 1953. When the cowsheds were reroofed to comply with milk hygiene regulations the valuable old stone roofing tiles were bequeathed to Saint Mary's Llanfair Waterdine in memory of John. These have been incorporated into some of the crazy paving church path - hence the peg hole in each stone.

A visitor and his dog 1908

Before the 1950's childhood days on the farm were particularly busy, happy and carefree. The whole family helped with the haymaking, turning, cocking and loading hay on to wheel carts (commonly called Will Cars) and then the hay was tossed with pikles in through the shutter holes of the tolants. The children had great fun playing "hide & seek" behind these old fashioned hay cocks.

The corn too was cut by horses and binders and put into stooks and left to dry for three weeks. Children and dogs chased and tried to catch the rabbits as they bolted through the corn.

During the War mechanisation slowly began to creep in, horses were replaced by tractors, binders by combine harvesters. The hay was made into oblong bales which were approximately two feet by one foot and could still be stacked by the family. Now with the large round bales the children's haymaking days are over. The farm has become a hazardous place, although lambing time can still be enjoyed by the family.

Years went by - Jim married Jocelyn and lived at Brackenway, a house on the lower end of the farm. Margaret and Betty married and their mother died.

In 1982 Mr. Lawton Williams and daughter Glenys exchanged homes with Jim and Jocelyn and their children Sally, Simon and Kate. Jocelyn continued teaching at Chapel Lawn school until it closed in 1985, and then began bed and breakfast at Monaughty Poeth. Jim and Jocelyn also kept geese which were dressed for the Christmas market but owing to strict hygiene laws brought in in the early 1990's they had to give up. Feathering days used to be very enjoyable with all the family, friends and neighbours coming to help.

For the first two decades of this century the River Teme which flows under the bridge fifty yards from the house was used by Knucklas Baptist members for Baptismal purposes.

Monaughty in 1999

Monaughty Poeth house has a real family atmosphere and is frequently visited by Sally, Simon and Kate and their spouses - John Bright (farmer, mixed arable) - John Russell (fruit farmer) and Claire (nee Meredith), not to mention the seven grand children Thomas, Lucy, Joanna, Hannah, William, Jessica and Rosie, whose laughter and voices can be heard above the twitter of the many sparrows in the ivy wall. Worthy of a mention are Knighton races which are held annually in May on the big flat field on the farm. On the riverside meadow "Dol fawr" is a caravan club site, and the Abraham Darby School Telford bring pupils each year for a summer school. In conclusion, Monaughty Poeth is a mixed farm rearing sheep and cattle. Jim is the shepherd and manages his flock with the help of his six faithful sheepdogs. The dogs, who would greet even thieves with wagging tails, work as a pack and can often be seen with Jim riding around the fields and roads on the truck, either inside or on top or chasing along behind.

This autumn will see big changes at Monaughty. Harry Davies, the cowman for over thirty years retires in September, and Jim, who has not been well recently has decided to have a reduction sale on October 2nd as Simon at present is pursuing his livelihood as an Accountant at Wye Vale Nurseries, Hereford. The sale will be organised by McCartneys, the local auctioneers.

Jim and Jocelyn Williams, and Patsy

This is where we leave Monaughty Poeth - the summer of 1999. What changes the future holds....... Who knows?

To quote the latest edition of Farmers Weekly, September 1999, "The hill farmers (such as in this valley) are an endangered species - and the National Farmers Union estimates that this year Hill farmers earnings will average just £5,300, many in Wales and the border counties will be lower!!!.

Will the Government give adequate support for these farms to survive ???

Myrtle Cottage

This is the stone cottage adjoining Rose Villa which is popularly known as the old post office. Owner/occupier of Myrtle Cottage: Mrs. Rosemary Naylor. I moved into Myrtle Cottage on January 6, 1998, ie very recently as I write this.

I am retired, as from late December 1997 and now live alone. I am divorced. Age 67.

The cottage previously belonged to the Gwilt family, who still own the cottages on either side of Myrtle Cottage. Several generations of the Gwilts have lived in Llanfair parish as far as I can discover. The previous residents of Myrtle Cottage in recent years had rented the cottage from the Gwilt family.

The cottage is reputedly eighteenth century but the title deeds go back only to earlier this century.

Previous owners as shown on the deeds:

Conveyed to	Date	Price
Mr. J. H. Evans	6.8.1921	£45.00
Mr. W. N. Price	24.4.1945	£540.00
Mr. T. E. Coulthard	15.10.1958	£640.00
Messrs W. & J. C. Evans	3.2.1966	£800.00
Mr. W. J. Bridgwater	7.5.1970	£1,000.00
Mrs. D. A. Gwyther	8.7.1970	£800.00
Mr. & Mrs. P. J. Goddard	18.8.1970	£700.00
Mr. & Mrs. R. H. Gwilt	12.7.1978	£14,500.00
Mrs. R. C. Naylor	22.12.1997	

At some stage, 25 to 30 years ago the old cottage was extended to include a single storey extension consisting of bathroom and kitchen with a flat roof. The original cottage probably had two living rooms downstairs. There is now a single room here with a disused chimney breast on the western side. The garage is integral and supports one of the three upstairs rooms. There is no central heating as yet but a wood burning stove in the living room gives out plenty of heat. Otherwise the house is warmed downstairs by night storage electric heaters. The newer extension receives ample sunlight in season but conversely can be cold in winter.

To the back of the house, the land, which I am transforming into garden, is 30 metres long by 10 metres wide. It slopes gently towards the southern boundary and then very steeply to the River Teme. This river comes dangerously close to my neighbour's property on my western boundary but the present meander takes it slightly away from my land. I do hope that it remains so, though my knowledge of physical geography tells me that meanders move downstream with time. The garden is bounded on either side by hedges with a mixture of hedging species including mahonia, symphocarpus, lilac, holly, hazel and hawthorn. A very tiny specimen of Myrtle struggles to survive under a massive holly.

Myrtle Cottage

Though I have no animals of my own, the building plays host to house martins who nest on the house walls beneath the eaves and to swallows who nest inside the garage. The garden is visited by a variety of birds and I shall do my best to make future generations of birds welcome here. The buzzards hovering over the hill opposite are a regular sight and part of the pleasure I gain when looking up the Teme Valley to this lovely bit of Welsh borderland.

I have made one major alteration to the house during 1998. Evans Windows of Newtown have erected a conservatory on part of the existing patio which I now use as a greenhouse, happily growing new plants to be bedded out next year in the garden. Gardening is a passion with me.

My greatest passion, however, is astronomy and this is the reason that I chose this part of Shropshire for my new home.

Most of the UK is well illuminated at night; so much so that seeing the stars is exceedingly difficult. A photograph of Britain taken from space at night, on one of the rare occasions when it was totally cloud-free, shows the problem. There are few areas where the land is in darkness at night. South west Shropshire, and neighbouring parts of Wales are the few remaining areas where motorways and city lights do not ruin the night sky for would-be stargazers.

So far I have not been disappointed with the quality of the night sky, except that more often than not it is cloudy. This is the price one pays for living amongst hills, but that is something which I would not want to give up.

My great hope is that future generations in Llanfair Waterdine will be able to step out of-doors on a fine night and readily see the Milky Way, as is possible in 1998. That is a pleasure denied to most of the inhabitants of the UK except when they go overseas for holidays etc.

I am finding the people of Llanfair very welcoming and hope that future generations will continue to do so too. The pace of life in the countryside is reputedly slower than in our great conurbations, and this is something I am finding to be the case here. Long may it remain so.

Rosemary Naylor 4.11.98

Nantiago

Nantiago was a Welsh Longhouse. Little is visible of the original timber framed building other than parts of four couples of medieval cruck beams exposed in the kitchen and stairwell. In 1672 a Hearth Tax of two shillings a chimney was levied on Mr. Henry Davies then living at Nantiago in the township of Trebirt who paid eight shillings. A large crumbling tomb in the corner to right of the church porch is the Davies tomb, it has on it an 18th century date.

The Reverent Kinchant was the vicar and owner of Nantiago from 1834 to 1884. In 1837 he owned 26 acres of meadow, arable land, the house, garden and pond on which he paid £3-7s-9d in tithe. He was born in 1805 in India and was married to Maria who came from Ireland. The census in 1851 shows three unmarried daughters, two sons, a governess from Camberwell and a servant from Bromsgrove. By 1871 one daughter, Rose was married to W. Trevor Roper a merchant from Flintshire and they had a daughter Ethel. The Reverent Kinchant is buried in Llanfair churchyard. The present church was built in 1854 and Nantiago was purchased as the new vicarage. Some of the church wall was used to renovate the house.

Nantiago 1916

Nantiago. The Present Day House

During the War, Nantiago held a school evacuated from Hill House School Hornchurch in Essex. The head mistress was Miss Northridge and the assistant mistress Miss Pyeman. Some local children also attended. The drawing room was the school room and the present dining room the staff room. The vicar's wife Mrs. Thomas also held evening classes in first aid and home nursing.

In 1950 the church sold the vicarage to Sarah Woodward, a concert pianist who renamed the house Llanfair Court. In 1966 she sold it to Mr. and Mrs. Gomer Bennett from Presteigne who did not live in the house but did carry out work on the pool. The Bennett's' sold the property, by then in need of extensive repair to Alastair Lyons in 1976. He carried out extensive alterations inside and out. It was sold to Mr. and Mrs. Anthony Mainwaring in 1985 and to the present owners Mr. and Mrs. Edward Phillips in 1994. An architectural student recognised the chimneys as the work of Repton, a contemporary of capability Brown. It has been impossible to find evidence of either the father or son working in this area.

New House

New House, Llanfair Waterdine, and its outbuildings, appear on the lst edition Ordnance Survey map of the 1885 survey, and also on the tithe map (apportionment maps) dated 1843. However, from some of the interior features of the house, and from the building practices known to date from earlier times, it would appear that New House is considerably older.

The house is constructed of rubble stone walls - presumably because the local stone is flat and friable - and is heavily beamed. It has wood floors, and lime plaster and wattle-and-daub walls! The width of the walls varies according to the house height; for example, at ground level the width is 56 cms. and this decreases, with increasing house height, to 38 - 46cms. on the third floor, depending in which room one is taking measurements (and, indeed, even which wall one is measuring too!), and to much less on the fourth floor. There is not a straight wall or correct right-angle anywhere in the house! Although in former days there must have been a loft or small attic, it is only since Victorian times that the attic stands as large and as high as it does now, and it must have been added at a later date.

Originally a farm with 77 acres of land, and named Cwm Brain, there is evidence that the house fell into disrepair and so a new (or renamed?) Cwm Brain was built further down the valley, and the original building was, much later, eventually rebuilt and renamed as New House. Part of New House has been clad on the outside with Victorian brick and we feel that this must have been done during the rebuilding phase..

New House earlier this century

We purchased New House in March 1988, prior to which it had (for some 18 years) been used as a holiday home. During our complete renovation of the house we found that several of the walls are wattle and daub and these remain still. However, as is the fashion these days, we removed the lime-plaster ceilings to expose the beams and it was quite heartbreaking to rip down all the laths which had been so securely nailed to them: two-hundred years on, and they could still bear the weight of a man without snapping. We couldn't but help think of the men who had carried out such excellent workmanship — only for us to tear it down! It seemed such a shame. There are two large inglenook fireplaces in the house, one in the lounge, the other in the kitchen. The latter has a beautiful dome-shaped bread oven to one side, and on the other side there used to be a stone copper for heating the water for the washing. The possibility of there being a third inglenook, in the lounge, often occupies our minds. . .

There are a few anomalies in the house. For example, it is traditional for floor joists to run from the front to the back of a house, and for the beams on which they sit to be placed crosswise, However, in what is now our kitchen, the beams run transversely. These beams, comprising lengths of timber sawn or lopped from oak and similar hardwood trees— one such beam comprises four equal quadrants of the self-same tree trunk or whatever — all of them knarled and in their original state without being planed or chiselled, have never been plastered and so it is obvious that the building of the kitchen was of a different style to the rest of the house — and, therefore, most likely of a different time also. It is pure speculation on our part, but one feels it is quite possible that the house was originally just a small two-room cottage with a dairy, and that it was later enlarged into the existing structure.

In our earlier days here we were fortunate enough to talk to Harold Gwilt, who had lived in the house during his childhood, and we treasure the stories he told us. Apparently, there was a dairy (now our utility room) adjoining the kitchen, with a well, whilst what is now our bathroom used to be the room where cheeses were kept to mature; sheep fleeces were stored in the attic to await collection. Harold told us he and his several brothers all slept in the same room, adding that it was the duty of the last one of them that jumped into bed to extinguish the candle by the somewhat dangerous expedient of throwing a sock at it! He also told how tractors used to drive into what was a yard on the north side of the house, and had to circle the chestnut tree in order to turn round (this manoevre remains a similar problem today!), and that there was a pig-cot at one edge of the premises. Opposite this, at the north side of the barn, there once were cattle stalls, or similar, but when we arrived these had been reduced to mere rubble, although the site is now a small lawn bordered by a stone wall and supporting a damson tree.

One can well imagine that life in New House was quite hard in days gone by, even though the rubble walls act as excellent insulators, retaining some warmth well into winter, some coolness in summer. We understood from Harold that the myriad snowdrops that now bloom in the garden used to be picked and it was his job to take them—little or no transport in those times of course — to be sold in Knighton market, and that someone used to make a weekly call to collect the rabbits which had been shot here, and which also would have been sold in the market. Harold explained that the old manual plough which we found in the attic (yes, the attic! !), on our arrival, was used to plough what is now our orchard. Also, we learned, what is now our sitting room used to be a general living room with an old 'Rayburn-type' stove, a partioned cupboard, and fewer, much smaller, windows. As a result, it must have been quite dark and depressing, especially on a winters day. I wish we had remembered to ask about the then water supply, which presumably came from the same excellent and natural-spring well that is currently in use now. Today, however, this supply comes to us via an electric self-operating pump; however, since electricity was not connected to the house until the 1970's, presumably, prior to that date, it must have been collected manually.

I would dearly love to meet the person who built New House (despite all my searching I have yet to encounter his ghost!) because, whoever it was, he certainly chose a perfect position; out of

Present day New House

the wind (albeit marginally!), sheltered by higher hills, always catching whatever sun nature gives us, having a constant source of water which never dries up, built on a slope to one side and the apex of a hill on the other, so that drainage or rain water always flows away from it, and surrounded by the most gloriously unspoiled countryside imaginable. . .

Today, in 1999, the property consists of just the house and barn, the latter also having been extensively renovated and which is used partly as a store and also for parking our cars, and a large garden. All the surrounding land is owned by adjoining farms, so, apart from our German Shepherd dog who died a few years ago, there have been no animals at New House for many years. We still have lots of snowdrops growing wild and we have planted many flowers and trees since we have been here. On our arrival here in 1988 we planted a beech and a birch tree to the south side of the house, an alder to the east and a chestnut tree and a walnut tree to the north side, plus a damson tree on the north side of the barn.

Although, for almost ten years, we were constantly rebuilding and/or refurbishing the house etc., we still strived to get, and retain, the garden in a satisfactory condition. In some ways, this has been one of our toughest tasks to date; for every bucket of earth that we dig over, we also manage to retrieve about half-a-ton of rock and stone.... However, now that most of our work on the house has been completed, and being keen gardeners, we have more time to improve and maintain the garden, and I am beginning to think that maybe, just maybe, we are slowly but surely succeeding.

New House, known then as Cwm Brain, was mentioned in the Llanfair Hills Enclosure Award and the tithe map of 1843 shows that a John Griffiths owned the property at that time; both the house and land was rented out as below. Note: the measurements were ***A***cres, ***R***ods and ***P***erches.

Owner	**Tenant**	**Plot**	**Type of land**	**Area A R P**	**Rent payable**
John Griffths	Edward Evans	693	House/ garden/fold	- 3 12	1s 6d
		692	Meadow	- 3 30	- 10d
		694	Pasture	2 - 7	5s 2d
		696	Pasture	2 1 26	6s 6d
		697	Arable	1 2 30	5s 5d
		698	Pasture	7 1 16	9s 5d
		699	Arable	2 1 30	7s 9d

In 1891 a Mrs. Susan Griffiths farmed at New House.

Other owners have been:

12 July 1906 **Fanny Elizabeth Craig** of Ludlow
sold to
Thomas Clee of Llanwolley (who died on 18 March 1927)
The property consisted of 61 acres 5 rods and 24 perches -- **more or less!** except for the mines and minerals, the rights of which belonged to the Lord of the Manor.

20 Jan 1950 **Gertrude Clee** of Noke Lane House, Pembridge (living in Berkhamstead, Herts),
sold to
William Philip Thompson Garrett of the Birches, Lloyney, and
Philip Thompson Garrett
The property then consisted of 77 acres O rods and 14 perches

10 Nov 1967 **Philip Thompson Garrett**
sold to
Evan Douglas Powell, Cwm Farm, Dutlas

March 1970 **Evan Douglas Powell**, Cwm Farm, Dutlas
sold to
Anna Dorle Horne of Northampton

23 Mar 1988 **Anna Dorle Horne** of Northampton
sold to
John and Dorothy Lee-Frampton

The tithe map of 1843 also notes that the surrounding land was owned and rented out as follows:

Owner	Tenant	Plot	Type of land	Area A R P	Rent payable
Duppa Thomas	John Syer	691	Pasture	2 3 34	5s 1d
		695	Arable	1 1 36	4s 9d
		642	Pasture	- 3 -	
		689	Arable	3 1 30	10s 0d
		690	Meadow	3 1 25	1s 8d

Nether Skyborry

Nether Skyborry was probably quite a small cottage built into the hillside. It was extended and modernised in the 1870's and then let to tenants. It was under the ownership of the Treverward Estate and had previously probably been part of barns used to store grain for the monks at Abbeycwmhir. In 1902 the property was let to Mr. Harold Matthews on a 21 year lease. When in 1920 the Treverward estate was sold at auction the house was withdrawn and sold later to Mr. J. Bowen who ran a chicken farm and had a bakery shop and grocery in Knighton situated at the bottom of Broad Street. His cakes were often iced in a violent pink colour which was known locally as Bowen' s icing pink. From 1960 to 1969 Nether Skyborry was owned by Mrs.

Nether Skyborry at the turn of the century

Freda Harroway. Miss Murial Jones bought the house in 1969 and divided it and the Coach House in the grounds into two separate properties. Mr. D. Harvey and Mr. M. Cranston took up residence in 1987 and remained there until 1999 while the Coach House passed into the ownership of the Nickerson family.

Nether Skyborry, the house as it is now

Oak Cottage

Oak Cottage is older than Skyborry Green farmhouse, appearing on the 1849 Tithe map. It was advertised as the "Service Cottage" , in the 1947 Estate particulars and was obviously intended for a farm worker. It was well constructed of stone with a slate roof. The kitchen had an open grate and pantry and there were two bedrooms. Outside was a coal-house and earth closet, water being obtained from a nearby spring.

Oak Cottage

Between 1920 and 1940 Mr. & Mrs. Dick Evans, Jack, Bill, Dai and Walter lived at Oak Cottage. Mr. Evans worked for several local farmers and for a carpenter at Knucklas. Jobs were very scarce at that time. Later he became a postman, a job he held until his retirement .

Mr. Tom James was the next occupant, working on Skyborry Green Farm, then farmed by Mr. Charlie Price. Other tenants included Mr. Dick Ruff, Mr. & Mrs. Ivor Smith between 1955 and 1957, followed by Mr. & Mrs. Charlie Davies. In 1959 Mr. Stanley Davies moved in and began work for Mr. David Matthews at Skyborry Green farm. Mr. Davies has retired but still lives at Oak Cottage.

Old School House

The Old School House was built sometime in the 1850s by the Diocese of Hereford and there is a record in an old Shropshire Directory of the first schoolmaster living here, named Theophilus Watkins. The building has walls of local stone with limestone surrounds to the windows and doors with some later replaced by brick. The internal partitions were oak framed, as are the floor joists. The roof is slated and of a very steep pitch. The design and layout is very similar to other School/Schoolhouses of the era, notably the one at Nantmel, nr Rhayader. There were originally 6 rooms, 3 on each floor. The upstairs had 12 ft high ceilings, so the bedrooms were all higher than they were wide or long. Although the house faces south with excellent views across the Teme valley it was only built with one small window high up on the South Side, and with all other windows pointing East and North. There have been at least 4 sets of extensive repairs and alterations to the building. A plaque on the north gable records: "This School and Schoolhouse were put in thorough repair in commemoration of the Diamond Jubilee 1897". Copies of the Daily Express dated April 1948 were used to stop up various cracks during a substantial rebuilding of the South Wall, (including a page featuring an article referring to one of the present occupant's father!). In c. 1960 the Schoolhouse was sold to Mr. Jones of Llanfair Hall for c. £1000 and a septic tank and new (lower) ceilings were put in upstairs. The house was rented out or used as a tied cottage for farm workers until it was sold to the present owner/occupier in 1988. In 1991 further alterations and very extensive repairs were carried out including conversion of the attic to 2 rooms, and the dismantling of the large Victorian chimneys. The house has a ¼ acre garden which was used for vegetables for the schoolmaster. According to Harold Gwilt pupils often did the gardening work. There is a very large oak tree in the N.E corner of the garden with a girth at shoulder height of c. 15 ft.. This gives an estimated age of at least 180 years. The structure of the tree indicates that it was coppiced at least once in the late 19th or early 20th century. The house is currently occupied by Hugh Colvin (51), his partner Anne Loughran (44) and their two sons John (7) and Joseph (1).

View of the School House, Jack & Bill Evans?

The School House 1999

Pond Cottage (Memories of Mrs. Julia Bright grand daughter of Mrs. Polly Evans)

About a mile from the village there is a hamlet called Melin-y-Grogue, it used to contain five dwellings, one farm, one mill where the farmers took their corn to be ground into feed stuff, or flour for baking, and three cottages. A few years ago one cottage was demolished, this was where my grandparents and I lived. It belonged to Mr. Jones from Llanfair Hall. It was called the Pond Cottage. It contained two bedrooms, the smaller bedroom had a fireplace, the landing was also big enough to hold a single bed. The stairs were very steep with a bend and three steps before getting to the bottom. Down stairs there was a pantry,

Melin-y-Grogue Cottage

The site of Pond Cottage

kitchen, back kitchen and washhouse. The kitchen had a black leaded grate with an oven one side where the cooking was done, the other side contained a boiler but there was a large crack in it so it didn't hold water. The floor was big stone flags. The back kitchen had a furnace in it but there were holes in that too so it didn't hold much water and it was rusty. My grandmother used to boil the clothes in a big pot over the fire. On the floor there were red bricks, on washday we threw the suds from the washing over the floor and brushed it outside. We threw clean water down to rinse it and it looked nice and clean. There were no mod-cons, the lavatory was a little distance up the road joined on to the pig sty and the garden still further on up the road. In summertime my grandfather used to lock the garden gate because I used to sneak in and pick the peas on my way to fetch clean water from the well in Mr. Clee The Mill's field. Water for other uses was carried from a brook that flowed down from Cwmbrain. Some things were delivered to the door. Mr. Bob Baker from Knighton brought bread once a week and quite often gave me a cake—I thought that was great. I have many happy memories of living in Pond Cottage.

Rose Villa

Rose Villa

Rose Villa opened as a shop in 1921 and later became the village Post Office. It closed in August 1994 and the last customer was Mr. Raymond Davies.

In 1871 John and Elizabeth Evans lived in the house and by 1921 Mr. & Mrs. Jordan owned the property, they ran the shop, he was a tailor and later they also had the Post Office. In 1952 it was sold to Mr. A. Scrivens. In 1960 Mr. and Mrs. Bunn moved in but they only stayed for a year. In 1961 Harold Gwilt from Cwm Collo with his wife Ann bought the property. Their daughter Pauline was already 4 years old having been born in 1957. Robert was born in 1961 and Anthony in 1964. Harold and Ann ran the shop and Post Office and delivered groceries to outlying houses until 1994. Robert inherited the property and lives there still. He has made a flat where Brian O'Higgins lived in 1996 and Trudi Hayward and her son Joseph in 1998. Robert works as a local builder as his father did and takes a full part in local community activities. Pauline teaches in Knighton and Anthony is a builder and carpenter.

Selley Hall

After farming a small farm with a modernised house in Llangunllo we moved to Selley Hall in February 1964 in a snowstorm. There was no mains electricity, power was from an engine from which we could iron, have one bar of the electric fire, or run the fridge at one time. The water was pumped to the house by a water ram, which frequently broke down. Luckily these were soon rectified especially with three young sons, Terry, David and Robert (Michael arrived five years later) to look after.

Polly Evans,
Pond Cottage

SUMMARY OF THE LLANVAIR-WATERDINE ESTATE.

Lot.	Description.	Tenant.	Area.	Outgoings. Tithe Apportionment	Land Tax for Year 1918-19
				£ s. d.	£ s. d.
1	Pound Farm	Mr. T. A. Price	281.401	22 5 5	4 8 0
2	Wernygeufron Farm	Mr. G. Turley	218.829	17 5 0	3 6 0
3	Lower Goytre Farm	Mr. A. Davies	62.456	7 11 8	1 2 11
4	Goytre Wood	(In Hand)	9.106	Nil.	Nil.
5	Lloyney Mill and Land ..	Mr. Robert Davies ..	21.117	1 12 5	Nil.
6	Mellin-y-grogue Farm	Mr. Percy C. Beavan ..	162.562	10 6 6	2 6 1
7	Mellin-y-grogue Mill	Mr. A. Clee	13.548	1 4 10	19 0
8	Cwm-colla Farm	Mr. R. Swancott	146.791	6 0 7	1 15 7
9	Cwm-Mawr Farm	Mr. J. M. Price.. ..	126.871	6 14 3	Nil.
10	Mountain Tenement	Mr. H. Clee	15.545	1 1 2	Nil.
11	Bwlch Farm	Mr. T. Price	93.564	(Tithe Estimated.) 4 13 2	1 6 3
12	Llanvair Hall Farm	Mr. T. S. Jones	668.536	27 11 1	7 13 6
13	Hirgin Land	ditto	36.490	3 0 9	1 0 0
14	Red Lion Inn	Mrs. Evans	16.786	2 5 1	6 5
15	Brynedin	Mr. A. Bufton	5.943	10 0	Nil.
16	Smithy and 2 Cottages ..	Messrs. C. W. Farmer and C. Evans	.296	1 5	Nil.
17	Cottage, Mellin-y-grogue ..	Miss A. Jones	.144	Nil.	Nil.
18	3 Cottages, Cwm-Cold	Mr. J. Price, Mrs. Davies (and one void) ..	.262	Nil.	Nil.
		A.	1880.247	£112 3 4	£24 3 9

About 1919

Sampler sewn by Mrs. Julia Bright

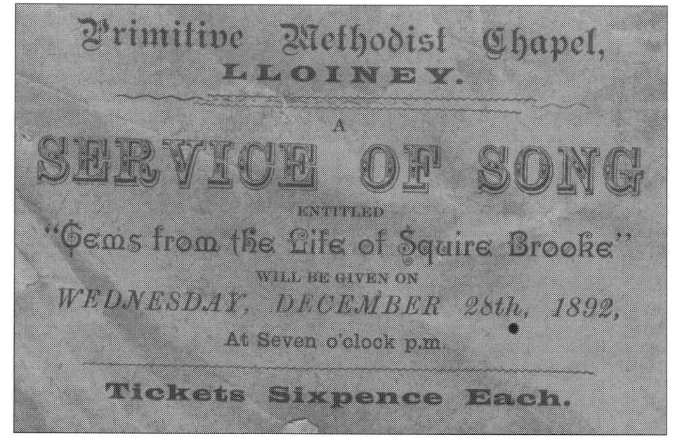

Primitive Methodist Chapel,
LLOINEY.

A
SERVICE OF SONG
ENTITLED
"Gems from the Life of Squire Brooke"
WILL BE GIVEN ON
WEDNESDAY, DECEMBER 28th, 1892,
At Seven o'clock p.m.

Tickets Sixpence Each.

We bought Selley Hall from Mr. W. E. Lewis, although it had been farmed for many years by Mr. George Bright and his sister. Mr. Bright was noted for his farming and his Clun sheep. He and his sister played a prominant part in the parish, with Mr. Bright acting as Church Warden at St. Mary's, Llanfair Waterdine, for a number of years. The farm was approximately 440 acres, but looking at the census the acreage had varied between 250 acres in 1841, to 600 acres in 1871. The very hilly land runs between 700 ft and 1200 ft.

Selley Hall

Mr. Penry Powell and his family farmed Selley Hall for nearly 100 years, and we believe he built the present large three storeyed house (plus a cellar) around 1880. The original farmhouse was on the other side of the road with the farm buildings. A water well and pump in the backyard supplied water for the house, and are still in situ but not in use. Also off the yard were the earth toilets (three in all) and two wash houses, in fact the day we looked at the farm prior to buying, Mrs. Lloyd who lived at Brynorgan and was 80, was doing the weekly wash in one of the boilers and had collected sticks the previous day to heat the boiler.

We believe previous owners lived in the front of the house with the servants in the back rooms, where there is a large attic room probably used for storing the wool. There is a large coffer in this room which must have been built in situ, for no way will it come down the stairs.

In 1881 the Powells employed a servant, a housemaid, a herdsman, a waggoner, under waggoner, and a boy servant. Today Llewelyn, David and three tractors, with the assistance of Mary and Lynda at lambing time, manage the farm.

Mr. Bright had employed Onoff Tortoriello, an Italian prisoner of war, during the war years and later in time he made his home nearby. Onoff was a most interesting and helpful worker who stayed with us for many years. In the 1960's and 1970's we had our groceries, meat and bread delivered to the door. Nowadays we have to travel to Knighton for such items.

In 1964 a working water wheel was used for shearing the sheep and pulping the roots grown on the farm. Electricity soon made the water wheel obsolete, and we used the stone from the pillars carrying the shafts to build walls around the garden, and the wheel was dismantled. During excavations for a new building in 1969 a number of clay pipes were unearthed, which seems to indicate it was the site of an old gypsy settlement, which could be the camp referred to on the tombstone of Herbert Locke, buried in Llanfair Waterdine churchyard.

Michael, Robert, Llewelyn, Terry and David 1974

The late Frank Noble was instrumental in getting the Offa's Dyke footpath recognised as a National footpath, and spent many hours walking the path which passes through the farm land. He also encouraged us to create a Bed and Breakfast business during which time we met some most interesting and famous people. We now run a self-catering unit instead.

In 1970 we purchased the adjoining farm, Little Selley, from Mrs. Watkins, and this is now farmed as one unit with Selley Hall.

Mary Morgan kneading bread

Farming has changed greatly during our time at Selley Hall, for instance hay harvests involved the whole family helping to stack, load, and unload small bales - now it is all big round bales. Ewes were lambed out in the fields in all kinds of weather, day and night. Now we have the luxury of a shed and electric light, but there are still lots of problems! Sheep, cattle feed and fertiliser are now delivered in bulk, or big bags, and milk fresh from the 'house cow' has gone forever.

Llewelyn & Mary Morgan

Selley Hall Cottage

Selley Hall Cottage

Originally known as the Old Workhouse for Selley Hall the cottage was built by 1859. Pauline Sprakes, the great great granddaughter of Evan and Elizabeth Lewis called at the house recently. Pauline White also called at the house in search of her family history.

Selley Hall Cottage was at first two joined cottages each comprising one room downstairs and two bedrooms above. Each cottage was about 20 feet by 13 feet. A well was located on the south side with the earth closet further down. The water supply which comes from across the road follows the same path today. The same water supplies the garden plots where the families would have grown vegetables. The size of the cottages is important as at one time there were 9 children and 2 adults occupying one cottage. The first family to live in the cottage were Evan and Elizabeth Lewis. They worked for Mr.

1 Selley Hall Cottages before renovation

CERTIFIED COPY of an ENTRY OF BIRTH
COPI DILYS O GOFNOD GENEDIGAETH
Pursuant to the Births and Deaths Registration Act 1953

CK 226

Registration District / Dosbarth Cofrestru: Radnorshire East

1859 BIRTH in the Sub-district of / GENEDIGAETH yn Is-ddosbarth: Knighton in the / yn: Counties of Radnor Hereford and Salop

No.	When and where born	Name, if any	Sex	Name, and surname of father	Name, surname, and maiden surname of mother	Occupation of father	Signature, description, and residence of informant	When registered	Signature of registrar	Name entered after registration
231	Thirteenth April 1859 Old Workhouse Llanfair Waterdine	Charles	Boy	Evan Lewis	Elizabeth Lewis formerly Humphreys	Agricultural Labourer	X The mark of Evan Lewis Father Old Workhouse Llanfair Waterdine	Second May 1859	James Davies Registrar	

I, Edmund M. Kelcher, Superintendent Registrar for the District of Radnorshire East in the Powys do hereby certify that this is a true copy of the entry No. 231 in the Register of Births No. 7 for the above-named Sub-district, and that such Register is now legally in my custody.

Witness my hand this 28th day of September 1996

E. M. Kelcher, Superintendent Registrar

CAUTION:—It is an offence to falsify a certificate or to make or knowingly use a false certificate or a copy of a false certificate intending it to be accepted as genuine to the prejudice of any person, or to possess a certificate knowing it to be false without lawful authority.

Birth certificate of Charles 1859

1883 MARRIAGE Solemnized at the Parish Church in the Parish of Ludlow in the County of Salop

No.	When Married.	Name and Surname.	Age.	Condition.	Rank or Profession.	Residence at the Time of Marriage.	Father's Name and Surname.	Rank or Profession of Father.
219	September 2nd 1883	Charles Lewis	24	Bachelor	Keeper	Old Street (LUDLOW)	Evan Lewis	Farm Bailiff
		Emma Alice Smith	20	Spinster	—	Old Street	John Smith	Miller

Married in the Parish Church according to the Rites and Ceremonies of the Established Church by or after Banns By me, Geoffrey W Turner assist. Rector

This Marriage was solemnized between us, Charles Lewis, Emma Alice Smith. In the presence of us, John Smith, William Ross, Ellen Jane Co[illegible]

The above is a true Copy of the Marriage Register of the Parish Church aforesaid.

Extracted this [illegible] Day of September in the Year of our Lord One Thousand Eight Hundred and eighty three

By me, Geoffrey W Turner Assist. Rector

Marriage certificate Charles and Emma 1893

George Bright a farmer and had three children Charles born in 1859, George born in 1860 and Elizabeth born in 1867. The next family were the Sprakes: Edwin Sprakes was a gamekeeper and his wife was in service. Martha Sprakes was born in 1906 and was also in service until 1925. She was the mother of Pauline White who was sent to Llanfair from London as an evacuee in the War. She remembers the walk to school in Llanfair following the existing footpath. There was no electricity or indoor plumbing and 11 people lived in one cottage.

Charles Lewis born in 1859 at Selley Hall Cottage. Son of Evan Lewis (right)

The living room before renovation

Mr. and Mrs. Ted Lloyd lived in the cottage until 1965. There was a fire in the early 1950's and many people remember Ted Lloyd running down to the Matthews' to telephone the fire brigade. When a wattle and daub wall fell down recently part of a charred beam was visible.

In 1965 the Morgan family purchased the Old Workhouse and sold it to Mr. L. M. Smith. By 1969 Dr. and Mrs. M. R. Davidson lived in the house and they put on it's distinctive "Dutch roof" after adding another storey.

Andy and Melanie Roberton, with their daughters Helen and Claire moved in, they added the garage and workshop. In 1994 I arrived with my son David Llewellyn. Our contribution is a conservatory we built in 1996. Looking out in the morning and seeing the landscape, the stock and knowing the people who work to maintain this, I know how lucky we are. Thank you.

Antoinette Lansdell

Mrs N Cummins with her pony and trap

Skyborry

During the late 19th and early 20th century Skyborry was owned by the Edwards family for three generations. It was being let when Colonel E. J. and Mrs. N. M. Cummins took the tenancy in 1936. Subsequently they bought the house in 1947 from an investment trust. The Colonel died in 1952 and Mrs. Cummins in 1978 and since then it has been the home of James and Esther Cummins and Sarah, Bobby and Rachel.

Balls Cottage. Jim and Esther Cummins bought the very small cottage in 1974 and

Balls Cottage 1999

extended it and returned from Norfolk to live there in the very hot dry summer of 1976. On the death of Mrs. N. M. Cummins they moved into Skyborry. Balls Cottage was let to several tenants and then sold. Since then it has been used as a holiday cottage.

Dolly's. In the 19th century census mention is made of Dolly's and it is listed between Panpwnton and Skyborry. A small building can be seen on the Enclosure map for 1853 and was situated in the field we call Dials Close through which the lime tree avenue now runs.

This is an article and letter written by Jim Cummins for a magazine:-
CHRISM – CHRISTIANS IN SECULAR MINISTRY.
Ministers at Work. Number 68 Jan 1999.
It tells us a great deal about Jim's life in 1999.

'Editor: Would you write about your current work and ministry, Jim, for CHRISM? Jim: I don't really DO anything ...', Jim said'.

Editor's note: Jim provided an article but he also wrote a letter. I have taken the liberty of printing it before the article because I believe that it provides the context for Jim's ministry more clearly than anything else could and brings it alive.

Dear Dorrie,

12th Nov. I have been interrupted already and must now begin again. It's been a bad day - two days, really. Yesterday we had one ewe on her back, fortunately seen by a neighbour who got her upright again but she'll be a bit wobbly for a day or so. (Sheep usually do this in the spring, before shearing. They lie down and roll over and can't get up again - then their tummies put pressure on their lungs and they can't breathe). Then Esther found one of the 'store' lambs dead on the hill for no particular reason. It's not a great loss since no one wants them but we don't like to see them turn their toes up before their time.

Today has been worse. I opened a new bale of silage for the cattle and found it contained almost as much soil as grass. That's bad news; the cows don't like it and there is a serious risk that they may contract 'listeriosis' (which can be fatal) from bacteria in the soil. Bless those dear little badgers who rip up the grassland after we've put it up for harvest. But worse was to follow. As it was getting light, Esther went to let the ducks out and found that a fox had managed to get through our defences in the night. He'd killed three and the remaining six had been 'necked'. They may survive but they are badly wounded, very gory and deeply shocked. All this happened before breakfast - and it's only Thursday 12th. If I was of a superstitious turn of mind I would go into hibernation until Saturday! It is a daily paradox that God's destruction walks hand in hand with his creation, and often very cruelly - like the Cross?.

Anyway, after that start I drive over the hill to Clun for a day punctuated with visits from gloomy customers who are increasingly anxious about the whole future of farming. They are not poor or hungry but they carry a grave burden. They are the spearhead of a huge industry. Their wisdom and knowledge has been amassed over many generations. Now they have to recognise that, as the value of their produce is halved, they are dependent on the will or the whim of distant politicians. I've had old men in here who reflect on the last major crisis in farming - in the Thirties. I would expect them to say "The trouble with you young men nowadays is, you've had it too easy; you just don't know what it's like." But they don't. There's a general consensus that this is worse, but in a very different way.

In those days "money" meant very little. There were no electricity bills, no 'phone bills, practically no rates or taxes - in short, expenses were minimal. And there was a pig in the sty down the yard, there were hens a-laying and a cow to milk and rabbits abounded on the hill. Few farmers from round here ever crossed the threshold of a bank. Now, every tractor, every piece of machinery, is valued in thousands - or tens or hundreds of thousands - of pounds. Not much goes out in wages, (more's the pity) but the overheads are colossal.

Most people around here own their farms. Most have used the better times to modernise their buildings and machinery and are able to weather even a really severe storm for quite a long time. But will the next generation want to carry on with the new style of farming - where they have to plough through more paper than land in order to get the tit-bits tossed to them by the none-too-civil servants? It's not a happy prospect.

Maybe I'm getting away from the purpose of this screed but two things I feel I should add. One is that when two or three of these sad people arrive in the shop I notice how they get together for a chat and before long they are making a joke out of some particular disaster, pulling one another's legs and all of a sudden its quite like 'old times' again. The underlying spirit is indomitable. The other thing is that the decline in values of livestock at auction is real. Lambs are making less than half what they were a year ago and so are cattle. We sell cows and calves. Before the BSE crisis we could expect between £650 and £850 for a young cow and calf. Last Spring I took three to auction and let them go for £560. A fortnight ago I took another five and they made from £300 to £335. The costs of production have *not* declined to any comparable extent. That's a measure of what we are up against.

And then there's the weather - the farmer's eternal whipping boy! It's been a rather gloomy summer and the 8.5 inches last month (it will have been a lot more than that further up the valley) may be very good for sales of wellies and waterproof clothing but it leaves a sea of mud for Mr. Farmer to trudge through. Grumble he will - it's his privilege - but he also sees his telly (that's another change from the Thirties) and even when the floods of China and Bangladesh have subsided from the screen the horrors of Honduras and Nicaragua allow us - the grumblers - a different perspective. That is not lost on my customers.

I lead a rather trinitarian sort of life. **First, I am a conscious Christian - ordained** in 1960 and doing more or less the traditional thing until leaving to explore other ways. That was in 1976. A lot has happened since then and so, **secondly**, we (Esther my wife, and self) now live in my old home where we are partners in a farming business. We have never tried to make a living out of the farm but it has been responsible for paying the rates and keeping the roof on, so to speak. That has become something of a joke over the past year or so and I am deeply thankful that we are **not** dependent on it - it's more like having a very big garden with a lot of pets in it. What it does do is to allow us to share at first hand, to some extent, the anxieties and problems of the local farming community.

That brings me to the **third** sphere of action in which I am involved. That is the business known as Clunside, or to give it its full title "Clunside Sales and Services". There I spend my days. Esther looks after the 'pets' (a bull, 20 cows and their offspring of the last two years and the flock of 100+ sheep and, unfortunately, a lot of their children as well - these last should have been sold before now but the trade just isn't there). I commute about seven miles over the hill into the Clun valley. Four people are involved in that business. We are "Agricultural and Motor

Skyborry in early Spring

Engineers" and that side of the business runs in parallel with a general "Stores" which aims to provide almost all the needs of the local agricultural community. Agriculture, or farming if you prefer, is the backbone industry of the area and most of the farming is concerned with breeding and rearing sheep and beef cattle though there is a fair acreage of arable, mainly barley and wheat, on the lower end of the valley.

There is also an increasing population of commuters and retired people living in the area and these too have an amazing assortment of machinery and cars not to mention dogs and cats who like the food we provide. I could go on and on about the odd things which Clunside has to offer and the joys which derive from working among such people. But you may well ask - maybe this is what you would ask - where does Christian Ministry fit into all this? I'll have to put in a little bit of background here, I think.

When I first came back to this part of the world, it was with an acute awareness of the changes taking place in rural ministry. Funds and manpower were, quite rightly being directed increasingly towards the inner cities and other neglected places. Might it not be possible, I thought, for a single country parish to be cared for by a minister who earned his bread in some undemanding job without being a burden on the church at large? I got a job as a dogsbody assistant storeman with a local agricultural engineering firm and offered my services to the Bishop. He was very amenable - he saw me as something of a bonus - and asked me to take on a local parish through a longish interregnum. That was fine; I was happy, the parish was happy and it proved the point, at least to my satisfaction. But it quickly became apparent that there was another sort of ministry developing. Pastoral ministry has to do with relationships. In Church these may focus in our communion around the altar. In the stores it is across the counter. That grew.

Other things happened over the years. Following the death of my mother we moved into the farm and that has grown, too. The old boss died (and I had the privilege of conducting his funeral); the firm was taken over by a bigger outfit and before long they shut us down. That was how we came to start up Clunside. So much for the undemanding job'! But the three elements of my present life interweave very constructively. Through the farm I share the joys and anxieties of the farmer customers at first hand - and I have the opportunity to try out most of what I sell. Equally it is known that I am a clergyman - by customers, reps' and others - and as such I am used, which is, I suppose part of what we are for. Then, I am very aware of the 'services' part of our title - but it has to be said that my partners are every bit as involved in providing our services as I am and they aren't ordained. So what'?

When trying to think, in preparation for the Birmingham Conference back in the summer. I wrote, *'If our perspective is theological, everything we do becomes theologically motivated. Without that perspective it is all too easy and too common for the likes of us farmers to take an awful lot for granted..."* Lately I have been especially aware of a need to recognise the holiness of the mundane and as far as possible to encourage others to do the same. By way of just one example of this I was confronted a few months ago with a questionnaire - a pilot survey for clergy - about 'the therapeutic use of oil'. I don't like being negative and my response to the questions was rather depressing. 'Was the use of oil for anointing incorporated into your ordination service as deacon or as priest? Do you currently use oil for Baptism? Confirmation for the sick etc.?' It was all 'No, No, No,' Then "Is there an increase or decrease in using oils in your ministerial practice within the last ten years?" Wow! After all those negatives here was a "Yes, Yes, Yes!"

I'm not sure about ten years, but in the fifteen since we started in Clun a quick glimpse at the turnover shows clearly that our use of oil has gone from nothing to just about ten thousand pounds worth last year. While those figures might not be quite what the researcher required to obtain her MTh. in applied theology they are for real. The oil services the tractors and machinery which in turn serve the farmer - customer and all is well.

Now it's time I went and sorted out cows again so I must stop.

Skyborry Green

Skyborry Green farmhouse was originally two cottages, tied accommodation for farmworkers. The landlord obviously cared about his employees as the cottages were spacious and well built. Whilst we may find them somewhat primitive now, in 1869, when they were probably built, the scullery, bread oven and salting slab were the latest mod cons! The cottages were built of local stone, with the more expensive brick reserved for the chimneys.

Skyborry Green Farmhouse

Water was supplied from a spring, and the two families probably shared an outside earth closet, but by the standards of the time the farm-workers were quite well housed. Times were harder and people were necessarily self-sufficient, baking bread, keeping pigs and poultry and growing vegetables. Most people kept a pig and in the sale particulars of 1947 we are told that Skyborry Green farmhouse had "two galvanized iron pigs cots with pounds. Timber and galvanized wainhouse and trap house with lean-to tool shed adjoining. Stone, timber and galvanized range forming cart stable for 3, loose box, cow house for 10 with byng and 2 calves kits and lofts and tallets over the whole".

In 1920 Skyborry Estate was broken up and sold in various lots. Prior to 1944 Mr. & Mrs. Price farmed Skyborry Green farm, followed by their son Charlie and daughter Gladys. By 1944 when Mr. David Matthews took on the tenancy, Skyborry Green cottages had become one house. He and his wife Peggy farmed 279 acres which must have been hard work. The lambing, shearing, haymaking and driving of sheep to market continued in their age old ceaseless round. Neighbours were always ready to help one another at busy times or times of illness or trouble. Threshing had long been carried out by the Lloyd family. This was quite labour intensive so neighbours helped one another and were helped in turn. Life was not all work however. Llanfair Waterdine W.I. began in 1931 (and is still going strong today), the Y.F.C. in 1944 and the Llanfair Waterdine village choir in the 1960's. In the early years travel to social events was slow, often by pony and trap, bicycle (with solid tyres!) on foot or by motorcycle if you were lucky, but, despite this, concerts, whist-drives and dances were popular. People enjoyed the refreshments of tea, cake and sandwiches, not expecting the alcohol usually served today.

At Skyborry Green, Mr. Matthews kept mainly sheep and a herd of 12—14 friesian cows. They were milked twice daily, and Cadburys would collect the 10 gallon churns every day and transport them to Leominster. Mrs. Matthews in common with many farmers wives of the time, relied on the proceeds of pig and poultry keeping for her housekeeping money. Making her own jam and cakes made the money go further. Sometimes she was lucky enough to obtain domestic help when particularly busy. Housework in those days must have been hard labour indeed and wash-days, especially wet ones, a daunting task. As well as the family, Mrs. Matthews would sometimes have to cater for various farm-workers including Mr. Jim Powell, Mr. Ron Phillips and Mr. Frank Calvert who would sometimes live in. It was not uncommon for men to call offering their labour in return for food. Gypsies would also call, selling clothes pegs and their caravans were a familiar sight, parked on the grass verge as the travellers gathered around their camp-fire making clothes pegs.

Raymond Matthews on an early 'Fergie'

The coming of the second world war showed how dependant the towns were on the farmer. The War Agricultural, a government authorizing body made it compulsory to grow certain crops, such as potatoes, sugar beet, grain and cocksfoot for seed at a fixed price. On the bottom fields, then farmed by S.W. Brisbane, such crops were grown and then taken by rail to the cities.

For generations Skyborry Green farm had been owned by The Edwards family but in 1954 Mrs. Cummins of Skyborry purchased it from Bandas Investments Ltd., and became Mr. & Mrs. Matthews' new landlady.

Other changes had taken place too. Mr. & Mrs. Matthews now had two sons, John and Raymond. A bus now came up as far as Selly Cross to take country folk into Knighton, where, no doubt, they spent their hard earned cash. Prices seem ridiculously low to us now, £9 for a ram (1950) and £115 for a bull in 1959, but wages, and incomes too, were still very low. However times were changing for the farmer. By the mid 1950's the coming of electricity must have lightened the work-load considerably, although todays farmers tackling Ministry of Agriculture forms on their computers, might consider it a doubtful privilege. Cars became more common, Mr. Matthews bought his first car in 1954, a Hillman, and his first brand new car, an Austin Cambridge (AFO 732) in 1959. In the same year he purchased The Brinney which is in the hills above Skyborry. It was the home of Mr. & Mrs. Robert Davies who had bought it in 1921.

In later years Mrs. Matthews did more work outside the farm, catering for funerals and private functions. She still worked at home and her sons remember her taking sheep fleeces to Newtown to be made into blankets for her family's own use. Mr. and Mrs. Matthews regularly attended Knucklas Chapel, the services and anniversaries connected with the Chapel were an important part of local life, as was harvest time. Everyone lent a hand and John Matthews remembers Lady Hunt calling by and readily joining in to help. Lord Hunt was the leader of the 1953 Everest expedition, and he was transported home to Weir Cottage from Knighton station in a pony trap, drawn by his many friends, amongst them Mr. Matthews. The Matthews family remember the many celebrations marking Lord Hunts conquest of Everest. The village hall, previously the school attended by John and his father is now called "Everest Hall".

His school days behind him, John worked the farm with his father, now assisted by a full-time worker Mr. Stanley Davies. When Raymond left school in 1964 he started his own business repairing vehicles in the wainhouse at the front of Skyborry Green house. In 1966 he purchased a second-hand Massey Ferguson combine costing £200 and in 1968 a Twose digger to fit on the back of a M.F. tractor. He married Elizabeth in 1969. In 1974 they built a bungalow in Lloyney, where they still live, called Riverdale. In 1985 John and Raymond purchased Skyborry Green farm and continue to farm it between them. John's other interests include the invention and development of such agricultural equipment as a cow lifting cradle. Raymond continues to run his business at Skyborry Green which has developed into heavy plant hire, Landrover sales and repairs and is also involved in haulage, building and a builders' merchant. His office stands on the site of the Wheelwrights shop — mentioned as lot 10 in the 1947 sale particulars. It was occupied by Mr. Robert Davies of The Brinney and later by his sons Robert and Leonard. Of course a large part of their work involved the making of cartwheels and coffins in the shop, but they travelled around the countryside as well. The local community depended on their many skills in repairing buildings and implements and often John Matthews as a young boy would go with them for the ride. Robert and Leonard would buy oak or elm trees from local farmers and "tush" it in with a horse-drawn timber wagon. Then they would spend a whole day sawing the wood with a circular saw. In later years the wood was bought rough cut from the Radnorshire Company, which must have saved a great deal of time and labour.

Leonard Davies

The photograph shows Leonard Davies making a wheel at Skyborry Green in the early 1950's.

His daughter Beth Williams describes how a wheel was made. In the photograph, one of the five felloes has yet to be put in place. (Felloes is pronounced to rhyme with jellies). Two spokes go into a felloe and the felloe makes up the circular rim. It then has the hot iron hoop or tyre fixed on.

The machinery at the shop was powered by oil in the 1950's , but the tools chisels, hammer and saws (behind Mr. Davies in the photograph) could easily have belonged to earlier times. Leonard died in 1956, Bob retired and the workshop closed, another link with the past was broken. By the end of the 1950's most wheelwrights shops had gone and the skilled craftsmen became few and far between. The wheelwrights busy shop may now belong to the distant past where almost everything needed, from cradle to grave, was made locally, but work goes on as it always did at Skyborry Green. Mr. Matthews died in 1988 and Mrs. Matthews in 1996 and they are buried at Knucklas Chapel, so much a part of their lives. Skyborry Green farmhouse stands empty now awaiting renovation.

The world has seen many changes since it was built but locals still travel the lanes to market and May Fair as did their great grandparents before them. Offas Dyke path running across Skyborry hill, will no doubt attract many tourists to the area well into the next millennium.

John, Raymond & Elizabeth Matthews and family

Stoney Pound

Stoney Pound

In 1943 Arthur Parry of White House, Whitcott Keysett owned Stoney Pound and about 77 acres. On his death he left it to his son, also Arthur, and it was let to Cyril Jones from 1943 until 1978 when he retired and moved to Bishop's Castle. From 1978 to 1982 Stoney Pound was again farmed by the Parry family. In September 1982 it was sold by public auction at the Castle Hotel Bishop's Castle. Stoney Pound and eight and a half acres was bought by Mr. Kingsley Price of Newcastle. Later that year he sold the house and three quarters of an acre of land to Mr. Kevin and Mrs. Sylvia Garvey from Beckenham in Kent. In July 1985 the Garvey's sold Stoney Pound to Mr. Norman and Mrs. Josephine Steedman and their son Michael from the Crown Inn Newcastle. In November 1990 they bought an extra acre of land to the West side of the barn. Roger Tydeman bought the property from the Steedmans in May 1997 and moved in soon after. Stoney Pound is quite an old house probably built in the late 18th Century. Farm buildings were connected to the house but have now been used as an extension. Roger Tydeman says that he has much enjoyed his first 18 months at Stoney Pound and hopes to be there for many years to come. He retired from a busy professional life in London where he lived for over 25 years and he finds the peace and tranquillity a great joy. As Stoney Pound is one of the northern most properties in the Parish and closer to Newcastle than to Llanfair he has come to know a number of people in Newcastle and not yet had much contact with the residents of Llanfair.

Teme Cottage

The history of Teme Cottage is a bit vague as the deeds to our house were mislaid by our Bank in the mid 1980's. From the Census records we can trace 'Bridge End' and 'Bridge Cottage' back to 1871 but we do not know if these refer to the small building on the bridge (affectionately known in the family as 'The Mansion') or Teme Cottage itself, but we assume the latter. It is still shown as Bridge Cottage on the 1903 O S Map and probably changed to Teme Cottage during the early 1900's.

The Mansion

Throughout the late 1800's the house was occupied by Joseph Miles and family whose occupation was shoemaker so maybe 'The Mansion' was his cobblers shop and he lived in Bridge Cottage.

Grandmother Sarah Davies

Our grandparents Sarah and Alfred Davies bought Teme Cottage in 1931 when they moved from Lower Goitre Farm. They lived here until the early 1940's when our parents, David and Mary Davies moved here from Tyn-y-Cefn, Dutlas with their firstborn, our eldest brother John. Four more children completed the family, Leslie, Ruth, Robert and Ann.

Teme Cottage was originally just a dwelling with a very small amount of land adjacent but over the years the family have acquired additional farm land making a total area of some 48 acres. Our parents were dairy farmers with some sheep. The tradition of milking was carried on until 1995 when we gave up producing milk and concentrated on beef cattle and sheep. Over 50 years of getting up early everyday to milk the cows, and again in the evening, in all weathers is hard work and such a tie. Mum used to deliver milk to both villages of Llanfair Waterdine and Lloyney, carrying the milk in a heavy churn and using a pint ladle to fill customers' jugs. She also delivered milk daily to the village school. We were the last farmers in the Teme valley to sell milk - in the 1950's and 60's there were as many as 20 farms producing milk to be collected daily in churns by the Milk Marketing Board lorry. We were forced to convert to bulk tank storage during the 70's but even so, eventually it just was not viable for 'small' farmers to continue to produce milk following privatisation of the Milk Marketing Board in 1993.

Mary Davies delivers milk in the village 1940's

The Davies family 1959

Teme Cottage

As children we were expected to help on the farm and in the house and garden, especially at lambing and harvest time. Families got together and helped one another at busy times, we made our own entertainment with youngsters gathering on the bridge to chat, mess about in the river, play football or whatever. It was a very special occasion when the otter hounds came up the river, the huntsmen in their blue coats caused great excitement. It was a rare treat to be allowed to go to Knighton on a Saturday afternoon, on Owens Motors bus, to go to the pictures, then up to the chip shop for three penneth of chips and home on the 8 o'clock bus.

Mum took in paying guests for holidays and when the house was full up we used to sleep in The Mansion, it was in much better condition in those days, although maybe no more comfortable!

The River Teme flows through the middle of our land, it is one of the fastest flowing rivers in Britain. It used to flood regularly and during 1947 the water rose up to the front door step of our house. That was a bit scary! Nowadays, it still floods most years but, with some help, the river bed is now much deeper and the banks are able to contain most of the flood waters. Over the years it has frequently changed its course due to the fast flowing flood waters washing away large chunks of the river banks on either side.

John, Leslie and Ann have moved away and have homes of their own, leaving Robert and Ruth to run the farm and house. Modern farm machinery and household gadgets, all things that our parents couldn't afford with five children to raise, have made life much easier for us than for Mum and Dad. Gone are the days of haymaking by hand, of washing in the tub and using an old boiler! Over the years the house has been modernised, re-roofed, some new floors and windows and a few changes inside but the exterior has remained very much the same for many years.

We have always kept dogs, mostly sheepdogs, as part of the family. As children we had a springer spaniel; who was a great family favourite and now after many years we have two spaniels, mother and daughter, well known for riding around in the back of the landrover and also for barking at everyone and everything that goes by!!

Dad died at the early age of 56, leaving Mum and Robert to carry on the farm business until Mum's death in 1988 at the age of 73.

Today, Robert runs the farm more or less single handed with Ruth as head cook and bottle washer and with both involved in and enjoying the local community life.

The Barn Melin-y-Grogue when renovation began in the 1980's

The Barn Melin-y-Grogue

In 1987 my husband Paul and I moved into Melin-y-Grogue Farmhouse. The lovely old barn was much in need of rescue and Paul thought we should repair it and convert it into a property for holiday letting. We did this and let it for nine years, but after my husband's death in 1996 I decided to move into it. I had found that looking after the main farmhouse, the garden, the few acres of land and the letting business was too much for me to do alone. I have lived in the barn since November 1997 with my cat Bede and it is a happy place to be.

Mary Simmons

The Barn in 1999

The Brinney – Memories

From about 1948, when I was five years old I often used to go during school holidays with my father, Leonard Davies, from our home in Knucklas to the wheelwright's shop at Skyborry Green, first on the carrier of his bike and holding on to his 'bait box' and later having my own bike, outgrown by Doris Swancott, The Lawn, and bought for 10/-. Whilst my father and Uncle Bob worked in the shop I would walk up to the Brinney to see my grandparents and Auntie Bertha who had recently retired from nursing to care for them.

The Brinney

Shortly after passing Miss Jones lovely aromatic garden at Herb Cottage and the large oak tree at Oak Cottage the lane narrowed and became steep and sunken, the fields on either side much too high to see into. In summer one length was dark with overhanging trees, dog roses and honeysuckle. Robins and blackbirds nests were at eye level and at one point the roots of an ash tree twisted above my head.

Finally the pigsty came into view on the left. First stop was at the well just above the house for a drink; a ladle hung by the back door for the purpose. Then in to see grandmother who was totally blind and used to identify the flowers I had picked for her by touch and smell. I had to stand before her so that she could feel my legs and shoulders to see how much I'd grown, assuring me walking would make me strong. Auntie Bertha insisted good fresh food was just as important and would send me out to the barn to find myself a bantam's egg whilst she made a loaf, which she called a 'baxon' on a griddle on the black leaded range.

Grandfather, retired but still gardening, was always ready to lean on his spade and point out linnets, goldfinches or a crane (heron) flying down in the valley. He was proud of his garden, maybe his success with growing carrots was due to the fact the Brinney was too high up for the carrot fly to travel!

The journey back down to the workshop was quick and easy except for one steep part which was rocky, slippery and often running with water. Walter Evans remembers, as a young boy being frightened watching his father Dick struggling to keep his balance on top of a hay load being brought down the lane as the horses slipped on the bedrock and a wedge called a slipper had to be used to slow the gambo. The condition of the lane, cut up by winter rain, proved difficult again in January 1955. Charlie Davies and his brother Stan of Oak Cottage tell me that when grandfather's coffin was being brought down with Mr. David Matthews' tractor and trailer they had to come down the fields instead.

For me there was always one problem at the bottom of the lane before reaching the safety of the shavings pile in the workshop. Would Peggy Matthew's geese and the old gander be out in the lane?

Beth Williams

The Bwlch when it was occupied by Ted Owens

After the fire 1985

The Bwlch

In 1881 The Bwlch was owned by Richard Gwilt. It was sold to Theodore Price in 1920 and to Jim Owens in 1934. Ted Owens took over from his father and ran the farm at first with the help of a housekeeper and then alone. He farmed with a horse and kept beef cattle and sheep. As he got older he found the work harder but he was an old fashioned farmer who did his best to keep things going. Sadly in 1985 the house caught fire and Ted died in the blaze. The property was then sold to the Gwilt family and Trevor continues to farm the land keeping sheep and beef cattle as Ted did.

Ted Owens. 'Ted the Bwlch'

The Coach House

The Coach House before the renovations

The Coach House was originally in the grounds of Nantiago (The Old Vicarage). It was called The Coach House or The Hearse House. The hearse was kept in it with accommodation above, for servants to the Vicarage, a gardener / hearse driver perhaps.

When Nantiago was owned by Alistair Lyons, who was married to Shauneen, née Rhodes, daughter of Joan and Jimmy Rhodes, landlords of The Red Lion Llanfair Waterdine, Alistair suggested that Jimmy and Joan build a retirement home on the site of The Hearse House. As The Hearse House was a derelict building it had to be pulled down to almost ground level and redesigned to make a cottage containing entrance hall and stairs, large sitting room, kitchen and toilet on the ground floor with two bedrooms and a bathroom upstairs, work on this was completed in 1985. As Jimmy and Joan were not ready to retire Mr. & Mrs. McMorran, Joan's parents from Northern Ireland moved in.

The present day Coach House

In 1987 when Joan and Jimmy decided to sell The Red Lion, they decided to build on a wing containing a kitchen dining/sitting room and upstairs a large bedroom a bathroom and airing cupboard/dressing room. On completion Joan and Jimmy moved from The Cave which they had rented, to The Coach House. Mr. McMorran died in 1989 and Mrs. McMorran in 1991, Joan and Jimmy then utilised the whole house turning the dining/sitting room into a full time dining room. A carport was added in 1996 and the porch in 1997. The bridge was made when the house was built giving private access apart from Nantiago.

The Croft

The Croft

The Croft was built by Mr. Raymond Matthews and his business partner Mr. Bill Preece. It was begun in 1982, originally intended as a retirement home for Mr. & Mrs. David Matthews, and completed in 1985. Sadly Mr. Matthews died in 1988 and Mrs. Matthews preferred not to live there alone, remaining at Skyborry Green farm.

The bungalow is built of brick and is double glazed. It is in a very attractive situation with a large garden at the front and beautiful views. The Croft is now occupied by Selwyn Wayne-Smith and his family. Anika, the eldest daughter, born in August 1984, Jenna, the younger daughter, born in July 1986, and their brother, Harry, born in September 1994 and of course , their mother, Gina.

Selwyn is a qualified tree surgeon and chainsaw trainer/assessor. He lectures at Walford Agricultural College in Baschurch on all aspects of woodland management and surgery etc., as well as training and assessing chainsaw users.

In his youth, Selwyn studied and received a diploma in sculpturing and turned this talent towards wood. He now carves various animals and birds out of trunks of wood using a chainsaw. He has carved owls, crocodiles, a gorilla, grizzly and polar bears, a wolf, an orang-utan, a fox, eagles and many others.

He is also a handle-maker for axes and bill hooks etc. He is a keen team member of the Mid-Wales Axe Racing team and enjoys participating at shows all over the country.

The girls, Anika and Jenna, both currently attend John Beddoes School in Presteigne. Their hobbies are their horses. They are both keen members of the Pony Club and enjoy attending Pony Club events and shows.

Anika follows in her fathers footsteps with a talent for Art, whereas Jenna, enjoys looking after her chickens and Jack Russell dog. She is hoping to become a Veterinary Surgeon. Then there is Harry. He enjoys his days at Beguildy Village Primary School, which he has attended on a full time basis from the age of 3½ years. He loves books and like most boys, enjoys football.

Gina is kept busy as a domestic engineer (a housewife) looking after both home and family. The sort of job that keeps most women busy!

The Graig

The house was built in 1740. Local stone was used. The outer walls consisted of two walls filled with rubble. It originally had a stone tile roof though it is now slated. It was built right into the bank, so on one side there was only one layer of walling. At some stage, probably when the roof was slated, storm slates were added to the house.

The Graig early in the Century

The inside of the house was constructed in two parts with a very heavy lockable door between. The back part consisted of a kitchen, dairy and wash house. All the way around the dairy there were very large stone slabs supported on huge wooden legs. The kitchen had a black lead range in it. The wash house had a copper which was heated with sticks for the washing. A very large heavy mangle was used and flat irons were heated on the range.

In the dairy there was the separator, the churn and the butter maker. One large slab in the dairy was used for salting the pig, and is still there with the groove around it for draining the water away. The food storage cupboards, perforated zinc to allow air in, were also kept in the dairy as it was the coldest room in the house. Above the kitchen and the dairy there were two large bedrooms which were approached from the kitchen up the back stairs.

The front of the house consisted of the hall with a beautiful oak staircase. On one side there was a living room and pantry and on the other a parlour which had a wooden floor over the cellar. All the other ground floor rooms had stone flags until the 1960's. Upstairs there were two large rooms and one little room over the hall. Above this there is the attic. The cellar used to lead from the living room and also had an entrance from the yard.

The Graig

We believe that the table we now use in the kitchen is the original table that was used when the house was built. Between then and now it has been used for shearing lambs on and mending grain sacks. This shows how little such pieces of furniture were valued in the intervening years.

The Beavan family have been around this area for a great number of years. We know that in 1861 Fred's great uncle was at The Graig and in 1871 his great grandfather went to The Graig aged 80, probably to be looked after. At the same time Fred's grandfather started farming at Lower Trebert with a housekeeper. By 1881 he was married to Maryanne Bubb and had three children.

Lower Trebert before rebuilding

The Graig water supply was originally a hand pump in the back yard, and the toilet, always called 'parliament', because it was the place you went to sit, used to be at the bottom of the garden with three holes of varying sizes! Arthur Powell, who lived at Graigwood, used to clean it out once a year and put it under the runner beans.

About a hundred years ago there seems to have been some sickness in the Beavan family which was traced to the water supply and a fresh supply of water was piped from a spring about three quarters of a mile away.

Lower Trebert after rebuilding

Lower Trebert is very much older than The Graig and is listed as 14th century to early 15th century. It is an ancient cruck house, and the area around it was the Township of Trebert.

Graigwood Cottage is also an interesting old house. From 1841 Matthew Thomas a tailor lived there in one half with his wife and they reared eight children. Matthew Powell and

Charlotte his wife were living in the other half of the cottage in 1861. He was a groom and gardener. He and his wife had seven children, one of whom was Arthur who became quite a well-known personality. He lived with his blind sister who had been run over by a cart when she was a child. The older generation had moved across the valley to The Cote (Matthew had spent much of his time working for the Vicar, and is described on a brass plate in the church as 'a worthy man'). Arthur was well known as a person who could charm illnesses away with his homemade ointments. He could cure warts and bleeding. He was a knave of a fellow, one day when Fred was a little boy riding his pet billy goat in a field of mangolds Arthur came up and put a nettle under the goat's tail and off it ran with Freddie out through the gate and down the road. Another story has it that the orchard behind Nantiago (the Old Vicarage) was a favourite place for young boys to scrump apples, and one day Arthur, a good shot with a catapult, scored a bulls eye through an open window on the vicar in his shirt tails. Arthur lived to a grand old age with his niece in Craven Arms.

Fred, his pet goat and his sister Mary

In 1936 Isy Hughes married Mary, who had been working at The Vicarage. They set up home at Llandinshop for Isy to work at The Graig for Fred's father, Frank, as shepherd. Previously he had been working for Mr. Noel Price at Black Hall. Isy's brother, Fred Hughes, came to Lower Trebert with a young family in about 1940. He soon started at The Graig as cowman. In 1941 Frank Beavan died and left his son Fred to manage the farm with his mother. Both the Hughes's stayed on at The Graig for nearly 50 years and were presented with Long Service Medals at the Shropshire and West Midland Show. Isy's son John also worked at The Graig after he left school for a while and then came for another spell after he got married. He and Sue lived in one of the new Graigwood cottages and had three boys. Isy, who was born in 1910 has a wealth of knowledge of conditions as they were in the 20's and 30's, having lived in Llanfair all his life, and retaining a really remarkable memory.

Another Hughes family connection was that Pryce Cadwallader married Rhoda Hughes and moved into one half of Trebert and also worked at The Graig. This was after Trebert was done up.

A wonderful character who worked at The Graig for many years was Jack Miles. He and his wife 'Galloping Ann' lived at Graigwood Cottage. Everyone who knew him will remember him with great affection as the regular doorman at all the 'do's' in Llanfair. Later on Bert Williams and Edward Bright worked for many years at The Graig.

Driving stock to market used to be an eventful occasion for us all. Polished boots, clean britches and well-shaved whiskers were the order of the day. To get your sheep into the right pen, without any mishaps along the way, was a major achievement. There would be sheep coming into Knighton from all directions, including the railway. Whatever the weather, it was always gave great pleasure and feeling of anticipation to walk one's flock down the road to market. Even the Kerry Hill sheep had their faces scrubbed. Daz and Reckitts Blue were used, for the occasion. The cattle were also walked from The Graig which was just as eventful if not more so. Now stock lorries do the work and Knighton market is quite different.

While we were growing up ponies were, and always had been, very important on all stock farms. Everybody was used to managing with a pony and a dog. They were hardy and sure footed and able to carry a sheep or a bag of corn on their backs as well as their owner. Now all the horses sadly seem to be for leisure only.

Some animals have very strong instincts. In the late 1940's Isy noticed in the 'Lost and Found' column in the Wellington Journal a ewe and lamb with The Graig Hill mark advertised. She was on a farm above Rhayader. It was after the autumn cattle sale in Knighton and Fred decided he must investigate. He had bought a bunch of ewes from Rhayader the year before. He went to look and there was the ewe in her favourite meadow. She had taken her lamb all the way from The Graig Hill back to Rhayader. Fred brought them back home in the back of his old car.

Memorable Winters

In 1939 there was an ice storm, when the rain froze as it fell and everything was covered with a layer of ice. Throughout the night branches broke off trees with the weight of the ice, and the sound of cracking was really frightening. The next morning was quite amazing. The damage was horrendous. Clifford Morris managed to get up to The Graig, having tied sacking over his hob nailed boots. It was impossible to walk without. To get around the stock was virtually impossible. Horses couldn't walk on the ice of course. It remained on the fields for several days. The ice was like little round marbles wherever you went and was very dangerous.

SCHEDULE.

DISTRICT CLUN

Parish, O.S. Map No. and Edition	Area	Description	Required Cultivation
	Acres		
LLAN-FAIR-WATER-DINE 1902			
1417	2.971	Permanent	Fields No. 1338 and 1314 must be ploughed by 1st October 1940, cultivated, brought to fertility and sown with Wheat for the 1941 harvest.
1475	5.070	Temporary	
1338	10.393	do	
1325	2.800	do	Fields 1417, 1475, 1325, 1238, 1478 and 1270, must be ploughed by 15th February 1941, cultivated, brought to fertility and sown with an approved crop for the 1941 harvest.
1238	6.522	do	
1314	7.369	do	
1478	4.923	do	
1270	11.178	2 year ley	
		Owner:- Occupier.	

W.A.C. 100

(34318) Wt.21588/1704. 600M. 8/40 51-7517. M.& S., Ltd.

Schedule 1940

1947

Heavy snow started on January 26th and it didn't melt until after Easter. It was a complete tragedy, with animals dying of starvation and fodder in barns which could not be reached. In March a tremendous gale blew up and tore off several roofs and blew down the only hay barn that The Graig had at that time.

1963

There was a very hard frost which went deep into the ground and froze the pipes which meant getting water for the animals was extremely difficult.

It is worth mentioning there was no mains electricity up the valley until the early 1950's and the last farms to have electricity waited until the early 1980's. This meant that we all relied on oil lamps, oil cookers and candles. We also used a lot of elbow grease!

Disasters sometimes happen on farms and our most distressing one was in the 1960's. One morning, Harold Gwilt who was our postman at the time came to tell us that our little bitch 'Lassie' who was in season had gone off with a dog and driven a bunch of lambs into a corner where they had smothered. Over 160 had died and only a few damaged ones recovered. It was a dreadful loss and Lassie had to be put to sleep as well as the other dog. It was something we will never forget. Another great tragic event for many people was the outbreak of Foot and Mouth disease in about 1968. It did not directly affect us but enormous care had to be taken with buckets of disinfectant everywhere for the washing of boots etc. The nearest outbreak to us caused the movement of animals to be stopped on a Monday morning, but we had been lucky enough to move about 200 lambs the day before which was a great help.

In 1971 Black Hall joined The Graig. It is another very old and interesting house. Maybe it is worth mentioning that in 1961 at the age of 40 Fred decided maybe he had better get married. No sooner said than done. Mig Cummins joined the team followed by Andrew, Paddy and Derek. Later editions were Anne at Black Hall producing Amy, John and Alice and Paddy married David Brick to produce Esme, Toby and Freddy at Lawton Farm and so on and so on ...

Mig Beavan

The Green Farm

Mr. J. Davies the father of Mrs. Alma Lloyd bought the Green in 1920 from two brothers called Price. Mr. and Mrs. Davies and their two daughters lived at The Green until 1930 when they rented it out to Mr. John Davies who was the father of Mrs. Mary Morgan who now lives at Selley Hall. They were at The Green until 1935.

In 1935 Mrs. Alma Lloyd and her husband Mr. Walter Owen Lloyd came back to the farm and Mrs. Lloyd has lived there ever since.

The Green, some of the original farm buildings

Mr. and Mrs. Lloyd had three children Lavinia, Margaret and John. Margaret still lives in the parish at Lower Tregodfa. John married Elizabeth and farms The Green with their two sons Roger and Roy.

The Bungalow

Roy Lloyd with his favourite 'Welsh Black'

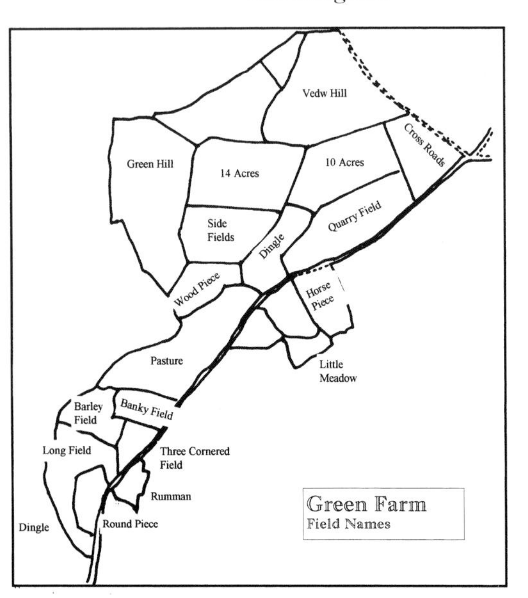

Roger married Ann Roberts from the Forge at Felindre and they have a baby girl called Zoe. Roy is married to Louise Richards from The Garn and they have a baby boy called Graham. The original house at The Green was of the same style as several other farmhouses in the parish but owing to movement in the stonework it was replaced by a modern bungalow, built by Deacons of Kington in 1955.

The Old Forge

The Old Forge was built in about 1857. The last blacksmith to work there was Bill Farmer who moved to the Forge at Lloyney (which was later knocked down for a road widening scheme) and later to the Builders Arms (now The Lloyney Inn). Mike and Liz Lockey moved into the Forge in 1998. They write:- Our first impressions are of a valley where lives are well lived and where people are happy and fulfilled. The land seems greener, lusher and more fecund than anywhere we lived before and we feel that there is a richer and more varied animal and plant life than we have ever come across before. Having said all this we are sorry that there is no shop or school or public transport. We wonder what the children find to do and are worried that there is no large local hospital. We feel there must be many elderly people living alone in cottages without transport and we wonder how they cope. If people can cope however and have enough income to survive and access to transport Llanfair is a wonderful place to live.

The Old forge and The Old Shoppe before renovation

All one house since 1999

The Old Shoppe

The Old Shoppe was built in 1857. Throughout the War and for many years afterwards it was a holiday home belonging to a dentist called Stammers. His daughter Sue Phillips remained in Knighton all her life after coming to Llanfair on holiday as a child. She organised a highly successful local holiday group known as Sceneseekers. The house was more recently owned by John and Ruth Tiller. This year it has been sold to Mike and Liz Lockey who live next door.

The Runnis

John Bevan, Julie and our children Danny, aged 6 and Sarah 7, live at the Runnis. We moved across the valley from Vedalewydd in 1991. My family had owned the Runnis for over 20 years. Many renovations were done before we moved in. The house seems to have been built in three sections. The middle part is the oldest. We removed a black leaded grate in this middle section to find a large stone hearth complete with beams and a granny seat. We think the old buildings across the road from the house, which are now in ruins, may also have been a house at some time. We have made one set of barns into stables. Most of our farming is still done on the other side of the river. We hope to build a bungalow near the farm buildings in the near future. We shall then be moving back into Beguildy Parish.

The Runnis House

I was born at Vedalewydd, my Mum and Dad having moved there from Felindre in 1943. Julie is from Glascwm. I left this area and went to live in Malvern for about 15 years. I certainly realise how lucky I am to live in this area since I've been away. We have grown our own vegetables for the past couple of years and Julie has half a dozen hens. Danny says he hopes to be a farmer. Sarah likes to spend as much time as she can with the sheep, but she thinks, at the moment she would like to be a nurse. We have 15 horses all of them are Pacers. We've won some races and we also breed them. We're trying to reduce their numbers gradually and have managed to get down from 20 this year. We keep a thousand breeding ewes and have lambed them indoors for several years.

The loss of some birds and animals seems very sad to both of us. Curlews and lapwings seem almost to have disappeared as do hedgehogs. We think badgers have a great deal to do with this as there are many of them and they are becoming very destructive.

Tom Jones known locally as "Tom the Dut" (short for Dutlas) lived at the Runnis until about 1972. It was at this time owned by a family called Bywater.

The Runnis Chapel

The Runnis Chapel was a Methodist Chapel attended by people from a wide area. It was built in 1837 but as its congregation dwindled in the 1950's it was no longer used. It stood empty for some time before being sold to be converted into a house. The first owners did very little conversion work and in 1971 the chapel was bought by Herbert Spencer and his wife Marianne. Its conversion was sympathetically carried out as can be seen from photographs and an article which appeared in Ideal Home Magazine in 1974. The Spencer family owned the Chapel until 1998 when they sold it to Dr. John Hill.

While it was owned by the Spencers their niece Annalise and her husband Bernard from the Netherlands visited almost every year and stayed for at least a month. While in residence Bernard always flew the Netherlands flag from the chapel flagpole. They loved the local countryside and made many friends over the years in the vicinity of the chapel. When they took their final holiday in 1998 and the Spencers joined them for the last week it was the end of an era! A party was held at the Red Lion where the famous flag flew over the door for one last evening and a maudlin little group gathered inside to say "goodbye".

The Old Chapel

This article appeared in Ideal Home magazine, Oct 1974.

Have you ever thought of making your home in a Church?

When church buildings are no longer needed, what happens to them? Should they be allowed to fall into disrepair? Or could the House of God become the home of man? We have discovered an old Welsh border chapel which has been beautifully converted by graphic designer Herbert Spencer and his family.

In 1837, year of Queen Victoria's accession, they built Runnis Chapel. In 1973, the Spencer family converted it to make it a beautiful bolt hole from London life. And to understand why anyone should build a chapel miles from the nearest village, or anyone else should choose to convert an ecclesiastical eccentricity, you simply have to stand on the steeply-pitched hillside and look.

Down below, the infant River Teme winds through a lush valley, separating England from Wales, Shropshire from Radnorshire, backed by wooded hills and bordering the least populated county in the United Kingdom. If chapels should be symbolically sited, Runnis Chapel does itself poetic justice indeed, for it is in a heavenly setting.

The Spencers—Herbert, his wife, Marianne, and their 16-year-old daughter, Mafalda— came across it in 1969. They were spending a weekend in mid-Wales and stopped to photograph the chapel because they were struck by its superb position. "But at that time we were not looking for a chapel to convert. In fact, we didn't think we'd ever find a country retreat to suit us. It had to have light and space and be easy to run. We were not interested in a cottage because we would have to gut it to start with. All we really wanted was a big, empty space we could do things with."

It was nearly two years before they saw Runnis Chapel again. By that time an escape route from the pressures of running a design business in London had become more urgent. And, somewhere, in the Spencers collective subconscious, there lingered the enticing thought of that chapel in the valley.

It was not for sale. In fact, it had been used for services until quite recently. But that didn't daunt the Spencers. They enquired who owned it at the post office in the nearest village of Knucklas and discovered—by a friendly coincidence—that it was one of the professors at Leeds University, where Herbert had a design contract. Gently, they persuaded him to sell.

Three months later—in July 1971—the contract was signed for the chapel and a scoop of land out of the hillside to go with it. Then came a year's delay while permission, plans and estimates went through. The local authority in Shropshire was most concerned that the outward appearance of the chapel should be retained. Herbert Spencer drew up his own plans and assured them that he was as adamant on that point himself.

There were no services whatsoever. Bringing the water turned out to be a major feat of engineering, with three-eighths of a mile of pipes and steel tubes carried under the river bed from the other side of the valley. By September 1972, the builders were ready to begin, with the guarantee that they would finish by Easter 1973. They did—ten days early. "And there was no coming back to put the finishing touches to the letter box— or other fidgety things like that."

The Spencers have been lucky in their local allies. For the young builders—Sidney Stevens and James Watkins of Knighton—it was one of their first jobs, and their very first conversion. They entered into the spirit of what the Spencers wanted, soon picked up the feeling of the home they were creating. "We wanted something more than a weekend retreat but not so formal as our London house. It had to be simple and casual but still very comfortable. We wanted to retain as much as we could of the original appearance of the building, but still make a real home out of it. And we wanted to use natural materials and textures set against a few brilliant, theatrical colours."

In spite of having such a clear notion of their needs now, the Spencers didn't start with any rigid rules. The picture emerged as they went along. 'We knew fairly well what we wanted from the structure, but the furnishings just grew around us. When we saw something we thought would be right we bought it on the spot—nothing was worked out in advance."

And so, within the light and airy shell of the building, copies of Marcel Breuer's classic 1930 chair for Isokon (now obtainable from John Alan Designs) rub shoulders with a bentwood rocker. An Arts and Crafts movement dresser from a local antique shop and a beautiful-but-bizarre shotblasted hallstand ("from the rough end of the King's Road") share space with a desk that looks (appropriately) like a chapel harmonium, and Welsh tapestry bedspreads happily live alongside Spanish rugs and flower-bowery handpainted chests from Marianne's home near the Zuyder Zee. It all works beautifully because the visual interest of the furniture is offset by plain white walls and natural wood plus basic comforts such as Christien Sell's stacking beds and stainless steel Swedish kitchen fittings.

The main living room occupies the total pew-and-pulpit area. The porch makes a tiny square entrance hall which opens into the vast space dividing simply into a kitchen area, left, and a dining area, right. Straight ahead, beyond the cast iron spiral staircase which creates a visual break, the sitting space is grouped round an open log fire. Structural alterations were simple here. The Spencers were fortunate to find a chapel with enough roof space above the points of its gothic windows to put in an extra floor—and still keep the windows intact. "Sadly we had to take out the red and blue stained glass borders because we needed the light, and we have extended the length of the centre window—but otherwise they are as they were, except for white wooden shutters and Habitat blinds."

The Chapel as a house

Originally, the width of the cast iron staircase they ordered from the Lion Foundry in Glasgow was determined by the need to obey the fire regulations. But when they discovered the problems of getting their furniture upstairs (trapdoors?) they hit on the brilliant solution of building a bridge across from the hillside at first floor level and making another entrance upstairs.

This now opens into an upper hall/landing, which also doubles as a study (Herbert Spencer brings design work with him and Mafalda uses the desk for swotting) and—at a pinch—an extra bedroom. And it meant that they could have a narrower, more elegant spiral staircase, because of their second exit. Slanting dormer windows were put in upstairs to flood the two bedrooms and bathroom with light, and a single circular window in the end gable of the main bedroom was inserted as well. "In fact, we seem to have established a new Teme Valley building style with the round window— several houses now being built are following suit"

Another local contractor they employed, stonemason John Thornton ("Big John"), has also become a friend who keeps an eye on things for them when they are away. John and his wife, Judith, terraced the garden down from the hillside, and planted out the rockeries. Like the builders, they were sensitive to the Spencers' needs. "So much so that when the telephone people came to lay cables and sited them badly Big John noticed and told them to think again."

The Spencers are already much-liked members of the local community. When they rigged up a time-switch to put the lights on while they weren't there, the landlord of the pub across the valley got worried. So he made a long-distance phone call to St. John's Wood to let the Spencers know he suspected funny goings on at the chapel. Nice to know your neighbours care—especially when you are second-string home owners on the Welsh border.

The Upper Wain

Sylvia Lloyd lives at the Upper Wain with her sons Albert and Leslie (Bert and Les). She lived at the Lower Wain as a child and walked to school at Llanfair every day. She writes:-

I walked to Llanfair school in the 1920's and 1930's carrying my bag on my back containing my lunch. If we were late we were given three "tingles" with a strap across the hand. The tingling kept your hand warm for the rest of the day! The distance to school was over three miles in each direction along a rough track and over the fields. We walked down to the Cwm, and then down the valley to New House and on to Cwm Brain. We walked along to the barn near Melin-y-Grogue, then down past The Old Shop and through the village. School started at 9.00am and finished at 3.30pm. I left school at the age of 14 and went to work. If I was lucky I earned a shilling a day (five pence). If money was scarce, and it often was, I worked for my food which was very acceptable. A well earned shilling bought half a pound of Golden Stream tea plus a two pound bag of granulated sugar.

Sylvia Lloyd

The Upper Wain

I married Edward Lloyd of the Upper Wain who died in 1990. We had two sons Albert and Leslie and my husband's brother Pryce lived with us until his death in 1987. Bert our older son walked to Coed-y-Hendre each morning and was picked up there by car and taken to Beguildy School. Les rode his bike to Coed-y-Hendre and was also picked up there. The old house at the Upper Wain fell into disrepair. We built a new bungalow in the late 1970's. The Lloyd family has lived at the Upper Wain for over a hundred years. My husband and his brother didn't ever know about the beef crisis which has made farming so difficult and closed many auction yards. I look forward to the future and hope to be at the Upper Wain for some time yet.

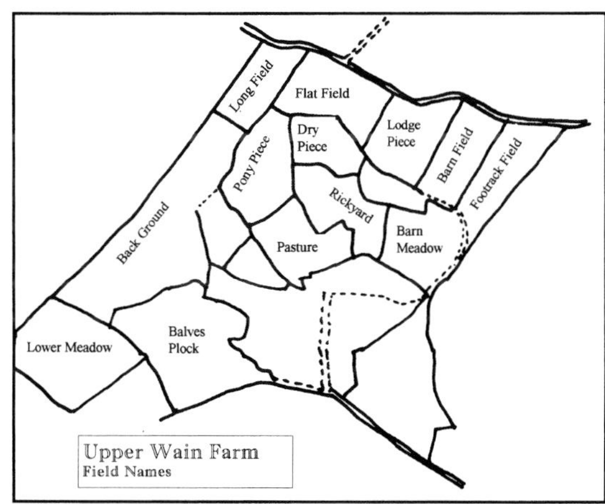

Thistledown

Thistledown

Planning permission for the construction of "Thistledown" was granted to Dr. Margaret Hilderbrand of "Fairfield", Llanfair Waterdine, on the 7th of August 1972. The proposed bungalow was to be built for the purpose of housing Dr. Hilderbrand's long standing friend, Miss Hilda Jones. It was to be located to the South West of "Fairfield" but within the same plot of land and sharing a common entrance.

Harper & Sperring, Chartered Architects of Dudley, were engaged to design and supervise the construction. The builder, H.A. Tipton, completed the work and handed over the property on the 8th of February, 1975.

Miss Jones owned "Thistledown" thereafter until her death in 1996. She lived alone apart from her beloved Labrador, "Floss". She sadly suffered a stroke in 1994 and as a result was forced to take up residence in a Nursing Home located in Kingsland, she never returned to Llanfair Waterdine.

In June of 1996 Mick and Judy Richards moved into "Thistledown", having purchased it from Miss Jones' executors. They had previously lived in the village and had owned the "Red Lion" Inn for some seven years (1988-1996). They occupy the house with their two dogs, "Bill" (an aged black Labrador) and "Ben" (a border Collie — bred at Llanfair Hall).

"Thistledown" sits in half an acre of secluded garden just above the river Teme. An idyllic spot to escape the crowd.

Upper Panpwnton Farm

Upper Panpwnton Farm is situated to the extreme east of the parish about half a mile from Knighton, with the River Teme, Offa's Dyke Path and the Central Wales Railway Line passing through the land.

The farmhouse and surrounding farm buildings, of barns and traditional cowhouses are included in a list of buildings of special architectural or historic interest compiled by the Secretary of State for the Environment. Built in the late 17th to 18th century it is one of the older properties of the parish. It is a three storey stone house, coloured white with a slate roof and two gabled dormers. The interior includes two oak staircases, large oak beams and wattle and daub panelling. The front door has the original Queen Anne head knocker. The barns and traditional cowhouses are from the same period.

Upper Panpwnton Farm

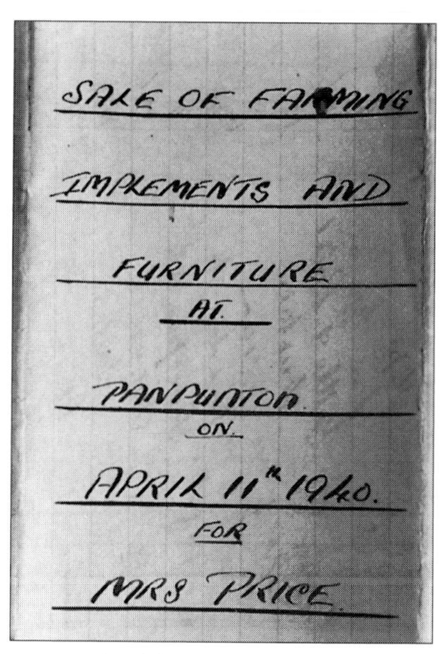

SALE OF FARMING
IMPLEMENTS AND
FURNITURE
AT
PANPUNTON
ON
APRIL 11th 1940.
FOR
MRS PRICE.

Sale of farming implements

Around the middle of the last century, the farm consisted of 148 to 150 acres of pasture, meadow and arable land including three acres of orchard. The farmer at that time was Mr. William Parr aged 30 who employed Mary Phillips aged 20 a house servant, Benjamin Edwards aged 20 a waggoner, Edward Beaumont aged 18 a cowman and Griffiths Rogers aged 65 a shepherd. Soon after this time when the Central Wales railway line was built, the farm was split and when it was purchased by Mr. and Mrs. Edward Price from the Skyborry and Treverward Estate in 1920 it was only 33 acres. Mr. and Mrs. Price continued to farm until 1939 when sadly, Mr. Price fell from a load of hay causing his death due to broken neck. Mrs. Price stayed at Panpwnton until her death in 1957.

From 1939 to 1950 Panpwnton was farmed by tenants who also lived in the farmhouse. From 1940 to 1945 the tenants were Mr. and Mrs. Robert Price and their family, Iris, Howard and Winston. From 1945 to 1949 Mr. and Mrs. Stanley Knill and their family, Olwen and Gwen lived in the house. After 1950 the land was let as grasskeep until 1960. Between 1957 and 1962 the

Item	£	s	d
Old Iron		7	-
Cider Cask }		1	
Barrels }			
Barrel & Tubs		1	-
Benches }		5	-
Rat Traps }			
Riddle etc.		2	
Pikles & Rakes		3	6
Pulleys		11	-
Pikles & Rakes		4	-
Bit		1	6
Pick etc.		1	-
Saws Axe.		4	-
Scythe etc & Ladder.		3	
Ladder.		5	6
Netting		4	6
String			6
Spray.		5	-
Iron Bar etc.		3	6
Lantern		4	-
Do		4	-
Spade & Fork.		3	6
Hay Knife		2	6
Do.			6
Steel Rake.		19	-
Iron Bar & Mallet		3	6
Grindstone		1	-
Do.		8	-
Wheelbarrow.		16	-
Troughs & Iron Trough		1	-
Chicken Coops		2	6
Gambo	1	-	-
Horse Rake.	6	7	6
Sheep Cratch		17	-
Harrows			6
Chicken Coops.		7	6
Carried Forward.	15	4	

Item	£	s	d
Carried Forward	15	4	-
Chicken Coops		10	-
Do		11	-
Coffer.	2	7	6
Do.	1	11	-
Bench		2	-
Bed		2	-
Trap Lamps		7	6
Trap		6	-
Saddle.		6	-
Timber Chain.		4	-
Saddle.		3	-
Collars Bridle }		14	-
Set Harness }			
Cart Saddle		12	-
Set Shaft Gear	1	5	-
Ropes.		2	6
Saddle & Bridle		18	-
Steps.		4	6
Fire Screen		4	-
Kettle & Paint.		1	6
Fountain		12	-
Drum		8	-
Fender etc		4	-
Saucepan etc		4	-
Firescreen			6
Scales.		10	-
Churn		1	-
Mit & Pails		7	-
Bucket.		5	-
Strainer		5	-
Bench.		3	-
Separator.	3	2	6
Scales	4	15	-
Incubator.		10	-
Fire Grate		1	-
Chicken Feeder.		6	-
Carried Forward	51	9	6

Item	£	s	d
Carried Forward.	66	15	-
1 Bag Feathers		3	-
2 Do.		2	-
1 Do		1	-
Meat Cratch		10	-
Knives		1	6
Ornament.		3	-
Bed Pan etc.		2	6
Tea Set.	1	10	-
Table.		16	-
Pr Candle Sticks		12	
Do		-	-
Do	-	-	-
Basket & Contents.		1	6
Dishes etc.		2	6
Glass.		1	-
Teapot etc		1	-
Dishes			6
Vase.		1	-
Forks & Spoons		1	6
Tea Spoons		3	-
Milk Pan etc.			6
Do			6
Jugs.			6
Tea Pot		2	-
Lamp		3	6
Table.		2	6
Treadle		2	-
Carpet		8	6
Brace & Bits		4	-
Box Tools.		7	-
Sewing Machine	4	2	6
Table	1	-	-
3 cpls Hens. 12/	1	10	-
3 - Do. 9/-	1	7	-
3 Do Do 7/6	1	2	6
3 Do Do 8/-	1	4	-
Carried Forward	83	5	1

Item	£	s	d
Carried Forward	83	5	-
2 cpls. Hens. 8/6		17	-
3 Do. 7/-	1	1	-
1 Do. 6/-		6	-
2 Do. 8/-		16	-
2 Do. 8/-		16	-
2 Do 8/-		16	-
3 Do 7/6	1	3	3
2 Do. 8/-		16	-
Wash Stand		17	6
Eiderdown.		10	-
Chest	1	2	6
2 Chairs		9	-
Clock.		15	-
Feather Bed.		4	-
Weather Glass.		11	-
Bedstead		7	-
Fenders.		2	-
Toilet Ware.		3	-
Oak Box		4	-
Cupboard		12	6
Bath		5	6
Bag Potatoes }		2	-
Do. }			
Do. }		3	-
Do. }			
Gun.		6	-
Box Potatoes		2	-
Do		2	6
Do		2	-
Do		3	-
Bag Do		2	-
Do		2	-
Do.		2	-
Do.		2	-
Do.		2	-
Do		3	-
Total £	97	13	

Schedule

house was empty and underwent general repairs and improvements until the present owners moved in. Since 1962 John and Betty Williams and their family Susan and Janet have lived at Panpwnton. Susan attended Agricultural College and trained as a farm secretary. Janet joined the QARANC (Queen Alexandra Royal Army Nursing Corps), and they have both married and moved away from the area. In 1976 an additional 50 acres of land was purchased from a neighbouring farm making 83 acres in all.

The Black Bridge. Between 1850 and 1860 when the Cenral Wales Railway Line was built the farm bridge over the River Teme was demolished and a new farm bridge was erected a short distance away, this was known locally as the black bridge. In the mid 1930's this bridge was washed away by floods and was not replaced until 1962.

Betty Williams 1999

Upper Redgate

George Jones, his father and brother, Upper Redgate

Upper Redgate

Upper Redgate is quite an old stone house and has a traditional range of farm buildings. It was owned and farmed by Mr. Bill Lloyd and his family for many years until his death. It now belongs to his niece and the land is mainly rented out as grass keep to local farmers.

The Jones family lived at Redgate from about 1860 until it was bought by the Lloyds. Doris Jones was the last member of her family to live there. She died in Knighton at the age of 95 in 1998. Doris was the daughter of Clara and George Jones. She had a brother called George and a sister Beatrice. They all attended Llanfair school Mr. Matkin being headmaster. They walked the three miles to school and home each day across the fields. On leaving school Doris went to work for the Matthews family at Cwm Sannum. George went into insurance later becoming the manager of a branch office. Beatrice went to work at Twitchen. When her father became ill Doris returned to Redgate and helped to run the farm for several years. She remembered baking bread and huge rice puddings in the black leaded range and making butter. She enjoyed outdoor work and rounded up the animals on her pony. The evenings were passed playing cards once the work was done. When her father

Doris Jones, born at Upper Redgate

Mr. George Jones in 1909 with a horse and foal

George died her mother Clara went to The Runnis to housekeep for her step brothers Phillip and Alan Jones and Redgate was sold. Clara was a methodist and while at the Runnis she cleaned and cared for the Chapel for many years. As children George, Beatrice and Doris walked to Beguildy Church every Sunday and were all confirmed there. They remained keen churchgoers for the rest of their lives. As an old lady Doris lived with her daughter Ruth in Knighton. Throughout her life she enjoyed looking back on her farming past at Redgate and often said she regretted the family leaving there.

Upper Tregodfa

Geoffrey and Valerie Smith bought Upper Tregodfa and two and a half acres of land in 1979. They came from Six Ashes, Bridgnorth. The present Upper Tregodfa is a very old dwelling and there were probably others on the site before it. Geoff and Val say of their house:- Tregodfa was built around 1550. The roof is of the Queen Post type and originally carried stone tiles. We still have some of them. Our sitting room has a large open fireplace with a 16 inch square oak beam 14 feet long spanning 10 feet.

Upper Tregodfa

Herbert and Mrs. Clee, parents of Aubrey at Tregodfa

To the side of the fireplace is an oak screen. This should really be part of the plank and muntin partition which divides the two ground floor rooms. The screen has a Tudor doorway with a triangular top. The ceiling is quite rare being heavy oak cross beamed. On the first floor there is an original timber framed partition pegged to the beams and another Tudor doorway.

Geoff repaired and restored the old barn to form two loose boxes for his hunters. He hunts with the Teme Valley Hunt on a regular basis and this makes for a very busy but happy retirement. There were other barns on the property one of which was thatched. The buttresses and part of the walls are still there.

The previous residents of Upper Tregodfa were Mr. and Mrs. Aubrey Clee. Aubrey farmed here for 57 years before retiring in 1979. His daughter still lives in Knighton and his wife Dolly in Lloyney. We came here with our daughter Sara who now lives in America with her husband Philip and two sons Thomas aged 7 and Harry 2. They were married at St Mary's Church Llanfairwaterdine in 1990. Geoff and I visited them this year in Massachusetts a big adventure for me (Val) as I had never flown before.

The Vedw

The Vedw was built in about 1841. Victor and I bought it in early 1960, took possession in March and carried out extensive work before we moved in. We dug out a well in the cellar which was about 16 feet deep. We put in a mains water supply and one bedroom was converted into a bathroom. We added extra power points and switches in every room and renewed all the windows and made some of them larger. We made a hall through from the front door to the back and put a Rayburn in the kitchen. We built a driveway from the road up to the house and removed the back stairs which consisted of a ladder to one bedroom. We did away with the two seater lavatory in the garden which had a self flush system as it was built over a small stream. We moved in in October 1960.

The Vedw

Victor carried out mixed farming and kept cattle, sheep and pigs. He also did agricultural contracting such as spreading lime and slag. He ran lorries to deliver it. The lorries also carried other goods such as steel, hay and straw.

When we took over the electricity agreement we had to guarantee to use £14 of power per annum. We had no trouble at all!

Pricilla Davies lived at the Vedw in 1871 and donated two hundred pounds to the Llanfair Waterdine Parish Charity when she was about 63 years old. I now live at the Vedw with my Jack Russell Digger.

Joan Adams

Joan Adams

Weir Cottage

Weir Cottage

In 1841 Weir Cottage already appears to have been a substantial house. At that time it was occupied by John Thorpe aged 39 who was of independent means, he was married to Susannah and they had a child aged 14. By 1851 Thomas Hamar aged 65 from Clun who described himself as a landed proprietor lived in Weir Cottage with one servant. By 1861 the house was occupied by the Relieving Officer for the parish who would have had the task of taking care of the poor before the existence of the Welfare State. He was Richard Smith from Bromyard aged 38 his wife was Elizabeth and they had brought a servant Eliza Archer aged 16 from Bromyard with them.

A solicitor, Frederick Green from Presteigne had taken up residence by 1891. His nephew Ralph from Reading Berkshire aged 16 lived with him and acted as his clerk. They employed a servant and a groom. This century several people have rented the house and during the War it was sold to Joy and John Hunt. It was to Weir Cottage that he returned in triumph after conquering Everest in 1953, and it was at the house that he wrote his book 'The Ascent of Everest'.

In the early 1980s Doctor Gwyn Rosser sold Weir Cottage to Geoff and Linda Hall and their daughters Sally, Wendy and Marie. They have lived there since then. They run several shops in Knighton and Presteigne and Geoff is the local undertaker. The hearse is stored at the house as is a car Geoff uses for occasional weddings. They have done extensive landscaping to the grounds and modernised and improved the house.

New houses are built in the village 1999–2000

LOT 16.

(Coloured Yellow on Plan).

TWO Stone and Slate COTTAGES & SMITHY

situate on the Road from Llanvair Waterdine to Mellin-y-grogue,

and comprising an area of about

1 r. 7 p.

(Number 1161 on Plan).

ONE COTTAGE and the SMITHY with Forge and Pent house are in the occupation of Mr. C. W. Farmer, on an annual Lady day tenancy, subject to six months' notice.

The Cottage contains :—Kitchen, Pantry, 3 Bedrooms, E.C., Good Garden.

THE SECOND COTTAGE, known as "YE OLDE SHOPPE," has similar accommodation, with the addition of a Timber and Iron Toolhouse, and is let to Mr. Charles Evans on an annual Lady day tenancy subject to six months' notice.

The Tenants have the joint use of the stone, timber and slate Piggeries.

THE WATER SUPPLY is obtained from a Spring and Well at Nanty-y-twydy on Llanvair Hall Farm.

OUTGOINGS :—Tithe Rent Charge Apportionment, 1/5
Land Tax, Nil.

This Lot is sold with the right of obtaining a supply of water as heretofore enjoyed from the Spring and Well at Nant-y-twydy in field No. 1124, part of Lot 12.

Sale of Millington Estate, 1919.

Llanfair-Waterdine Y.F.C. Re-Union — Oct. 30th, 1970

Far Table:- seated - those visable:
Westall Price, Shrops Y.F.C. County Organiser; Jim Williams; Mrs. J.C. Williams; James Cummins; Glenys Williams; Rev. J.C. Williams; Mig Beavan; Stuart Deakin; Tommy Jones

Peter Davies; Jocelyn Williams; Brenda Davies; Harold Gwilt; Betty Williams; John Williams; Ann Gwilt

Centre Table:-
Margaret Worts; Edith Huffer; Lawton Williams; George Jones; Kathleen Jones; Mrs. Cummins; Aubrey and Dolly Clee; Margaret Swancott; Joan Davies; Trevor Gwilt

Jack Huffer; Raymond Matthews; Elizabeth Metthews; Giles Swancott

The hunt meets at The Red Lion, 1956.

Part Two

Lloyney

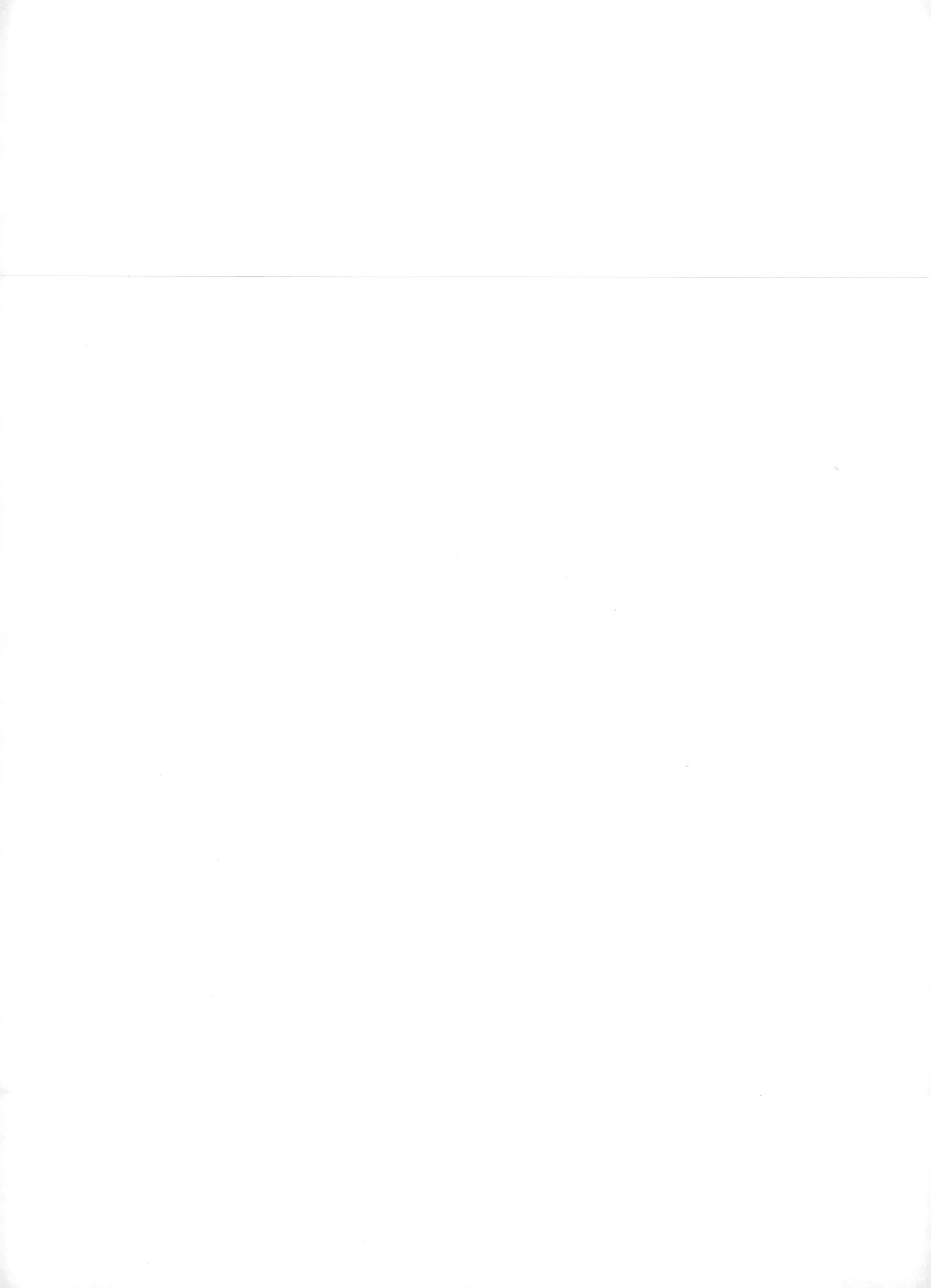

Reminiscences of a Lloyney Childhood

by Brenda Davies (née Jones)

Lloyney was, in the 1930s, a small hamlet – it had neither Church, Post Office nor School. It did have a primitive Methodist Chapel, built in 1851, a flourishing village shop, an inn, the *Builders Arms,* a thriving blacksmith's shop, and a carpenter and wheelwrights shop where my father

The Builders Yard, Lloyney (Fred Jones)

carried on the family trade inherited from Henry Griffiths. They had been the local Builders for 100 years and were responsible for the building of our village Chapel, other chapels, many of the large stone farmhouses existing in the Teme Valley today and the village inn.

The Mill

Lloyney also had a 'Mill,' which during the First World War 1914–1918 had worked night and day grinding corn for the local farmers. The big mill wheel was turned by the mill stream, or phlegm, diverted across the meadows from the River Teme.

The Tailor

Another small business was run by Mr. Bill Hammond the tailor, who sat cross-legged on a bench beneath his window stitching high class suits for the gents outfitters in the local towns of Knighton and Presteigne. Savile Row in London could not have competed with his workmanship.

Transport Pre 1930

Apart from these local businesses in the first half of the century there was the village shop – 12 other cottages and 5 outlying farms. The cottagers worked either as "roadmen" – roadside verges, ditches and drains, were always immaculate – on the local farms, or on the railway which since 1861 had passed through the neighbouring village of Knucklas en-route from Shrewsbury to Swansea. Steam trains chugged their way uphill over Knucklas viaduct towards Llangunllo with their thick white smoke billowing behind.

Sadly now in 1999 the line is used mainly for tourists and is known as the 'Heart of Wales' Railway. The grandeur of the steam giants has gone, their place taken by uninteresting, uncomfortable diesel sprinter trains, but thankfully the railway still exists.

Before 1930 only 9 households between Knighton and Cwmgwyn owned a motor car – all other inhabitants either walked, rode on horseback, bicycle, motorbike, pony and trap or on the Owens bus to and from Knighton on Thursdays (Market day) – and on Saturdays and Tuesdays to Newtown.

I am pleased to record ONE thing in 1999 that has not changed: Owens buses still run from Knighton to Newtown as they did in the 1930s, but their service has expanded to places outside the valley.

In the late 1930s more cars were in use, so my father installed a petrol pump. Serving the petrol was a laborious task involving winding a heavy metal handle to fill a glass gallon cylinder with petrol which then had to be emptied before a second gallon could be started. Petrol per gallon was then 1s.5d. – new currency 7p.

My father himself purchased a car, a secondhand Jowett with a 'dickie' seat, where my sister Jocelyn and I sat for many a hair raising ride – up and down over abundant pot holes along the narrow and twisting roads. Tarmacadam was a product of the future but I do recall the roads

Owens bus ready to drive up the valley

RADNORSHIRE BUS

By Joan E. Gillespie

PILGRIMAGE to a well-loved place is often fraught with disappointment when there has been an interval of a few years since the last visit. But on the rare occasions when I am able to return to my enchanted Radnorshire valley, its magic never fails me.

There have been few changes in this wild and lovely country which first cast its spell upon me fourteen years ago. Even the local bus has not changed and still goes "sounding on its way" among the lonely hills between Knighton and Felindre.

The busiest day of the week for the bus is Thursday, which is market day in Knighton, at the lower end of the valley, just as it has been since A.D. 1230. Unless they own a car, people from the remote hill farms and cottages have to go into town "by buzz," for this is their only chance of meeting friends and relations from over the hills.

FROM THE Felindre forge, the single-decker bus may be seen far away across the fields—a blue speck thrusting its way along the winding lane. When it arrives at the forge, Jack, driver-and-conductor, may have to deliver a letter at a nearby cottage and after a few minutes he turns the bus (for here the road widens) and starts back with a handful of passengers on the ten-mile run down to the town.

I have used the bus so often that the route has become very familiar, but never dull. Progress is slow, with Jack on the alert at every corner in case we overtake a flock of sheep or a drove of Hereford bullocks going to market; if this happens, they are jostled into a huddle at the side of the road by the intelligent Welsh sheep-dogs which no wise farmer is ever without. Jack slows down every now and again at land-ends and farm gates in case there should be anyone hurrying frantically across a field to catch the bus.

There is ample time to enjoy the scenery: on the Shropshire side, good red plough, and water-meadows with the river flowing shallowly over pebbly beaches, and probably a heron or a few black-headed gulls from the colony at Llyn Hylin; and on the Radnorshire side, reclaimed grazing land, tumps, twisted trees, for here on the foothills of Radnor Forest "the soyle is hungry, though not barren—rough and churlish and hardly bettered by painfull labour so that its riches consisteth chiefly in the brood of cattle" (and, one might add, sheep).

As the river broadens below into a small plain of fertile fields, our road still hugs the hillside, now steeply wooded, now gently sloping and cultivated—but away to the north the wild, tumbled hills of Clun Forest are most beautiful in their infinite variety of shape and colour.

AT last we reach Knighton, with a full bus load. Jack collects the fares as we alight—a leisurely business, especially when there is a shortage of change, or a long delay as an old granny searches fumblingly for her precious bit of money which is wrapped up too well in a screw of paper. All the time, there is talk—a sing-song "pobbling" flow of conversation which is so fascinating to listen to. Only odd snatches are distinguishable in the general hubbub.

"How be Mrs. Williams? . . . I've been upon go, fair play, since six this mornin' without one word of a lie . . . She hadn't been gone none when you come in. . . I didn't know no aim what to say . . . I wanna very well last night—I ruz in me sittin' and put me feet on the soller. Goodbye now!"

Jack drives off thankfully to the terminus. By 12 o'clock the usually sleepy town, now "bustling with slow activity," is thronged with women eager to buy fresh vegetables and fruit, fish and meat, and to exchange the latest news about babies and husbands and illnesses. Farmers, their business done, [illegible] and smoke and gossip, negotiating many a shrewd deal over a glass in the pub.

WHEN IT is time to return home, you can sit and wait for the bus on a conveniently low wall in the High Street, surrounded by other people's packages and baskets. Is there perhaps just time to run across to the greengrocer's? The bus always lingers for a few minutes while passengers inquire whether it really is destined for Felindre or is maybe a relief going only half way up the valley.

I remember Mrs. Lloyd bustling up at the last minute, hot and flustered: "Wait a minute!" she begged, "John's coming!" and away she went to find him, flinging handbag and basket on the seat.

The bus resounded with cheerful and kindly conjecture as to what had happened: "Well-oh! she's going up the Narrows. She must have missed to bring her meat, sure-ly," "John be at the fish-and-chip shop, I doubt . . ."

"These Johns are a nuisance, always barrin' the driver, of course," said a smiling farmer's wife with a wink at Jack—"'Ere they comes! 'Er's blowin!"

On the return journeys Jack seldom needs a reminder to stop at each homegoing passenger's corner or gate, but when he inadvertently misses one, there is much good-humoured banter about his failing memory. The women take so long to gather up their baskets and precious wireless batteries and to indulge in lingering farewells on the step of the bus that one cannot help speculating on the confusion they would cause (and feel) on a "hurry-along-please" city bus.

Jack will sometimes have a parcel to leave at a farm gate, which may be as much as a mile away from the farmhouse. Once I saw two t[illegible] skeins of wool, sent up by bus, balanced on top of a gate: someone would "fetch it up"—either a child dawdling home from school, or a labourer on his way from the pub.

But it is not only small packages that are carried—the bus has even coped with pigs and calves and bicycles, and on one occasion, a sack of live kittens.

I SHALL never forget the first time I went on the Saturday bus to Newtown, twelve miles over the hills. It was not difficult to realise that this had been a very wild and dangerous road in the days of long-ago and that travellers used to prefer a much longer, but safer, route.

We went up, up, through a mizzle—a light, drifting mist of rain—past isolated farmsteads, where the land looked poorer and the trees more stunted. The road twisted and turned and if you were at all subject to travel-sickness it was best to sit near the door, so they said.

I certainly felt unaccountably dizzy as we climbed—perhaps some dark deed of the past still haunts the road and bewitches unwary travellers. One is affected in these hills by an indefinable sense of old unhappy far-off things and battles long ago, of which there are many reminders in the numerous hill-forts, tumuli and standing stones scattered over Radnorshire.

Indeed, as the bus crawled slowly up over the tops, along the open road of the higher hills, I was transported into a faery world—the world of hills that change not with the changing years, where the curlew's haunting cry has echoed over the lonely places from time immemorial.

A RAVEN with a hoarse "*pruk-pruk*" slowly and with dignity made his way home to the distant purple of Radnor Forest; a mewing buzzard spiralled higher and higher. There were wild stretches of moorland where grouse and meadow pipits lurked amongst the bracken and whinberries, and tiny rills bubbled up to "sparkle out among the fern and bicker down the valleys," over grey pebbles and heathery tufts—for here is the source of the River Teme and of the Ithon, and not far away the Severn rises.

We passed a peaty tarn with the baleful name of Dead Pony Pond. The road narrowed and Jack, who knew its tortuous bends by heart after twenty years of negotiating it, had always to be ready for straying sheep which stood shilly-shallying in the middle of the road before making a sudden bolt for the bank. Small wild ponies, too

ACCOUNTANCY

The joy of youth is total—
Its woe, in turn, complete.
Each has a separate ledger;
Their entries never meet.
Time brings one consolation;
We draw a balance-sheet.

GILBERT THOMAS.

Memories 1959

being resurfaced by gangs of roadmen, during the summer months. They spread a thick layer of tar over the road followed by deep shovelfuls of coarse grit which was then rolled into the tar by a steam roller owned and driven by Mr. Dick Woolley of Bucknell. The tar splashed everywhere and for days it was glued on to our legs, shoes and 'white' socks!

The 1930's in Lloyney were happy, carefree, days for us children – not quite so for our parents, they were the years of 'the slump' and work and money was scarce.

The Blacksmith

After a disciplined day at school in Llanfair Waterdine, with the dominance of the three R's from which we all benefited, we would return home and head straight for our village's star attraction, 'The Blacksmith's Shop.' There we would crowd around the doorway of the dimly lit interior to watch the sparks fly as Mr. Bill Farmer, also the publican of the Builders Arms – shaped horseshoes into varying sizes. He often shod a waiting carthorse on the roadside, sitting astride the animal's upturned leg while he hammered in the nails.

The blacksmith also fitted the iron bands round the cart wheels made by my father at his timber yard just up the road. The wheels would be trundled along to the smithy, have a red hot iron ring put around them, and then get dipped into a purpose built narrow 'well' of water to tighten them on to the wheel.

From the left: the blacksmiths, the public house, Underhill, Top and Bottom Row under Lloyney Rock

In the evenings the blacksmith became landlord again, helping his wife in the bar of the inn. Few tourists had found the beauty and solitude of the Teme Valley in those days but the Builders Arms was host to a few dedicated fishermen who came to fish for trout in the Teme.

Unfortunately the old blacksmith's shop with other roadside housing was demolished in a road widening scheme in the 1960's – and the little village green, which 'fronted' the Builders Arms, was also a victim of the road widening.

The Carpenter

In those days the village carpenter was a man of many trades: not only did he build and repair farm carts and gambos, he made gates, stiles and fences, fashioned doors and windows for houses and, most importantly, he was the local undertaker. Like the blacksmith he had a young 'apprentice' to one day follow in his footsteps. To make a perfect coffin was my father's pride and joy.

The oak or elm boards were cut and carved into shape and polished by hand. The interior was lined with 'dowl,' white felt cloth, and the 6 brass handles and nameplate were fitted.

On the funeral day, the carpenter became the Funeral Director, his duties being to organise the journey to Church and afterwards to the grave.

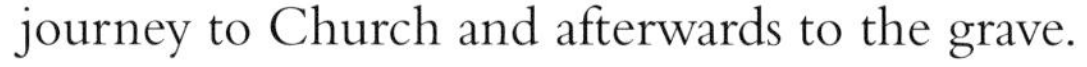

'Puffing Billy'

In winter time this could be difficult, with horse and cart the only means of transport, and farm and bye-ways filled with snowdrifts.

The timber for these various jobs was purchased from local woodlands and transported on the carpenter's timber wagon, drawn by 2 cart horses, to the timber yard. There he had a saw bench and the small sawmill was powered by steam. Another local business hired out a steam engine to farmers for the threshing season. In Lloyney and Llanfair Waterdine it was Mr. George Lloyd, and later his son Ted, who was 'on call', and it was his big 'Puffing Billy' that was sited in our timber yard periodically to drive the saw.

My sister and I loved playing with the mounds of sawdust created in the workshop – it made realistic ingredients for pies and cakes for the family of dolls etc that were part of our household.

Wash Day

The brick boiler had to be filled with water by bucket and then a fire lit underneath, 'whites' were washed first – boiled, rubbed on a rubbing board, rinsed, blued and then starched, with mangling between each stage. 'Whites' were followed by the coloured wash, but without boiling, blueing or starching. A hard long day for the housewife.

The Village Shop

This was a great source of pleasure for the children of the 20's, 30's and 40's. A big bell clanged as the door was opened and summoned Mrs. Gwilt, swathed, as all housewives were, in a large wrap-around pinafore.

On the counter were chunks of cheese, red or white, and a variety of large round loaves. "Loose" sugar and flour were weighed on scales which had brass weights – quarter ounce to 2lbs. – and then tipped into a coarse blue paper bag and the top turned down.

Along the back of the shop were jars of sweets, boiled, toffees and peppermints. These too were weighed in ounces and put into small cone shaped white bags. We did not actually ask for a quantity by weight, but by half pence, or pence (old currency). Candles and matches were sold and also packets of tobacco for the pipe smokers, 'Twist' for those who chewed it, and Woodbines, which were a small cheap cigarette.

Ploughing under Lloyney Rock. Alfred Davies and his father.

Other provisions were collected from Knighton on Thursdays – Market Day, when the road was crowded with horses and traps, weighed down with baskets of eggs, butter, poultry and rabbits for sale on the outward journey, and with provisions, not available in the village shop, on the return journey.

Also on this day slow noisy processions of sheep and cattle were driven through our village from hill farms many miles up the valley en-route for auction in Knighton. Some of the sheep had been "dipped and dyed", to enhance their appearance, in hues of orange and yellow. Each flock was accompanied by 2 or 3 "farm hands" and several dogs. Poor animals – if unsold, they had to make the return journey later that evening, when both man and beast must have been extremely tired.

Amenities

There were few amenities in the village during the first half of the century. Electricity arrived in the valley in the mid 1950's, and a water supply in the early 1950's.

Until then people used oil lamps and candles, and for cooking, oil stoves. Water was drawn from an old rustic pump which stood in the centre of the village by 'The Mill'; it stood on a blue bricked surface surrounded by posts.

From our home we would watch the villagers, buckets in hand, trundling to and from the pump, stopping to pass the time of day. Their buckets had noticeably rusty interiors – the water from the pump was always discoloured with minute rust particles, and it was generally believed

Fanny Price at home in Lloyney 'row'

to be 'full of iron' and therefore beneficial to the system! Whether it would have passed the stringent water tests of 1999 is doubtful - but judging from the age of its users no harmful effects have ever arisen – and it could even have helped build a natural immunity to the many bugs and viruses which seem to afflict us nowadays.

The Milkman

One amenity we did enjoy was the daily delivery of milk, 'warm' from the cowsheds of Mr. Dai Davies, Teme Cottage: lovely creamy milk – before the days of pasteurisation – brought personally by 'Dai' or his wife, and measured into our jugs with the pint measure hooked onto his milk bucket.

Christmas

Christmas in those days was a wonderfully simple happy time, we celebrated Christ's birth in all sincerity.

The week before Christmas holly and mistletoe were gathered, shopping for presents was done in Knighton, and garlands strung along the ceiling.

A goose was prepared, puddings and mince pies made, and the Christmas cake was iced and decorated. As a special treat for my sister and I, our mother made special small iced cakes and prepared jellies and blancmanges.

Of course the great excitement for us was choosing the longest stocking and hanging it on the hearth on Christmas Eve in readiness for the arrival of Father Christmas. Before bedtime our father always took us out to hear the sleigh bells in the distance - which we always thought we could.

On Christmas morning our stockings were unpacked – nothing expensive, but the simple contents – an apple, orange, a sugar mouse, some sweets, a book, a small 'wind up' toy, a handkerchief, a doll, or cuddly toy, and maybe a new card game, gave much pleasure.

After Christmas Dinner we listened to the King's speech (George V), pulled crackers, played a card or board game, and listened to carols on the wireless, or enjoyed a sing song around the piano.

Before bedtime all the Christmas cards were looked at and read, before being displayed on every available surface. We did not post our Christmas cards until a few days before Christmas, even Christmas Eve, hoping they would be delivered on Christmas morning when the postman cycled around delivering them.

New Year Gifters

Until noon on New Year's Day it was customary for children to visit all the houses in the village – and chant 'We Wish You A Merry Christmas and A Happy New Year,' for which they would be given a penny or two.

The child who would be the first New Year Gifter that morning would usually receive the huge amount of sixpence - this necessitated starting their 'rounds' at 6am. Some children were able to buy themselves a pair of shoes with their earnings on New Year's morning.

The Primitive Methodist Chapel 1851-1969

The Chapel adjoined the village shop (both are now converted into houses) and sadly closed in 1969.

In the 1930's and 1940's two services were held each Sunday at 3pm and 6.30pm and a flourishing Sunday school of 30 or more children at 2pm.

The highlight of the Chapel's year was the Sunday school Anniversary Services held on the first Sunday in August. Weeks of preparation went into this event which attracted country folk from near and far. The Chapel was packed to overflowing and most of those attending would have to sit on the roadside verges or stand in the road. Like the annual May Fairs, Chapel Anniversaries everywhere served as a social "get together".

The closing service of Lloyney Chapel, Summer 1969

Standing: Walford Jones, Jim Williams, Bert Griffiths, Mrs Bayliss, John Lloyd, Rev. Rose, Rene Griffiths and Elaine, Nancy Griffiths, Fred Jones, Brenda Davies, Harry Evans, Jocelyn Williams, Marjorie Swancott, Elizabeth Lloyd, Bert Williams, Margaret Hildebrand, Ivor Thomas, Ann Thomas, Mrs Thomas, Mrs Salmon, Mr Salmon

Seated: Kate Williams, Lily Jones, Rhoda Griffiths, Ada Jones, Harry Jordan, Mrs Marpole, Bessie Bevan, Alma Lloyd, Sara and Carol Griffiths, William and Louise Davies, Sally Williams, David Davies, Simon Williams

Lloyney Chapel anniversary 1924

A platform for this event was built around the pulpit and the organ and small bench seats hoisted on to it. The children sat on this 'arena' and felt very important as they surveyed their audience. The Sunday school teachers had for weeks beforehand been coaching them to sing 'sweetly' and recite 'clearly' – instructions often forgotten as stage fright afflicted them as they rose to their feet!

The crowning joy for the Sunday school was the anticipation of the Annual "Outing" on the Saturday following the Anniversary.

Before the war this was a trip by rail from Knucklas station to Swansea and the seaside - great excitement as this also entailed rumbling through the blackness of two tunnels. During the war they had to be content with the short train journey to the lake at Llandrindod Wells, but that too was exciting for children who never ventured further than Knighton.

Another memorable day was the Camp Meeting to honour the memories of John and Charles Wesley and in Lloyney this was always on Whit Sunday.

As children, we hoped the day would be fine and warm for us to carry the small Chapel organ and pews into the adjoining field of Lloyney House Farm where we could enjoy the distractions the open air would bring to a lengthy sermon preached from a 'Wheelcart' (pronounced 'Wilk-kyer'!)

The Club Room, Airgun Club

Air Gun Club

Before the war, men would meet on winter evenings for Air Gun practice in a small wooden room, known as 'The Club House' adjoining the village shop. Most men owned a shotgun in those days, to shoot rabbits, which were a staple diet on the weekly menu. The Club House disappeared with the road widening of the 1960's.

Demolition day, 1985

Lloyney Rock

A large rock looms over the village and is known as Lloyney Rock. As children we spent happy hours scrambling up it – and then on through the bracken (higher than our heads) to the grassy peak, which is called 'The Pinnacle.' From its summit there is a panoramic view over the Teme Valley and during the war we could see from here the glow of the fires in Liverpool resulting from the Blitz.

Lloyney Rock viewed from across the River Teme

The War Years

With the onset of war in 1939, a change took place in the village, and life was never so tranquil again.

Young men and women were "called up" to join the Forces, others had "compulsory" work in the local Ammunitions Factory in Knighton.

Our homes, and the local school, were shared with evacuees from Liverpool, and our roads were busy with convoys of Army vehicles. Petrol was rationed so none was available for social trips.

The older men, and those exempted by their work on the land, spent Sunday afternoons and 2 or 3 nights a week training with "The Home Guard" in preparation for a possible invasion.

'Land Girls' from the inner cities and local towns joined our community to replace the young men who had to leave their employment on the farms.

My father was the village ARP. Warden (Air Raid Precaution). He had to attend a weekly lecture in Knighton and patrol the village to see that no glimmer of light showed from any house. There was little danger of an air raid in our remote area, though we did get stray bombs as enemy aircraft retreated.

All the signposts were removed and stored for the duration of the war and we had to carry gas masks and identification cards wherever we went.

Food rationing was little more than an inconvenience. Most country folk had a well stocked vegetable garden, a few hens and a pig, providing essential veg., extra eggs, lard and meat. Rabbits were plentiful, but we did miss out on sugar for baking and jam making, sweets and chocolate. Oranges and bananas became a memory for the five years of war.

Clothing too was rationed and we had to "make do and mend".

The Black Market did flourish in this valley. Eggs, chickens, boiling fowls, butter and meat were sold at inflated prices to town dwellers who were desperate for provisions to augment their rations. These provisions, too, were useful to 'barter' for clothing coupons.

Post War Years

With the ending of the war in 1945 came a change in village and country life. The slow pace of pre 1939 was vanishing.

Farms were mechanised and more cars and vans appeared on roads. The colourful cavalcade of 'driven' stock got less as stock lorries could now be hired. With cars becoming a means of travel for all, it was soon discovered there was 'life beyond Knighton,' and journeys as far afield as Shrewsbury and Hereford became possible.

As already mentioned both electricity and piped water arrived in the 1950s and transformed the whole Teme Valley: paraffin stoves, candles and candlesticks were just kept for power cuts.

Old houses were modernised and had bathrooms with "hot and cold" and flush toilets. No more tin baths for Saturday bath night: and the old privy at the bottom of the garden, with its wooden seat and twin holes, became redundant.

Electricity, in the 1950's, also enabled some households to install television: to SEE pictures, albeit indistinct and snowy, of sporting and other events seemed nothing short of miraculous.

Kitchens, too, got a facelift. Out went the inglenooks, and dusty fire grates and in came Rayburns and Agas. Worktops, cupboards and sinks were 'built in,' also dishwashers and washing machines.

Washing days were revolutionised. With the aid of electric washing machines, spin or tumble dryers and electric irons, laundering was no longer a chore.

A float leaves Lloyney for Knighton Show, 1902

Old flagged stone floors were replaced with labour saving vinyl flooring. Sitting rooms and bedrooms were 'carpeted' and could be cleaned within minutes with a vacuum cleaner.

Other major changes have rapidly taken place in the last two decades of this century. Almost every household has a car, some more than one; some people have satellite and digital TV which is growing in popularity.

Every household has a telephone – no more running to the village kiosk, to ring the doctor, or a friend, and again many householders carry their mobiles in their pocket.

The children of the village no longer walk to school – they ride. With many rural schools closed, transport is provided to both the Primary Schools and the Comprehensive, John Beddoes School, for senior children in Presteigne. In 1939 a school car was provided to transport those who were to continue their schooling there. Prior to that they had no option but to stay at the local school and leave, with no qualifications at 14 years.

Of course the most incredible journey of all time was in the mid 1960's when America launched a spacecraft and put a man on the moon! The computer age has dawned and a letter can now be sent anywhere in the world by e-mail or fax and received within minutes not months.

These reminiscences of more than 70 years of the 20th Century, in which so many changes have taken place in my village and valley, will, I hope, be of interest to you who will be reading this book in the next millennium. I hope it will have given you a brief insight of the 'Good Old Days' of the 1900s.

Our only phone box!

Llanfair Village from Lloyney Rock

The Church gate looking towards Llanfair Hall wood

Refreshments at the Red Lion

Taking a break

A local letter box

A David Brown tractor

Speckled-faced ewes

Jenny Wakeman with pony and trap

Jodie Powell raises funds for the Youth Club

Roger and Katie Thomas at the Wakes

New arrival

Derwin Davies, Ruth Davies, Fred Beavan

Oak and birch trees above the Green

View of the Green Farm

Derek Beavan near the Dyke

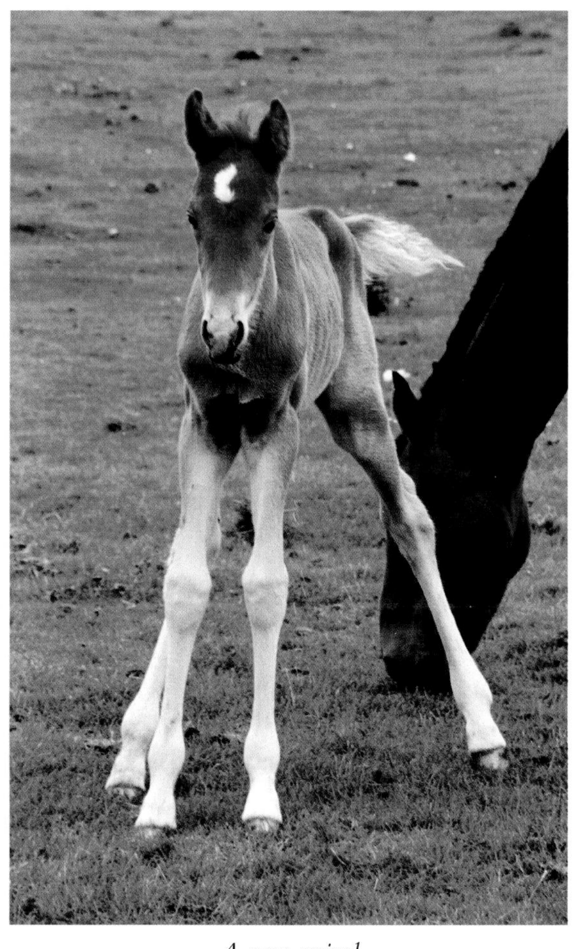

A new arrival

Tom Evans and Ben Swancott

Cow and calf

Roy Davies

Farm Sale, Monaughty Poeth October 1999

Jim Williams takes a last look at the sheep

Harry Davies watches the sale of the cows he worked with

Tom with a pulping machine

The flag at the Church

John and Billy Riddle near Lloyney Bridge

The winning design for the Parish Flag with its designer Alex Lewis

St Mary's, Llanfair Waterdine: Parish Church watercolours, 1856 (old and new church) – artist Mary Leighton

The Church

Interior of St Mary's Church

Dr Richard Townshend works on the barrel organ

Christingle service.
Danny Bevan with
mother Julie and sister Sarah

Rev. Eileen Lloyd rouses the congregation!

WI play
Anne Harroway Mary Chapman Vera Lenior Freda Powell Nora Barrett Mary Morgan Jean Gardener Barbara Carter Winnie Davies Mary Beavan Iris Leason

Ruby Thomas Joan Thomas ? Smith Joan Hobby Winnie Davies Amy Johnson Peggy Mathews Mary Morgan Vera Lenoir Freda Powell Francis Richards Angela Davies Maureen Bates Dolly Clee Ann Harroway Mary Davies Kathleen Jones Avril Nicholas Marjorie Hewins Iris Leason Mary Beavan Nora Barrett Freda Harroway

Tree planting, churchyard.
Llewelyn Morgan Mary Townshend Eva Mac Lauchlan Joan Rhodes Barbara Carter Mary Chapman Jean Gardener Mary Morgan Freda Harroway Dr Townshend Ann Harroway Ruby Thomas Joan Hobby Freda Powell Mary Beavan Rev. David Hayes

Paul and Mary Simmons at Melin-y-Grogue

Lower Graig in summer

Lower Skyborry garden provides a water interest for the Townshend grandchildren

Rudbekia

Ben enjoys the view!

Kingcups

Long Wood

View over a gate at Selley Cross

Andrew Beavan and Tom Adams Evans stack bales

Future farmers?

Silage cutting

A cattle crush – reading ear tags

Marking sheep

Footbridges were common when streams were allowed to flow over roads

Free range hens and ducks

A well-secured door

The Hunt

Brushes!

David Gardner starts a trotting race

Susie Lobell and John Davies make good speed!

Basketball at Youth Club

Tom Adams Evans and John Beavan supporting Shrewsbury Town

Youth Club, Philippa Boast and their newly finished mural

Lloyney

Crogue (1974 –)

Cyril and I moved into Crogue in November 1974. The bungalow took the name of the field upon which it stands. It seemed strange at first to have no staircase to climb but we realised the advantages of having all the rooms on one level as we grew older. For the first time we also had a view of all the traffic and pedestrians passing along the B4355 road and in our retirement this helped to keep us in touch with the world outside. Assisted by Winston, we laid out the flower and vegetable gardens. The lawns were laid by John Thornton, the local nurseryman. We grew a conifer hedge near the boundary with the road but unfortunately the very dry weather in 1975/6 caused some of the trees to fail. We replanted a green beech hedge in its place and this grew well. Winston, who had been running his own road haulage business since 1974, had converted a strip of land adjoining the road near our vegetable garden to form a lorry park and he would usually call to see us before and after a journey - he made many journeys all over Britain. Once he had made a particular journey, he never forgot the route. Although there have been minor changes, the layout of the bungalow and garden has remained basically the same since the late 1970s.

Mrs Williams at the Crogue

Tragically, Winston became ill with cancer and after a long and very courageous battle against the disease, he died in 1984, just 12 days after his 42nd birthday. During his illness he was cared for by his partner, Sylvia, and thanks to her efforts and those of family and friends he was able to remain at home until the end. Although Winston's life was cruelly cut short, he achieved much and is still widely and affectionately remembered in the locality. He was buried in Heyope Churchyard, in a valley of which he was always very fond.

Cyril and I tried to adjust as best we could to life without Winston. We busied ourselves in the house and gardens and still kept in contact with many friends in the local community. We were involved in fund raising for Heyope Church, I still enjoyed attending whist drives during the winter months and Cyril took great pride in cultivating the vegetable garden. Cyril had always loved horses and enjoyed attending race meetings; in his later years, he still occasionally rode, the last time being when he was about 76. He had a great sense of humour and was full of fun. Children especially loved him because he always made time to spend with them.

Ty Heulog

In 1989, six months after we celebrated our golden wedding, Cyril passed away after a short illness and was buried beside Winston in Heyope Churchyard. Following Cyril's death, I have continued to live as actively as possible at Crogue, I retain my great interest in gardening and keep in close touch with family and friends. More than 60 years have passed since Cyril and I came to live in Lloyney. Considerable changes have taken place since then but the beauty and tranquillity of this part of the Welsh borderlands remain to this day.

Dilys Williams
28 October 1999

Eagles Nest

Eagles Nest

The land on which Eagles Nest and Birches House (next door) were built was purchased from Mr. & Mrs. Hewin, Lower Goytre Farm, by Sarah Jane Turnbull in April 1988.

Sarah Turnbull then sold half the plot to Barry Green, from Cornwall, in September 1989, and he built Eagles Nest during the following year (naming it Sweetbrier) and subsequently selling to Mr. & Mrs. Holt, from Luton, in mid 1992. In the interim Sarah Turnbull built Birches House on the adjoining plot.

Peter Taylor, from Daventry, Northamptonshire, purchased Sweetbrier from the Holt's in March 1994 and renamed it Eagles Nest.

Why three owners of Sweetbrier/Eagles Nest in under four years, and all from well outside the local area? In a nutshell it was basically a reflection of the marital hiatus that manifested itself during the latter half of the twentieth century, resulting in an ever escalating breakdown of personal relationships, combined with a more mobile population, many of whom were seeking a better quality of life in a quieter and more appealing environment.

Barry Green's aspirations were thwarted by a partner who wished to return to Cornwall shortly after completion of the property, for her Elysium was not the Shropshire/Welsh border hills. For whatever reason the Holt's dream was shattered within a year of purchasing the house.

Conversely, Peter Taylor's purchase in 1994 was prompted by the failure of his marriage in late 1993 and a desire to start life afresh in a new location. For him the quiet beauty of the local area has proved to be extremely rewarding and therapeutic, and after nearly five years his love of walking in the solitude of the local hills, on turf manicured to perfection by the teeth of ten thousand odd sheep, remains undiminished. Although no stranger to living in the countryside, the close proximity of the local wildlife has stimulated conflicting reactions. The superb soaring skills of the buzzards and the aerobatic manoeuvres of the ravens almost daily bring pleasurable reminders of his personal aviating exploits, from flying fighter aircraft in the Fleet Air Arm to spending over forty years flying sailplanes on long cross country routes as a leisure activity. There is the occasional sighting of a red kite, confirming that bird's expanding population from a tenuous and near extinct enclave to the west in the mid twentieth century. Equally rewarding have been sightings of the occasional kingfisher along the banks of the river Teme and the odd polecat slipping through the undergrowth, surprisingly in broad daylight. Three hedgehogs have for two summers come nightly to consume their bread and milk from the dish at the back doorstep. A fox, however, caused some alarm; on a couple of occasions he/she? carried off the small milk crate and scattered its empty bottles across the lawn in the dead of night. Alarm because the implication was human vandalism before the mystery was solved. The sparrow hawks and the grey squirrels are less welcome, the former because they persist in skilfully plucking the tits from the nut feeders, the latter because they repeatedly tear the nut feeders apart. Squirrels have also demonstrated another destructive characteristic, each spring/summer they have stripped the rose bushes of flowers and carried them off into the woods. Do they eat them or use them to line their nests? That remains a mystery. Finally, the majestic herons, like the sparrow hawks, superbly skilful in seeking out and catching their daily rations, a magnificent bird when poised to snatch a brown trout from the Teme, but, again like the sparrow hawk, unwelcome at Eagles Nest when they turned their attentions to the fish in the garden pond. A permanent net has solved that problem.

All this is part of the excitement of living in the Teme Valley; adjacent to raw nature, but also in a scattered community, whose inhabitants tend to keep a low profile whilst undertaking their individual activities and pursuits. Locally born and those from afar harmoniously coexist, each prepared to come out from under their shells to offer help and guidance in times of need.

Peter A. Taylor

Greenlands

Herbert Charles Beaumont my grandfather was born in 1862 and died in 1953 at the age of 9l. He was a member of the Shropshire Yeomanry and my sister Ruth still has his helmet and other momentoes. He married Blanche who came from Monmouthshire. She died in 1948 at the age of 77 This was his second marriage, he had moved from Norton Street in Knighton to The Hobby on the death of his first wife Jane, in childbirth. Both he and Jane are buried in Knighton. Blanche left South Wales on the death of her fiancee who had been in the army. She was a housekeeper at The Hobby before marrying Herbert. They had three children Blanche born in 1904 (known locally as Bessie or Aunty B) Constance Mary (Connie) who died in 1983 at the age of 78 and Charles Herbert my father who died in 1985 aged 77. He married Gladys Mary Lloyd from Llandinshop in 1936 and she died in 1992 at the age of 80. They had three children myself, Ruth and Bernard. When my grandfather, Herbert first went to The Hobby he rented it and he worked hard for many years delivering coal, as a postman and running the farm in order to be able to buy the property and raise his family. He passed it on to my father, Charles Beaumont who lived there for most of his life. I married Idris Lloyd from Rose Cottage, Dutlas and we have lived in the area ever since. Idris is a builder and he built our home, Greenlands, where we still live with our dogs and a cat. We have one son, Steven David and a daughter Cheryl. Steven has five children of his own and four step children and lives locally. Cheryl has three daughters and lives in the house next door to Greenlands. Idris is the son of Pryce and Amy Lloyd nee Jones who were married at Llanfair in 1929. Pryce was from Black Mountain Bettws. Idris had one step brother Tommy who was in the Royal Marines and was killed in action in the Second World War at the age of 21.

Greenlands

My aunts, Connie and Aunty B returned to Lloyney to retire after full working lives, Aunty B in teaching and Connie as a housekeeper/companion in many parts of the country. On returning to the area they were both active in the community, Connie running the local Sunday school for many years.

My sister Ruth trained as a nurse, she is widowed, has two sons and lives in Ross-on-Wye. Bernard married Molly Virginia Bach and has a stepson Howard and two daughters Catherine and Rachel. I have always taken a full part in local activities and I played the organ in Llanfair church for 44 years taking over from Mrs T S Jones from Llanfair Hall and at first, sharing the task with Mrs Cummins, Skyborry. On special occasions Robert Davies who had been born at Melin-y-Grogue Cottage used to play the organ, he was an extremely talented pianist, organist and violinist and worked with Sir Edward Elgar at Shelton Hospital Shrewsbury. Elgar believed that music was very important to mental health. Robert's niece Beth Williams still lives in Knighton. The organ is unusual because it is a barrel organ and it also had to be pumped before it could be played. Bill Evans, (uncle of Joan Hobby) from the Vedw and later Myrtle Cottage did this job for many years, almost up until his death. My son Steven then took over and now electricity has been installed. I had to give up playing the organ when my working hours clashed with Church services. I work as a support worker taking care of adults with learning difficulties. I also raise funds for the local Samaritans.

I have many memories of Lloyney over the years. The first TV programme most of us saw was the Coronation in 1953. The first car I remember up the valley belonged to Marcus Francis who I think lived at Lloyney shop. He ran a taxi service from there. My grandparents generation walked to Knighton or paid to travel by pony and trap. They took produce to sell on a Thursday to supplement their incomes. Electricity did not come to Lloyney until about 1952. Before that candles and oil lamps provided light and cooking was done on an open range heated by wood or coal or on a stove heated by paraffin and later Calor Gas. Local people made their own entertainment and expectations were much lower than they are today. Now I feel we lead much fuller lives and I think nothing of travelling long distances for social and family reasons and am able to have many interests outside my home and the local community.

Margaret Lloyd.

Highfield

Highfield

Jan and Idris Williams live at Highfields and have two sons. The younger son Rhys takes a great interest in local wildlife. The family have one horse and two dogs and have managed to attract a group of woodpeckers to their bird feeders after two years of careful work. At first one great spotted woodpecker took nuts from their feeder, but as time went on a pair became quite tame and the following spring they brought two offspring along. By 1998 a pair of shy green woodpeckers joined the great spotted and Rhys his brother and parents are now visited by all of these on a regular basis. The whole family hopes that even more will be attracted as they breed each year and help to keep up the numbers of such beautiful woodland birds around Bwlch-y-Plain.

Spotted Woodpecker

Lloyney House Farm

Lloyney House Farm

Lloyney House Farm is owned by Edward John and Ethel Davies and their son Dennis. Edward is 81 and Ethel is 80 and Dennis is aged 49. They run a mixed farm with over 500 sheep and more than 50 cattle. They keep 2 farm dogs but no other animals. The farm is 174 acres and the land is situated around Lloyney. The Davies family bought Lloyney House from Mr and Mrs Cyril Williams. Mrs Williams still lives in a bungalow nearby.

Life at Lloyney House (1939 to 1974)

I was born at Llanhailo Farm, Hundred House, about six miles east of Builth Wells.

In April 1939 I married Cyril Williams whose family home was at Hundred House Post Office and Stores and we came to live at Lloyney House, some 20 miles from our home area.

The previous occupier of Lloyney House was a Miss Beavan who was assisted on the farm by Mr. Frank Gwilt and his sister. Sadly, Miss Beavan was quite ill during the last months of her life. When she became housebound, she was cared for by Miss Gwilt whilst Mr. Gwilt ran the farm. Miss Beavan died in the autumn of 1938. Fortunately Mr. Gwilt stayed on after we arrived and he proved a very trustworthy and respected employee.

When we came to the Teme Valley I remembered that Cyril remarked that he did not properly understand the broad dialect of the local people which differed from the more clipped dialect in the Hundred House area. However, we soon became accustomed to the differing language and customs in our new area.

Lloyney House in 1939 had none of the modern conveniences which we take for granted today. Water was pumped from a well at the foot of a dingle at the rear of the farmhouse and was then carried up to the house. In the house itself we had gas mantles to provide lighting on the ground floor and oil lamps for the bedrooms. In the kitchen there was an open grate with an oven and a boiler. In the rear kitchen we had a furnace for boiling clothes. There were small fireplaces in the dining room to the right of the hall and in the sitting room beyond that. There was also a fireplace in the bedroom immediately above the sitting room. The house had two staircases, one leading from the kitchen, the other leading from the dining room. The dairy adjoining the kitchen contained a huge stone slab and this room was very cool in summer. There was also a cellar which was entered via a flight of stone steps leading from the back kitchen. Our toilet was an earth closet at the end of the garden.

The farmhouse formed one side of a square with farm buildings on the other three sides. There was a rickyard and hay barn on the far side of the cattle shed opposite the house. There were flower beds in front of the house and a large garden on the south-east side.

The farm covered about 120 acres including land on an adjoining hill. Some fields bordered the River Teme. Some of the fields had names such as 'Crogue' and 'Jack Withers' but we never discovered the origin of these.

We had been living at Lloyney House for 4 months when the Second World War was declared. On that fateful day we received an urgent message from Cyril's mother who was very distressed after listening to Neville Chamberlain's broadcast. Mrs. Williams asked us to come at once and have a meal with the family as it might be the last occasion; she was sure that we would all be bombed by the Germans. We immediately set out on Cyril's motorcycle and with Cyril's father we tried to reassure her. Thankfully, the bombs never fell on our homes although at least one German aircraft did crash near Hundred House during the course of the war.

In 1939, our implements on the farm were horse-drawn. During the war we acquired a tractor. We were required by the government to plough at least three fields to produce wheat, oats, barley and potatoes. We kept cattle, sheep, poultry and usually a pig and we could therefore produce our own meat, milk, butter and eggs. This made the effects of rationing less severe for us in the countryside than in the large towns.

In April 1940 my father, Pryce Bufton, died. My mother (Mrs. Elizabeth [Bessie] Bufton) and my stepbrother John continued to farm at Llanhailo. In 1941 John married and my mother left Hundred House and came to live with us at Lloyney House. My mother had been involved in farming all her life and quickly adjusted to her new surroundings.

In January 1942 our son Winston was born. As a child he was fascinated by tractors and cars and was also very interested in animals. He used to construct cardboard 'houses' for the farm cats and kittens. He was particularly fond of a black cat with white markings on its feet and named it

'Whitesocks.' When he was a little older he had a pet corgi called Jenny which ran around with the farm dogs.

The end of the war in 1945 saw the beginning of many changes to our way of life and major developments in farming. We now had a tractor and a car. Mr. Gwilt continued with us until he retired in the mid 1950s. In May 1955 electricity was installed in the farmhouse. Shortly after, we had mains water and a Rayburn was installed in the kitchen. With its enclosed fire, it was much cleaner than the old black grate and the oven was very efficient.

In 1956 we constructed a 'deep litter' shed for our hens thereby improving egg production and making egg collection much easier. Although the hens were normally confined to this shed, it was large and they had freedom to run about within its walls. In the late 1950s and early 1960s the frontage of the cattle shed, which was wooden, was replaced by more substantial breeze blocks.

In 1960 the field known as The Green, which bordered our driveway, was acquired by Radnorshire County Council. The old properties in the village, below The Rock, which were known at Top Row and Bottom Row, had been condemned as unfit for human habitation. Six semi-detached houses and four semi-detached bungalows were built on The Green. The occupants from Top and Bottom Row, mostly elderly villagers, together with local residents from within the village and from Bwlch-y-Plain, moved into these new dwellings in about October 1961. The little estate became known as Rock View. The estate contained a rich diversity of characters, including Miss Gertie Evans, once employed as a housekeeper near Dolfor, who was renowned for her quick movements in spite of her portly frame. She was nicknamed 'Pirie' by the local lads after Gordon Pirie, the famous British runner of the 1950s.

For many years we took in guests. Some, like Dr. and Mrs. Gray and their daughter Sally from Kent, came each summer. Dr. Gray had retired and he loved the peace of the countryside and enjoyed fishing in the nearby River Teme. Mrs. Gray was an accomplished artist and she painted a small picture of Lloyney House in watercolours which I have kept to this day. Their daughter Sally also greatly appreciated the countryside and used to enjoy walking across the hills on both sides of the the Teme Valley.

Other guests stayed for longer periods and became part of the family. They included George Astbury who was a bank official at the Midland Bank in Knighton. He stayed with us during the mid 1950s and in his spare time used to enjoy fishing and golf. Sometimes he would practice his golf in the field immediately to the south-west of the farm building known as The Crogue. Later a young chap from Llanidloes, Graham Benbow, who worked for S. W. Brisbane in Knighton came to lodge with us. Graham stayed with us for several years until his marriage to a Knighton girl, Margaret Davies in 1967. Graham actively assisted us on the farm, particularly at harvest time. Following his marriage, he went to live in Knighton and he and his family have always kept in touch with us. His elder daughter, Sharon, is now married with a family and lives in Lloyney.

In 1968 Winston married and went to live in a bungalow which he had built on part of the field known as The Crogue.

In 1969 my mother died. She had been active in the community for some 25 years, especially in the local W.I. and the Church whilst at the same time being a great help to us on the farm. She was a wonderful character, whose love of gardening I have inherited.

In the early 1970s Winston decided that he would not pursue a career in farming and moved into road haulage. Shortly after Cyril's 65th birthday in September 1973 we sold the farm, together with the stock and the implements. The farm was bought by Mr. John Davies of Knighton. We retained part of the field adjoining Winston's bungalow and employed Dyke Construction of Knighton to build a bungalow on that land to which we could retire. The bungalow was completed in the autumn of 1974 and we left Lloyney House in November of that year.

Lloyney House always had a friendly atmosphere and I have many happy memories of my time there.

Dilys Williams

The Cote

The Cote

The Cote was built in 1821 by Richard Morgan, a sawyer. The land was part of the 'Hill Piece of the Cot Estate' owned by Andrew Davies. Richard Morgan appears to have had financial problems as he mortgaged the house twice and eventually sold it for a handsome profit after thirteen years. He presumably planted the small orchard through which runs the present day drive to the house. There were still a few elderly fruit trees in it when we moved in in 1981. We have partially replanted it and included a walnut and a mulberry tree. A fig and peach will be added in the near future when they are big enough to withstand the ravages of the sheep (we use the orchard for new born lambs). He also set out the vegetable garden which is in a very well sheltered spot and has very fertile soil. I often wonder what he would think of my organic methods and the green house full of peppers, melons etc. Beyond the garden is a small field where we used to keep goats. We now keep 16 sheep and have 6 hens and 3 ducks. We have 3 cats and a dog and we also keep bees. The fold is surrounded by various buildings, a barn which incorporates a two tie cow house and calf pen, a workshop where we both do woodwork, although Stuart has put in electricity and we use power tools these days. There is a privy which fortunately was converted when the mains water arrived in 1957. The original water supply was a spring which now feeds the garden ponds. There is also a pig sty and a coal shed, and where a building had collapsed I rebuilt it with the original stone to make a log and animal feedstore. The house looks much the same externally as it always did. We have double glazing now but the frames are replicas of the original ones. We have repointed some of the walls and repaired chimneys. Internally it has changed, one bedroom has been made into a bathroom, two small bedrooms have been made into one and the tiny dairy has been incorporated into the sitting room. The small front garden has been redesigned and now has two ponds and a crazy paving path and patio but the splendid holly hedge is still there and provides a welcome refuge for masses of birds.

A fox at the Cote

We bought the Cote from Mrs Gladys Jones who lived there for many years with her brother Charlie Price, who was quite a character according to local people who remember him. At the time of the sale some of the land was sold separately so in 1986, when we decided to keep sheep, we bought the Birches from Bernard Beaumont from The Hobby. It is approximately 10 acres of very steep, rough pasture and was once divided

Badgers

into 9 small fields. Before 1961 there was a farmhouse and outbuildings but in April of that year Knighton Rural District Council issued an order for its demolition as it was deemed unfit for human habitation. We don't know the date the farmhouse was built but it was mentioned in the will of Richard Tudge dated 6 June 1859. Before we bought the land all the hedges had been removed, quite a lot of trees felled and the lower few acres re-seeded; we attempt to keep the bracken at bay by cutting it and have planted about 50 trees, mainly oaks which we have grown from local seed. In the 18 years since we moved to Lloyney we have done a lot of hard work but we have had a great deal of satisfaction from our lifestyle. We have made many new friends and have had the opportunity to learn new skills, take up new hobbies and best of all we have a hands-on opportunity to pursue our interest in wildlife. We have carried out a polecat survey for the Vincent Wildlife Trust and a bat survey for the Bat Conservation Trust as well as studying the local badgers, foxes etc. and collecting data on several other species for various organisations. Hopefully the next 18 years will be as busy and satisfactory as those which have already passed.

About 1900 at the Birches

Stuart and Vera Howard.

Lloyney Mill – Stanley Davies

Stanley Davies was the son of Robert and Elizabeth Davies and was born at Melin-y-Grogue Cottage in 1912. He later lived at Lloyney Mill and The Brinney with his family. His father Robert Davies was a carpenter and joiner who did a great deal of work in the parish and in Dutlas and Lloyney. He worked at The Pound, Cwm Collo, The Red Lion, Cwmbrain, the Bwlch and many other places. Before the war Stanley worked for the India, China Tea Company near Knighton clock tower. During the War he was a prisoner of war for three years. His parents received four telegrams saying he was missing and they believed he was dead. A fifth telegram, much to the excitement of the local postman (who ran up the lane shouting "He's alive, he's alive!") said he had survived. He escaped via Italy and after the war lived in Wellington Shropshire until his death in 1995. He talked at length to his niece Beth Williams nee Davies and she wrote down his memories. Here he tells of life with his family at Lloyney Mill.

Moving from Melin-y-grogue Cottage to Lloyney Mill in 1916

I had only just turned four when, on Lady Day 1916, we left Melin-y-grogue Cottage to live at Lloyney Mill, so all I know is remembered conversations. We had outgrown the cottage, even though father had built a bedroom over the workshop. He needed land to start farming and was short of space for working and storing timber. He already knew Lloyney Mill well for he had kept it in working order for Mr. Evans and he hoped that by milling, farming and continuing the carpentry business he would be able to afford the much higher rent and eventually be able to buy a place of his own.

Two waggoners came to move us, John Simon from Llanfair Hall and Tom Jones the Runnis. The furniture was rather sparse but there was a large amount of timber, workbenches and tools. Father and Sam built a workshop between the house and the river which provided more room for wheelwrighting and coffin making.

We bought two cows and as time went on had pigs, sheep, some heifers, ducks and chickens. Mother sold milk for 1 penny per pint, measuring it out for villagers who brought their jugs to the house, and made butter and cheese, and sausage and brawn when we killed a pig, and took it, with eggs to Knighton market every Thursday, travelling with Charlie Hughes, Redwood, who charged 6d. fare and left his pony at The Plough with Harry Smith who had the hearse.

I remember I thought our new garden was large. It was a long way down the path, between box hedges, to the little house at the bottom! We saw many more people as the village pump was by the wainhouse across the road, and the mill, which brother Cecil helped to run when he left school in 1919, and the workshop were busy.

One visitor I remember with affection was Mr. Alfred Clee who used to call to discuss work with father. His brother also came to dress the grinding stones for us. The 200lb. sacks of grain were mainly for animal food, oats for horses, barley for pigs and crushed Indian corn for the hens. Father tried to produce a decent bread flour, filtering it through a fine Irish linen cloth, but with the exception of one hot dry summer during the first world war the climate was not suitable, being too wet to ripen the wheat satisfactorily.

Mr. Clee had a difficult time milling at Melin-y-grogue as his water came from Crochen brook. When the pond ran low he had to close the penstock until an adequate quantity had collected. That is why he often worked at night with a hurricane lantern, taking every opportunity to get his work done. At Lloyney we were fortunate to have plenty of water at all times, channelled out of the Teme beneath Melin-y-grogue, across the fields and through a pipe under the road. However, sometime in the 20's, after our time there, a severe flood changed the course of the river making it difficult to get water to the mill.

The Teme also played quite a part in our young lives. The older boys taught the young ones to tickle trout, and sister Bertha, a Queen's nurse, when she came home on leave – once bringing our first taste of bananas – taught us to swim under Graig Wood, near to where the gypsies used to stay. Harry Evans used to come to shoot and fish with my elder brother Sam and always took a keen interest in our progress – or so I thought. It was years later that he told me it was Bertha in her swimming costume which was the attraction!

The Mill, Lloyney

The Mill, Lloyney

John and Wendy were married in 1959 from their homes at Teme Cottage and Cwmjenkin and moved into The Mill in 1962.

The Mill has been on this site since medieval times, records show that it was still used to mill local corn well into the 1930's. It has always been a busy place and at one time in history charcoal was produced here and the area around was planted with bushes and coppiced for this trade. The village took its name from the bushes, that is what Lloyney means in Welsh.. We have been told that John's great great grandfather Thomas Davies lived and worked here in the mid 1800's. John's grandfather Alfred Davies lived here as a boy and then he and his wife Sarah bought the property from Llanfair Waterdine Estate in 1920. Alfred died at The Mill in 1961 .Granny (Sarah) lived with us until just before her death in 1964. When we first lived here, the house was very basic, a small kitchen downstairs. The living room (now the snug) the two original bedrooms and bathroom we have kept more or less the same but in 1974 we changed the "mill" part into living rooms. The main room on the second floor is the kitchen, living and dining area with bedrooms above and downstairs. The house is most unusual in that it has been built on five different levels. Other changes have been the addition of a stable, garage, studio, conservatory, outside loo and shower during the 1980' and 90's.

Wendy and John Davies, 1986

We have five children, Marion, Kevin, Suzanne, Yvonne and Derwin all born and raised at The Mill. John's Mum, "Nan" to all, played a big part in their young lives and they all used to sit on the wall and watch her helping with the milking twice a day. John has always grown our own vegetables and I love flowers and trees so the garden has always meant a lot to us.

Now we have eleven grandchildren who love to come and stay with us, spending a lot of their time playing down by the river, just like their parents did when they were little. We have always had lots of animals, dogs, cats, horses, hamsters, guinea pigs and so on but John's pride and joy are his trotting horses. He has bred horses since the 1970's and has raced in the Mid Wales Trotting Association with considerable success over the years. He now has just two horses, Morning Glory and Susie Lobell and spends most Saturdays during the summer months attending the local race meetings.

As the children were growing up Wendy started a small craft shop in the mill bakehouse, selling hand made local crafts and making soft toy animals, squirrels, badgers and so on, selling them to other craft shops for about twelve years. Wendy now paints in her studio and runs classes and exhibits other artists work and her own in the studio/gallery. John and Wendy run a very busy B & B business with holidays for art and horse lovers. They have a few more hopes and dreams for The Mill and hope that it will remain in the Davies family for the next one hundred years or more!

John riding Susie Lobell

LOT 5.

(Coloured Blue on Plan).

THE VERY ATTRACTIVE

Small Holding and Mill

known as

"LLOYNEY MILL."

Situate in the hamlet of Lloyney,

and comprising about

21 a. 0 r. 19 p.

with convenient

FARM HOUSE

substantially erected in Brick and Slate and containing :—Kitchen with Range, Scullery with Sink and Copper, Dairy, 3 Bedrooms.

LARGE GARDEN.

WATER POWER CORN MILL

in three floors,

with Overshot Wheel, 3 pairs of Stones, Dressing Machine, Shafting and Gear, Sack Hoist, Chains and Pulleys.

THE BUILDINGS

which are mainly built of Timber, Stone and Slate, comprise :—Workshop, Barn, Cowhouse (4 ties), Calf Kit, 2 Pigsties, Fowl-house. On the opposite side of the Road is a stone timber and slate Wainhouse and Cattle Shed.

THE LAND

About 12 Acres of Fertile Pasture and Arable Land adjoin the Mill, and are watered by the River Teme which runs through the Property.

At a short distance from the homestead is a detached portion divided into 4 fields and comprising 6 Acres, chiefly Pasture.

SCHEDULE.

No. on Plan.	Description.	Area.	No. on Plan.	Description.	Area.
	In Llanvair Parish :		Pt. 15	Garden and Orchard	.973
1448	Pasture	.188		(Estimated)	
1458	Do.	2.486	16	Pasture	2.474
1459	Do.	.880	19	Pasture	.700
1518	Do.	2.859	256	Pasture	2.375
Pt. 1522	River (Estimated)	.875	257	Arable	1.168
			261	Arable	1.677
	In Beguildy Parish :		437	Pasture	.944
1	Pasture	.618	438	Pasture	1.309
3	Pasture & Buildings	.318			
3a	Pasture	.009		A.	21.117
4	Pasture	1.264			

The Holding is let to Mr. Robert Davies on a yearly Ladyday tenancy, except Fields Nos. 1518 and 19 which are at present let to Mr. Alfred Davies, of Lower Goytre Farm.

A year's notice to quit, expiring at Ladyday, 1920, has been given to the Tenant of this Lot.

OUTGOINGS.—Tithe Rent Charge Apportionment, £1 12s. 5d.

Land Tax, Nil.

In consideration of the Purchaser of Lot 12 maintaining in good order and repair, the Weir on that Lot and the Mill Race to Lloyney Mill so far as the same passes through that Lot, the Purchaser of Lot 5 shall pay to the Purchaser of Lot 12 an annual sum of £5. The Purchaser of Lot 5 shall have a right of access to the said Weir and Mill Race so far as it passes through Lots 12 and 3 for the purpose of inspection.

Under an Agreement made 4th July, 1907, between the Vendors of the one part and the Knighton Rural District Council of the other part the Inhabitants of the Lloyney have the right of taking water from a Well in Field No. 4, part of this Lot, the said Council paying an acknowledgment rent of 1s. a year.

Sale of Lloyney Mill, 1919

The Old Farmhouse

The Old Farmhouse (The Hobby)

The Old Farmhouse used to be known as The Hobby. The house deeds only go back as far as 1922 when the house and nearly 41 acres of land was sold by the Reverend R C George to Mr C H Beaumont. In 1973 the house and land were transferred to Mr Beaumont's son Mr B H C Beaumont. He sold the house and a small piece of land to Mr and Mrs P Doran in 1983. In 1987 the present owners bought the house from them. Subsequently we bought two small pieces of land from Mr Beaumont. We have built a garage and added an extension at the rear of the house. Mrs M Lloyd nee Beaumont who was brought up at the Hobby thinks that the house is about 150 years old. She also believes that a previous house existed in a slightly different position.

Andrew and Eva MacLauchlan.

The Olde Shop

The Olde Shop, Lloyney

We, Bernard and Vi Dodd, purchased and came to live at The Olde Shop following our marriage in 1970. It had previously been the village shop run by the Gwilt family for many years but closed as a shop in 1970

The 'shop' was converted into a kitchen and over the years various other improvements have been made, including conversion of the cellars into living quarters.

The sister, aunt and mother of Mona Cadwallader outside Lloyney Shop about 1912

A wooden garage and shed next to the 'Shop', demolished in 1985, was used as the village club / hall for many years. The main Knighton / Newtown road used to run right outside our front door but road improvements in the late 1960's now mean that we have a 'private layby' instead.

We run a Round Timber merchants business, a family concern since 1969, operating in the Border Counties. Both of us enjoy sports, having being involved with playing and umpiring in rounders games. Bernard plays golf and is a past captain of Knighton Golf Club. Vi is a keen squash player and currently works at Knighton Sports Centre. We have two sons, Simon and Stephen, born in 1972 and 1975 respectively, who were educated at Beguildy Primary School and John Beddoes School Presteigne. Simon went on to Llandrindod Wells College of Further Education and obtained a B Tech National Certificate in Business Finance before joining the family business. He is a keen rugby player, playing for the Tref-y-Clawdd 1st team. He is married to Ann and they live in Knighton. Stephen obtained a BSc 2.1 Degree in Environmental and Mapping Science at Luton University and then spent twelve months at Swansea University to obtain his Teaching Diploma. He is now a Primary School Teacher working in London. Our family pets are Honey, a yellow labrador and Smokey, a grey tabby cat!

Honey and Smokey

Riverdale

We purchased the land on which the bungalow stands from Mr. & Mrs. Cyril Williams in 1973. We built the bungalow ourselves with the help of sub-contractors, the total cost being approximately £10,000.

It is partly rendered, and partly constructed of Forest-of-Dean stone and has double glazing. The same stone was also used for the garden walls and as a feature for the lounge fireplace and surround.

Riverdale under construction 1973

Riverdale 2000

We moved in in 1974. Lloyney is conveniently close to Knighton, where I worked for a firm of Accountants, and to Skyborry Green where Raymond's business is situated. In 1977 when our eldest daughter Lynne was born I gave up my job. Our second child Kate was born in 1982. I now help Raymond to run his business at Skyborry Green. Lynne is presently working and living away from home. Kate is attending Bishops Castle 6th form College where she is doing business studies.

Raymond and Elizabeth Matthews & Family.

Ty-Saer, Lloyney, Knighton, Powys

Ty-Saer is owned and occupied by Glyn and Sharon and their young daughter Eleanor.

The house was built in 1994. A local builder got the house water-tight then Glyn, Sharon and other family members completed the house in their spare time and moved in following their wedding in August 1994.

Ty-Saer under construction 1994

Previously the land was owned by Mr & Mrs Williams of Crogue, Lloyney who at one point was the owner of Lloyney House Farm. This plot of land was originally part of the farm.

The name Ty-Saer was chosen by Glyn and Sharon because Glyn is a carpenter and this means 'Carpenters House' in Welsh.

Glyn age 30, Sharon 27, Eleanor 16 months

Mike and Gillian Edwards

The Lloyney Inn

We came to The Lloyney Inn in June 1996. We think it was built in about 1760 and it was always called The Builders Arms. The licensee who was here before us changed the name but we have no idea why.

My wife Gillian was born in Cefn Coed, Merthyr Tydfll in April 1946 and moved as a young girl to a farm in Penderyn near the Brecon Beacons where she lived until we got married in 1967. Most of her father's family are farming people from around the Brecon area, her mother was in service in a family in a village near Merthyr.

I was born in Hirwaun near Aberdare in 1948. My father was a Merchant seaman before and after the last War. He spent four years of the War as a prisoner of war in Germany then he worked in heavy industry until his retirement in 1984. My mother was in the RAF during the War, she married my father in 1945. I am the second eldest of five children and I worked for most of my life for Civil Engineering companies until we took over The Lloyney Inn. We have two grown up children and one granddaughter. Janice is married and lives in Stoke-on-Trent and Katherine lives in London and works for the Bank of New York. Since being in Lloyney we have made many friends and from the very beginning we have felt very much at home.

Michael and Gillian Edwards.

The children from Chernobyl plant a Horse Chestnut tree outside The Lloyney Inn

Part Three

Everest Hall and the Old Village School
St Mary's Church
The Red Lion
A Typical Farm

The Everest Hall

and Recollections of the Old Village School

Brenda and Jocelyn - nee Jones

The Tithe Barn and the Red Lion
In the background Hawthorn Cottage,
the 'Dame School' used before the Village School opened

The Everest Hall was originally the village school at Llanfair Waterdine, and served a large area of outlying farms and cottages, together with the villages of Lloyney and Llanfair. At the turn of the century (1900) over 80 pupils attended and a new classroom was built on the West end in 1901.

The first school in the village was a 'Dame School' at Hawthorn Cottage, the house next to The Red Lion, and here a Mr. Edward Bright educated for 1/2d. per day, the children who could afford to pay. (He also provided music in the church on Sunday with his bassoon).

Dolly Clee
(née Setterfield) sitting
on the Tithe Barn steps

When we grew up in the 1930's childhood days were different from today. Living in Lloyney we walked to school, half a mile, meeting up with other children along the way. We would often find the first robin's nest up the 'Vicarage Pitch', or lean over the bridge and

Llanfair Waterdine School children 1929 approx

Fred Beavan Dennis Price Jim Price Dick Price Alec Gwilt Clifford Morris Claude Baigent
Annie Swancott Nancy Jones Julia Evans Doris Breeze Sylvia Parry Bessie Hughes Doris Breeze Miss Jordan
Winnie Price Bessie Barnett Mary Beavan Freda Jones Greta Howells Marjorie Jones
Tom Evans Ron Morris John Wellins? Stan Hughes

watch the trout swimming in the river Teme, sometimes picking a bunch of wild flowers which grew in profusion on the roadsides.

In the early part of our school days Llanfair had three teachers. The building itself dates back to 1854-55 and was built for 110 pupils at the same time as the 'New' St. Mary's church was erected. They are similar, in that both have stone walls and a black beamed roof.

In winter time we arrived at school to be welcomed by roaring coal fires, burning halfway up the chimney! Bill Evans (known as Uncle Bill) the caretaker, would have lit them hours earlier. The children who walked to school through the fields, often on rainy days, arrived wet and bedraggled, with sodden boots and clothes. Their coats would be hung to dry on the guards surrounding the open fires and the wet shoes arranged in the hearth.

The School

The old stone building was draughty and the tall windows rattled in the wind and if you were unfortunate enough to sit at the back of the room you shivered for most of the day! However, one highlight was that each child was permitted to take a potato to school and this was baked in front of the fire for mid-morning break! Miss Priddy, the infant teacher, would turn the potatoes around from time to time to ensure even cooking - with a pair of long black tongs, normally used to stoke up. These potatoes had a two-fold delight - for cold fingers were warmed, before they were eventually eaten! Fresh milk was supplied for "elevensies", from the cows that grazed on the meadows at Teme Cottage. The farmer Dai Davies or his wife brought it around in a large pail and ladled it out with a special measure. Children who wished could buy 1⁄3 pt. for half a penny (old pence). This is 0.208p.

Much of the education was based on repetition of tables and phonic sounds: what our former Conservative Prime Minister, John Major, described as "The Basics". Sounds were chanted with rhythmic movement e.g. "A for Apple", "B for ball", "T for Tiger" etc. Quite often the chants became quicker and quicker reaching runaway speed, resulting in "T for Tiger" becoming "Tiffer Tiger!" etc. Miss Priddy, who later married and became Mrs. Bufton, was an expert at sewing and the needlework girls (aged up to 14 years) produced many beautiful garments, also baskets were woven in cane. Miss Jordan, who taught the middle class, was a gardener and she, together with the boys and the Head Teacher, cultivated the school garden and flower beds, and also did craft work.

The playground was divided into two and the boys used the one half for playing football etc. and the girls played games like "Gathering Nuts in May", on the other half - called "the bricks".

Playtimes ended with the blast of a shrill tin whistle and the classes formed lines and led quietly into school.

The school had just two rooms, divided by a glass partition. Miss Priddy and the infants had the smaller room and Miss Jordan shared the big room with the Headmaster.

For lunch, the children who lived near ran home, these mainly lived in Lloyney and Llanfair. Those from a distance took sandwiches in a linen satchel and ate them in the classroom. On more than one occasion mice were seen popping out of a satchel – no Health and Hygiene Laws then!

1933 Dolly Priddy with Mary Beavan, Nancy Jones, Freda Jones, Joan Evans, Annie Swancott, Marjery Jones

Summer was always welcomed – the girls shed their long black stockings and boots were kicked off. Afternoon lessons took place outside, sitting on an old tree trunk in the playground. Sometimes teachers and pupils bathed and paddled in the river Teme.

Being a Church School the day began with a hymn and prayers followed by scripture. A scripture exam was held annually and on days such as Ascension Thursday, after a brief service in church the children were given the day off!

During the war numbers increased considerably due to the influx of evacuees, mainly from Bootle, a suburb of Liverpool. The classrooms were now overcrowded – desks for two accommodated three; bulky gas mask boxes, plus luncheon satchels added to the discomfort. Not many homes remained undisturbed by this infant invasion. The school windows were dimmed by criss-crossing sticky brown paper tape, to prevent the shattering of glass should an air-raid occur.

The headmaster Mr. Barraclough, of whom we were all "afeared!", left for active service, and his place was taken by his wife, assisted by Miss Priddy and Miss Dalton, the evacuee teacher. Prior to this the school had been reduced by one teacher, Miss Jordan being transferred to Brownhills. Apart from the evacuees from Bootle who were placed by the Liverpool Education Authority, a few private evacuees came from Kent and Merseyside. The local brogue was now intermingled with a "scouse" accent and the emphasis was on the war. We listened to the daily News bulletins

Llanfair Waterdine School children 1949

John Lloyd John Davies Norman Ellis Marston Gwilt
Vera Hughes Marion Ellis Marlene Hobby Joan Evans David Johnson Rosemary Hobby Margaret Hughes Ruth Beaumont Margaret Price
Ruth Davies Beryl Hughes Jennifer Clee Mrs Bufton Miss Diamond Mary Cadwalader Barbara Cadwalader Joyce Hughes
Colin Swancott Winston Williams Ben Ellis Clifford Price John Hughes Leslie Davies Trevor Gwilt

on the war and recorded events in diaries. We practised air-raid drill and fled to our given shelters in the classroom - such as the 'kneehole' in the teachers desk and beneath the piano etc. As children we lived in fear - at night we heard the German bombers droning over to bomb Liverpool; and the glow from distant city fires could be observed from the hilltops, while in the daytime we feared invasion.

Llanfair School had its own war effort, and adopted a Merchant Navy Ship, for which we knitted socks, scarves and mittens, and wrote constantly to "Captain Rue and his crew". Captain Rue was very appreciative and corresponded regularly. We also knitted for the Army and Air Force. In 1945 the war ended and social functions could now once more take place. A great asset for the youth of the area was the formation of the Young Farmers' Clubs, and in July 1944 one was formed at Llanfair. The school came into its own and served as a "Village Hall" in the evenings.

Llanfair Follies, December 1953: The Seaside
Fred Beavan Ron Morris Elsie Gough Jim Williams Westall Price
Jocelyn Jones Betty Williams Brenda Jones Glenys Williams Marjorie Moorman

From the onset this brought the youth of the area together (Lloyney, Knucklas, Heyope and Dutlas) for social events and interesting educational evenings, both practical and informative. Everyone had some form of transport, mainly bicycles, but most farms now sported a secondhand car or van. Entertainment was top of the agenda and created light relief after the "dirge" of the war years. The country lads and lasses and staid older members of this farming community were pleased to let their hair down as they cavorted over the well worn planks of the rickety platform in the school. We were fortunate in having a vicar, The Rev. J. C. Williams, who had the interests of the youth at heart. He became Y.F.C. "Leader" and we were delighted to be "led!" He not only produced our first one-act-plays but also gave demonstrations on icing the Xmas cake etc.

In due course we were fortunate to have living amongst us, in the early fifties, at Weir Cottage, John and Joy Hunt and their young family. John was away from home, as already recorded in this book, leaving Joy with time on her hands and she was only too pleased to help develop the talents of the would-be actors and actresses of the Y.F.C. She decided to produce 'The Llanfair Follies", a musical show based on one which had been produced by her sister in London's West End. At that time, early 1950's, oil lamps were still being used, so one can imagine the gasps of incredulity and utter amazement when Joy announced that she intended having footlights, spotlights and coloured floodlights on stage. However, Joy's wishes were always the clubs command and all knew instinctively that somehow the impossible would be achieved.

Llanfair Follies, c. 1950
Arthur James, Hazel Gwilt, Rev. J.C. Williams (producer)
Brenda Jones Harold Gwilt Betty Williams

Looking back it was a story of ingenuity, hard work and lucky escapes - but all was fulfilled!

Regular dances organised by the Y.F.C. were held in the school. The Victor Sylvester of the Valley, was Wilf Gough,

Lower Panpwnton, and his Scarlet Troubadours - and often we danced to his band. Another popular band was The Bucknell Dance Band under the leadership of Nesta Price. Both bands were marvellous to dance to and with plenty of ballroom wax sprinkled on the floor one did not even notice all the knots in the floorboards! Llanfair Y.F.C. was also keen on Square and Country dancing which was very popular at the time, and used to join in the big Folk Dance Festivals in Ludlow Town Hall. Sadly this thriving little club closed in the early 1960's due to rural depopulation and therefore lack of support; it was a great loss to the community.

Wilf Gough's Dance Band
Dave Lewis (Kingsland) Gary Davies (Knighton) Wilf Gough (Panpwnton) Peter Tranter (Knighton) Keith Broadhurst (Bucknell) John Francis (Milebrook) George Tippins (Presteigne)

End of the Village School

Sadly too the school closed in 1960, and it was unanimously decided at a Special Parish Meeting to purchase it for a Community Centre. An offer of £200 for the building and yard was made to the Diocesan Board on Aug. 26th 1960 and a letter of acceptance dated Oct. 4th 1960 was received. A house to house collection was made which raised over £921. This allowed for purchase and repairs i.e. re-roofing etc. In 1961 it was agreed to call the building "Llanfair-Waterdine Village Hall". However in 1967, at the annual meeting, it was decided to rename it "The Everest Hall" and to plant a horse chestnut tree in the old school yard to commemorate the Conquest of Everest by John Hunt's Expedition (1953). The hall was officially opened by John Hunt (Lord Hunt of Llanfair Waterdine) on June 22nd 1968. Today it is in constant use by the many committees and organisations in the Parish.

The School attends a religious meeting

As the old school fades into history we feel a pang of regret, but with the birth of The Everest Hall the building still lives on and serves a useful purpose to the community.

"If those walls could only speak, what revealing tales would be told!"

Llanfair Waterdine Church of England School

Shropshire Records Office hold the original plans for the school and School House – these were drawn up by Mr. Nicholson, the Diocesan architect in 1853 and agreed to by the Rev. Kinchant and John Evans Sept. 1st 1854. The building fund was partly supported by £5.00 from the Earl of Powys and £10.10.0 from Millington Hospital (St. Mary's new church was built at the same time). It was a Public Elementary School under Bishops Castle Attendance Committee. The new wing was built on in 1901. (W. end of school) and the building finally closed as a school in 1960.

Past views of Llanfair Waterdine village

History of the village and church

The history of the village and church of Llanfair Waterdine has been shaped by its location. The area has been fought over for centuries. It saw the last stand of the great Celtic chief Caractacus against the Romans, and lies in the shadow of Offa's Dyke, built by the Saxon king of Mercia in the 780s as a bulwark against the Welsh. Three centuries later, the Normans attempted to conquer Wales, arousing fierce resistance. At the time of the Domesday book, the area of Llanfair Waterdine was described as 'waste'. This probably reflects the destruction caused by attacks from the Welsh between 1052 and 1055, after which we know the nearby town of Knighton was deserted for over 30 years. The area was again devastated following the Welsh rebellion of 1069. Though Edward I conquered Wales in the thirteenth century, this border area continued to be the scene of conflict, notably during the rebellion of Owain Glyndwr, in 1400.

The first of St Mary's churches in Llanfair Waterdine (1012?)

Church interior before 1854

Perhaps the need to survive in the midst of conflict bred in the people of the area a spirit of compromise. The name Llanfair Waterdine is itself an interesting mixture of Welsh and English. Llanfair in Welsh means the Church of St Mary; Waterdine is probably derived from the Saxon Woeter - Denu meaning 'water valley' or 'wet valley'.

Charters show a place of worship has existed at Llanfair Waterdine for at least 800 years, though the present building is only 150 years old. For most of the medieval period the church, as part of the Deanery of Clun, was under the control of Wenlock Priory. In 1539, during Henry VIII's dissolution of the monasteries, Clun and her chapels passed first to the crown and then to the Walcot family.

The church at Llanfair Waterdine was but a small outpost, and apparently it was to some extent neglected. In 1582 there were complaints that the incumbent had not visited his parish for six years, no sermons were preached on Sundays and the roof was in need of repair.

There are few very old graves in the churchyard, and this is probably due to the fact that bodies were for many years interred inside the church. A document dated 1676 complained that the flooring and seats had become 'disordered' and there were 'unsavoury smells' as a result of 'persons of all sorts and degrees being usually buried within the body thereof and very few in the churchyard'. The paving was repaired and no further burials were allowed within the church without the permission of the minister and churchwarden. By way of further discouragement, a charge of three shillings and fourpence was also payable for a burial inside the church, to cover making good the flooring.

By 1852, the church was obviously badly in need of renovation. There was a fashion at that time of demolishing and rebuilding small churches, and the Rev. Kinchant, the then incumbent, was obviously a a follower of this trend. The parish was by then quite prosperous, Welsh incursions being a thing of the past, with a population of around 600 (the present population is approximately 200). After some dispute, for some of the parishioners wished to repair and preserve the old building, the church was entirely rebuilt in 1854. A village school was built at the same time.

There are photos in the church of the previous St Mary's. Bagshaw's Gazetteer of 1851 describes it as a stone building without a steeple, consisting of a nave, chancel and south aisle. This aisle was separated from the body of the church 'by a row of oak pillars beautifully carved". The present altar rail is made from material from this original rood screen.

There were three enclosures of land in the parish, Clewilsey in 1859, Skyborry in 1872 and Llanfair Hill in 1891. The latter was the last enclosure in England.

The present church and the Everest Hall

The new church of St Mary's was built in 1854 at a cost of £1,000. Records show it has been in constant need of repair ever since (perhaps proving the parishioners who had opposed the demolition of the original church right, after all). The new church differed in an important respect from the earlier building in that it had a spire. However, this only lasted just over 120 years - it was removed in 1975.

Inside the church the middle and south side pew ends carry the names of the farms to which they belonged. The north aisles are 'free'. A font, believed to be Saxon in origin, stands between the pulpit and the front pew. The lectern is inscribed to the memory of parishioners who died in World War I. The organ is very unusual because it incorporates a barrel organ, still capable of playing a number of hymn tunes.

The church was the scene of a great parish event in 1870. The winner of the 1869 and 1870 Grand Nationals was a horse called 'The Colonel', owned and trained by John Davies of Cwmsannum, a local farm. Following his second victory, the horse was led into the church for a special service in his honour.

The last vicar exclusive to Llanfair Waterdine seems to have been the Rev. Robinson in 1947: subsequently the benefice has been shared.

The elementary school, built at the same time as the church when the parish was booming, originally had 110 pupils. It closed in 1960 and became a community centre. After refurbishment in 1967 it was renamed the Everest Hall, in honour of Sir John Hunt the leader of the 1953 Everest expedition, who lived in the parish for many years. The Hall continues to be used regularly for parish events, notably 'the Wakes', a traditional summer fair, held every August.

This is an abridged version of 'A Short History of Llanfairwaterdine and St Mary's Church,' by WI Harper.

The Red Lion Inn

Llanfair Waterdine

Outside The Red Lion before 1920 (Owens Motors?)

Believed to have been built circa 1570 (advised by the President of the British Vernacular Architects Association).

Over the last 30 years the role of the country inn has changed dramatically. No longer can one rely on local drink trade to support such an establishment. Drink driving laws enforced by Central Government have all but destroyed the drinks-only trade.

In 1999 the trade of the Inn is roughly split into 3 categories -

1. Immediate Local Food & Drink

A regular, but small core of drinkers, largely centred on the Tap Room, supplemented by sports night activities, chiefly Darts and Dominoes. The pub now runs 2 darts teams in the local Teme Valley league and 1 Dominoes team in the Knighton and district league.

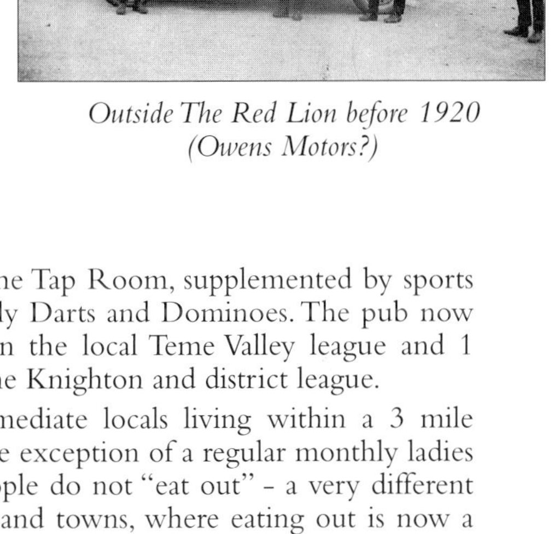

The Red Lion

Food sales to immediate locals living within a 3 mile radius is low. With the exception of a regular monthly ladies night, most local people do not "eat out" - a very different trend from suburbia and towns, where eating out is now a major feature of everyday life.

2. The Diners' Radius

An important source of business is gathered from a 3 to 20 mile radius of people who do eat out on a regular/semi-regular basis. This trade comprises both middle-aged and retired folk.

Retired people primarily make up the lunch-time dining trade, with a wider spectrum of people at weekend evenings.

Regular diners come from Knighton, Clun, Teme Valley (Bucknell to Ludlow) Leominster, Bishops Castle and over to Craven Arms. Very few come from Newtown; the hills being a geographical and culture barrier.

3. Visitors to the Area

An extremely important sector of business is the tourist industry.

From spring through to late autumn visitors come from towns and cities to enjoy the peace and beauty of the South Shropshire countryside.

The Inn has an excellent reputation with local and intermediate Bed & Breakfast establishments and enjoys a large amount of trade through the recommendations of B&B/Guest House owners.

The Inn is also listed in a number of national and international guides to high quality inns and eating houses.

Noel Price outside the Tithe Barn

What do People Eat and Drink?

Real Ales

Traditionally brewed and cellar conditioned, the genuine hand-pulled draught bitter is the most popular beer sold in the Red Lion.

We sell our own brand 'Lionheart' bitter (3.8% alchohol by volume). This is brewed for us by a small local brewery in Hereford and is made with Marris Offer Pale and Crystal Malts and uses Target and Goldings Hops, many of which are grown further down the Teme Valley in the Tenbury Wells area.

Our other main draught beer is the Dorothy Goodbody range of Seasonal Ales - a different brew for each season.

Other beers in our current line-up include - Carling Lager, Guinness Stout, Worthington Smoothflow Keg Bitter, Bass Mild and also Strongbow Cider from Bulmers in Hereford.

Wines

A copy of our current wine list is attached and the reader will readily see that wines from around the world are enjoyed regularly by our customers.

Bottles of wine are usually sold to accompany meals; a range of draught wines are also available. White wine on its own or diluted with soda or lemonade is gaining popularity as a ladies drink.

Spirits

Our spirit trade is relatively small compared with the sales of wines. Whisky would be the Number 1 choice, followed by Gin and Vodka. The following list indicates the range of spirits and liqueurs stocked in 98/99.

Food

Copies of our Bar Food Menu for 98/99 show the day to day range of foods popular with visitors to the Red Lion.

At weekends we always have a range of 'specials' available, primarily for the evening dining trade; again sample menus are appended here.

An approximate guide to the balance of food and drink is a 50:50 split. As we commented earlier, a country inn can no longer survive on just the sale of beers. Food plays an increasingly important part of our trade, particularly for the visitor segment.

Tourism is playing an increasingly important part of our business. Without tourism Llanfair Waterdine's pub would certainly not be viable and would close its doors for good.

The balance of population in Llanfair does not make for a balanced trade. The lack of young and middle-aged family groups does not bode well for the future of the village. From a personal viewpoint, the village could do with at least another 15-20 houses, making a core of variable socio/age groups.

In the bar at the Red Lion, late 1950s

Tourism to the area needs to increase by at least 50% to guarantee long-term viability for the Inn.

The current owners of the Red Lion Inn are Chris & Judy Stevenson, who moved to Llanfair in April 1996 from High Lane, a district of Stockport in Cheshire. Chris originated from London and Judy from Manchester.

The main attraction of South Shropshire for them as a place to live and work included beautiful countryside, quiet country lane with little traffic and genuine, honest and friendly neighbours.

The Red Lion Inn & Restaurant

Menu

Starters

Soup of the day £2.10
Vegetable Spring Rolls with hot chilli dip £3.50
Potato Skins, salad & blue cheese dip £2.50
Crispy Prawn Balls, salad & hot chilli dip £2.95
Deep-fried Mushrooms, salad & blue cheese dip £2.95
Pate & toast £2.60

Fish

Salmon Fish Cakes with salad & saute potatoes £4.95
King Prawns in Bed £7.45
Wholetail Scampi, chips & peas £5.95
Plaice Goujons, chips & peas £5.80
Fillet of Cod, chips & peas £4.95

Grills & Fries

Sirloin Steak with vegetables & potatoes of the day £8.95
Gammon steak & pineapple £6.85
Sausage, chips & beans £3.95

Pastas & Bakes

Cheese, tomato & basil Quiche with salad & saute potatoes £4.95
Pasta of the Day £5.50
Lasagne with side salad £5.60
Vegetable lasagne with side salad £5.60

Curries & Chillies

Pini Pini Chicken & Rice £6.75
Chicken Curry & Rice £5.95
Vegetable Curry & Rice £5.95

Sandwiches & Side Orders

Ploughman's Platter £5.10
Sandwich with side salad £2.30
Portion of Chips £0.95
Salad Bowl £1.60
Bread & Butter £0.30

Tonight's Specials

Chicken Sililiana

prime chicken breast fillet, finished in an onion, tomato, coriander and Marsala sauce. £8.20

Steak Chasseur

prime sirloin steak, grilled to your liking, then topped with a mushroom and onion sauce. £9.95

Fusilli Disperate

spiral pasta in a spicy tomato, peppers and chilli sauce. £5.50

Red Wines

Bluestone Ridge (12% abv) / **Australia**

The Shinaz grape dominates this lively dry red from down-under. Easy drinking with red meats on pasta dishes. £7.95

Errazuriz (13% abv) / **Chile**

Cabernet Sauvignon grape grown and vinified by one of Chile's best wineries. If you like a real gutsy red wine, this is the one for you. Bright red colour and intense berry fruit flavours.

Absolutely Fabulous, as Patsy would say! £10.80

Montepulciano D'Abruzzo (12% abv) / **Italy**

Gathered from the sun-kissed hills of the Abruzzo region of Italy, the Montepulciano grape gives a wine of deep purple colour with a wonderful, well-rounded baked fruit flavour.

Heaven in a bottle! £9.80

Vina Arisabel (12.5% abv) / **Spain**

A well-balanced Rioja wine, which hints of vanilla and dried fruit aroma. Smooth on the palate, yet full of flavour. £10.95

Bardolino (11.5%) / **Italy**

Light ruby in colour, you could say this was a little gem of a wine (sorry!). Dry, well-balanced, perfect for those who like a light red wine with their meal. £8.90

White Wines

Niersteiner Gutes Domtal (10% abv) / **Germany**

Light and fruity, easy-drinking medium white wine from the Rhine district of Germany. £6.95

Pinot Grigio (12% abv) / **Italy**

Dry, crisp and fruily, with a subtle spicy aroma. This is one of Italy's lesser-known white wines, but well worth finding out about.

Excellent with fish. £9.95

Trebbiano D'Abruzzo (11% abv) / **Italy**

Coming from the same area as the Montepulciano red, the Trebbiano grape bathes in the Italian sunshine, then vinifies into a refreshing dry wine of excellent character.

Perfect with pasta and white meat dishes. £8.95

Erruzuriz (12.5% abv) / **Chile**

Packed full of goosegogs, this is a stunning Sauvignon Blanc wine from our favourite New World producer. Well worth a try. £10.40

Villa Maria (13% abv) / **New Zealand**

This private bin wine from one of the world's finest Chardonnay areas, full of tropical fruit flavours, yet with tasly oak complexities.

An excellent top of the range wine. £12.95

Draught Beers/Ciders	abv %	£ per pint
Dorothy Goodbody's Seasonal Ales	from 4.0	1.70
Tetley's	3.8	1.65
Pedigree	4.5	1.76
Lionbeart	3.8	1.65
Carlsberg	3.8	1.75
Strongbow	4.5	1.80
Ansells Mild	3.2	1.50
Guinness	4.1	2.00

Bottle Beers & Ciders		
Holsten Pils	5.3	1.70
Budweiser	5.0	1.70
Matins Brown Ale	2.8	1.20
Old Rosie Cider	7.3	1.70
Cider/Ginger Punch	4.9	1.60

Spirits *(all 25 ml measure)*		
Bell's Whisky	40	1.15
Famous Grouse Whisky	40	1.15
Gordon's Gin	37.5	1.15
Bombay Sapphire	40	1.25
Courvoisier Brandy	40	1.30
Smimoff/Virgin Vodka	37.5	1.15
Absolut Vodka	40	1.25
Bacardi White Rum	37.5	1.20
Lamb's Navy Rum	40	1.20

Ports/Sherries/Vermouth *(all 50 ml measure)*		
Tio Pepe Dry Sherry	15.5	1.10
Harveys Club Medium Sherry	17.5	1.10
Harveys Bristol Cream Sherry	17.5	1.10
Cockburn's Port	20.0	1.10
Cockburn's Special Reserve	20.0	1.30
Noilly Prat Vermouth	18.0	1.15
Martini Dry	15.0	1.15
Martini Sweet	14.7	1.15
Citizano	14.7	1.15
Pimni's	25.0	1.80

Soft Drinks		
Baby Mixers	113 ml	0.75
Large Mixers	180 ml	0.80
Orange Juice	125 ml	0.90
Juice Mixers	113 ml	0.85

PLEASE REFER TO WINE LIST FOR PRICES OF WINES, LIQUEURS AND SPECIALITY DRINKS.

Brandies, Malts & Liqueurs (25 ml serving)

Why not finish off that special meal with one of our after - dinner delights?

Malts		
Glenfiddich	40% abv	£1.60
Glenmorangie	40% abv	£1.60
Macallan	40% abv	£1.90
Dalwhinnie	40% abv	£2.00
Bushmills	40% abv	£1.60
Brandies		
Courvoisier 3 star	40% abv	£1.30
Courvoisier VSOP	40% abv	£2.60
Liqueurs		
Cointreau	40% abv	£1.70
Grand Marnier	40% abv	£1.70
Glayva	40% abv	£1.90
Amaretto	28% abv	£1.30
Drambuie	40% abv	£1.70
Galliano	35% abv	£1.40
Benedictine	40% abv	£1.70
Chartreuse	55% abv	£2.95
Cream Liqueurs (50 ml serving)		
Baileys Original	17% abv	£1.95

Chris & Judy Stephenson.
The Red Lion.

A typical farm, 1900 – 2000

Bryn Bedw – A Hundred Years

Bryn Bedw was a typical farm for this area. At the turn of the century it had what was then considered an up-to-date five bedroomed stone house with a cellar. Several houses of similar size and style were built around 1850. Many of them probably replaced older houses on the same sites.

Cwmbrain, The Green and Melin-y-grogue were all of similar design and layout. All were about 150–170 acres and all had stone and slated farm buildings around a courtyard type farmyard. Bryn Bedw lost most of its buildings in a fire and the replacements were probably considered very modern when they were built in the early 1940s. The layout was certainly well designed and labour- saving. As machinery took over from horses and bales from loose hay however they became more difficult to use. The position of feed stores, hay lofts, calf pens and cow ties in relation to each other can still be appreciated.

Over a hundred years ago in 1891 John Hudson, aged 37, ran Bryn Bedw with his mother Elizabeth, a widow aged 60. John's brother Thomas lived at Cow Hall with his wife Margaret. Both families had moved from the Upper Wain between 1871 and 1881. John employed four workers to help him run Bryn Bedw.

By 1915 when John was 61 years old, he decided to sell most of his animals but continue to live in the house. The animals he sold and the prices they made were as follows:

John Hudson

	Kerry Hill Sheep	£	s	d
1	5, 3yr old Ewes @57/-	13	-	-
2	5 Do @50/-	12	10	-
3	6 Do @48/-	14	8	-
4	6 Do @49/-	14	14	-
5	6 Do @45/-	13	10	-
6	5, 2yr. old Do @55/-	13	15	-
7	5 Do @54/-	13	10	-
8	5 Do @52/-	13	-	-
9	5 Do @46/6	11	12	6
	Carried Fwd. £	119	19	6
	Brought Fwd	119	19	6
10	5, 2yr. old Ewes @51/-	12	15	-
11	5 Do @46/6	11	12	6
12	6 Do @46/6	13	19	-
13	5 Do @52/-	13	-	-
14	5 Do @53/6	13	7	6
15	5 Do @54/6	13	12	6
16	5 Do @50/-	12	10	-
17	5 yearling Ewes @47/6	11	17	6
18	5 Do @49/6	12	7	6
	Carried Fwd. £	235	1	-

		£	s	d
	Brought Fwd.	235	1	-
20	5 Ewe Lambs @38/6	9	12	6
21	5 Do @39/-	9	15	-
22	5 Do @35/6	8	17	6
23	5 Do @33/-	8	5	-
24	5 Do @37/-	9	5	-
25	5 Do @30/-	7	10	-
26	5 Do @30/-	7	10	-
27	6 Do @25/6	7	13	-
28	5 Wether Lambs @34/6	8	12	6
	Carried Fwd. £	312	1	6
	Brought Fwd	312	1	6
29	5 Wether Lambs @34/6	8	12	6
30	5 Do @27/-	6	15	-
31	5 Do @26/6	6	12	6
32	5 Do @24/-	6	-	-
33	5 Do @26/6	6	12	6
34	5 Do @21/6	6	9	-
35	5 Yearling Wethers @55/-	13	15	-
36	5 Do @52/-	13	-	-
37	5 Do @50/-	12	10	-
	Carried Fwd £	392	8	-

No.	Item	£	s	d
	Brought Frd.	392	8	-
38	5 yearling Wethers @ 51/-	12	15	-
39	5 Do @ 48/-	12	-	-
40	5 Do @ 44/6	11	12	6
41	6 Do @ 47/6	14	5	-
42	6 Do @ 44/6	13	7	-
	Ram Lamb	2	11	-
45	Yrlg. Ram	3	17	6
46	Do	3	5	-
	Carried Frd £	466	1	-

Cattle Etc

No.	Item	£	s	d
	Brought Frd	466	1	-
1	Barren Cow	10	5	-
2	Heifer Calf	5	5	-
3	Barren Cow	12	15	-
4	Heifer Calf	5	15	-
5	Barren Cow	14	15	-
7	Barren Cow	13	-	-
8	Bull Calf	8	-	-
9	Barren Cow	12	17	6
10	Heifer Calf	8	-	-
	Carried Frd £	556	13	6

No.	Item	£	s	d
	Brought Frd	556	13	6
11	Barren Cow	12	5	-
12	Bull Calf	8	-	-
13	Heifer	13	7	6
14	Heifer Calf	8	10	-
15	Barren Cow	15	17	6
16	Bull Calf	9	5	-
17	Barren Cow	13	15	-
18	Heifer Calf	7	12	6
19	Barren heifer	13	-	-
	Carried Frd. £	658	6	-

No.	Item	£	s	d
	Brought Frd	658	6	-
20	Heifer Calf	5	5	-
21	Barren heifer	12	2	6
22	Heifer Calf	4	10	-
23	Barren heifer	12	5	-
24	Heifer Calf	4	15	-
25	Barren heifer	13	5	-
26	Heifer Calf	3	12	6
27	Barren heifer	10	15	-
28	Bull Calf	5	10	-
	Carried Frd £	730	6	-

No.	Item	£	s	d
	Brought Frd.	730	6	-
29	Barren Hfr	11	10	-
30	Calf	2	12	6
31	Barren hfr.	13	7	6
32	Heifer Calf	5	7	6
33	Barren Hfr	13	7	6
34	Bull Calf	5	5	-
35	Barren hfr.	11	5	-
36	Bull Calf	5	10	-
37	Barren Hfr	13	15	-
	Carried Frd £	812	6	-

No.	Item	£	s	d
	Brought Frd.	812	6	-
38	Bull Calf	6	10	-
39	Barren heifer	11	12	6
40	Heifer Calf	6	-	-
41	Barren hfr.	12	2	6
42	Heifer Calf	6	5	-
42A	Heifer in Calf	15	17	6
42B	Barren hfr	17	-	-
43	2 yr. old hfr in calf	13	-	-
44	Do	12	-	-
	Carried Frd £	912	13	6

No.	Item	£	s	d
	Brought Frd	912	13	6
45	In calf Heifer	12	5	-
46+47	2 Barren hfrs. @ 11/12/6	23	5	-
49	Barren heifer	13	7	6
50	Do	10	15	-
51+52	Pair yrlg Heifers	21	5	-
53+54	Pair Do	20	-	-
55+56	Do	19	-	-
57+58	Do	19	-	-
59	Yrlg heifer	8	5	-
	Carried Frd £	1059	16	-

No.	Item	£	s	d
	Brought Frd.	1059	16	-
60+61	Pr. yrlg Bullocks	24	-	-
62+63	Pr Do	19	-	-
64+65 +66	3 Do @ 8/12/6	25	17	6
	Carried Frd £	1128	13	6

Horses.

No.	Item	£	s	d
	Brought Frd.	1128	13	6
1	Brown Mare	33	-	-
2	Filly Foal	18	-	-
3	Bay Geldg.	60	-	-
4	Bay Geldg.	72	-	-
5	Brown Geldg	50	-	-
7	Brown Colt	30	-	-
8	Bay Yearling Filly	24	-	-
11	Cream Filly	20	-	-
	Carried Frd. £	1435	13	6

No.	Item	£	s	d
	Brought Frd	1435	13	6
9	Cream ~~Geldg~~ Mare	19	-	-
10	Cream Geldg	28	-	-
	Total of Sale £	1482	13	6

In 1916 the decision was made to sell the remaining animals and all the small tools, machinery and furniture, the prices made were as follows:

Implements	£	s	d
Old iron		4	.
Thatching pegs			9
Sheads			9
Shead & Dung hook			9
Scythe			6
2 racks			6
2 racks			6
2 bill hooks & hay knife			6
Carry forward		8	3

	£	s	d
Brot forward		8	3
Grind stone		16	.
Belting		10	.
2 casks		1	6
Hogshead cask	1	.	.
Hogshead cask		13	.
Cooler & brewing tub		5	.
Small cooler		14	.
2 tubs		1	6
Tub		9	.
Carry forward	4	18	3

	£	s	d
Brot forward	4	18	3
2 ropes		5	.
2 ropes		4	.
10 sacks	1	.	.
10 do	1	8	.
10 do		15	.
10 do		12	.
Scales & weights		4	.
Heel rake		16	.
2 heel rakes			3
Carry forward	10	2	6

	£	s	d
Brot forward	10	2	6
ladder		8	.
ladder		1	6
ladder		8	.
ladder		1	.
ladder		4	.
2 Chains		4	6
Chain		6	.
Shearing Bench		6	.
Shearing Bench		2	.
Carry forward	12	3	6

	£	s	d
Brot forward	12	3	6
Shearing Bench		8	.
Shearing Bench		3	.
Pig bench		15	.
Pig bench		8	.
Bench		9	.
Bench		1	6
Bench		3	.
Bench		6	.
2 Benches		1	.
Carry forward	14	12	6

	£	s	d
Brot forward	14	12	6
Chaff Cutter	4	15	.
Turnip pulper	1	5	.
2 troughs		1	.
Sheep rack	4	15	.
Sheep rack	2	15	.
Sheep rack	2	10	.
Sheep rack	3	.	.
Sheep rack	1	.	
Landtrees		6	.
Carry forward	34	19	6

	£	s	d
Brot forward	34	19	6
Landtrees		5	.
Single plough	2	2	6
Plough		15	.
Plough		17	6
Scuffle		7	.
Chain harrows		13	.
Iron harrows	4	.	.
Harrows	1	12	6
Scuffle	4	10	.
Carry forward	50	2	.

	£	s	d
Brot forward	50	2	.
Drill		7	6
John Bull, Corn Drill	28	10	.
Roll	3	5	.
Reaper	2	.	.
Horse Rake	4	.	.
Lime Cart	1	12	6
Wheel Cart	10	.	.
do do	6	10	.
Cart	7	.	.
Carry forward	113	7	.

	£	s	d
Brought forward	113	7	.
Cart	5	10	.
Cart	13	.	.
Narrow wheel waggon	36	.	.
Waggon	13	.	.
Narrow wheel waggon	3	10	.
Iron bar		3	6
Grease jack		15	.
Rake & pikel		3	6
do		4	.
do		1	.
Carried forward	185	14	.

	£	s	d
Brought forward	185	14	.
Fork & rake		2	.
Spade & pick		1	.
pick & shovel			6
Rake, 2 forks, & shovel		2	6
Pick, 2 shovels & fork		3	6
Odd tools			6
Chain		8	6
Chains		10	.
3 Chains		7	.
Carried forward	187	9	6

	£	s	d
Brought forward	187	9	6
Back Bands		15	.
Chains		1	6
do		3	.
do		3	6
Breeching		10	.
Set of gears	1	17	6
Leading harness	2	2	6
do	3	5	.
do	5	.	.
Carried forward	201	7	6

	£	s	d
Brought forward	201	7	6
Lidding harness	5	.	.
14 hurdles		4	.
11 do		7	.
12 do		7	.
12 do		8	.
33 do	1	5	.
	£208	18	6

	Sheep	£	s	d
	2 Ewes @ 80/-	8	.	
	2 Theave lambs @ 66/-	6	12	
		£14	12	.

	Cattle	£	s	d
	Heifer in calf	22	5	
	Heifer in calf	24	17	6
In	Cow in calf	27	5	.
	Barren cow	28	.	
	Calf	8	12	6

	Horses	£	s	d
	Brown Gelding	82	.	
	Brown Gelding	89		
In	Dun Gelding	33		
	Dun Mare	28		
		£232	.	

	Keep	£	s	d
	Lot 1	40	.	
	Lot 2	25	10	.
In	Lot 3 Rick	18	.	
In	Rick of wheat	19	.	
		102	10	

	Sundries	£	s	d
	2 hen coops			6
	1 do do			9
	Goose house		1	6
	Fowl house		5	0
			7	9

	Furniture etc	£	s	d
	Mirror		1	1
	2 Windsor Chairs		7	.
	Mirror		1	6
	Clock		3	6
	Skip		3	6
	Skip		3	6
	Skip		3	6
	Skip		4	6
	Tin pail		2	6
	Carried forward	2	10	6

		£	s	d
	Brought forward	2	10	6
	Wicker Chair		3	
	Washstand		8	.
	Pig net		2	.
	Curtain pole		1	.
	8 cow ties		7	6
	11 do do		9	
	Cider cask		1	1
	do do		1	.
	Stove		2	.
	Carried forward	6	4	.

		£	s	d
	Brought forward	6	4	.
	Measure		7	6
	Cheese press		2	
	Table		19	.
	6 Cow Ties		4	.
	7 do do		8	.
	Chest of drawers	2	10	.
	Wardrobe	2	2	6
	Couch	1	7	.
	Corn bin	1	.	.
	Carried forward	15	4	.

		£	s	d
	Brought forward	15	4	.
	Hopper		2	6
	Table		4	.
	Washstand		5	6
	Saddle	2	15	
	Feather bed		18	9
	do	3	6	.
	do	3	15	10
	Snaffle bridle			9
In	Fender		1	6
	Carried forward	26	13	10

		£	s	d
	Brought forward	26	13	10
	2 steens		2	6
	1 steen		1	6
	2 dishes		1	9
	Tub & bottles		3	.
	Clock		10	.
		£27	12	7

Summary	£	s	d
Implements	208	18	6
Sheep	14	12	
Cattle	111	.	.
Horses	232		
Keep	102	10	
Sundries		7	9
Furniture etc	27	12	7
	£697	.	10

JACKSON & McCARTNEY
AUCTIONEERS, VALUERS & LAND AGENTS
CRAVEN ARMS & LUDLOW

In 1917 the farm was let to local farmers for grazing. Some of the tenants names can be recognised still:

Lot	Field	£	s	d	Tenant
Lot 1.	The Orchard Field 6-3-0 @ 33/- to March 1st 1917.	11	2	9	R. Price, Mardu Clun.
Lot 2.	The Corner Field 8-0-0 @ 30/- to March 1st 1917.	12	.	.	Thos. Meredith Llanbister Road
Lot 3.	The Dingle Field 6-3-0 @ 58/- to November 30th 1916.	25	7	6	Wm Price [illegible] Beguildy.
	Carried Forward £	48	10	3	

Lot	Field	£	s	d	Tenant
	Brought Forward £	48	10	3	
Lot 4.	The Moor Hill Field. 8. 3 0 @ 28/- To November 30th 1916.	12	5	.	J.J. Thomas [illegible] Llanfair Waterdine
Lot 5.	The Moors. 10 1 0 @ 32/- To March 1st 1917.	16	8		George Farley [illegible] Knighton
Lot 6.	The Main Road Field. The Top Knoll. 12 2 0 @ 33/- To March	20	12	6	Thos. Meredith. [illegible] Llanbister Road. Radn
	Carried Forward £	97	15	9	

Lot	Field	£	s	d	Tenant
	Brought Forward £	97	15	9	
Lot 7.	The Lower Black Meadow. 3. 3. 0 @ 52/- To March 1st 1917.	9	15		Thos. Hudson Cow Hall
Lot 8.	The Upper Black Meadow. 3. 1 0 @ 56/- To November 30th 1916.	9	2		G. Farley [illegible] Knighton
9	Second Wood Field 6 1 0 @ 48/- To November 30th 1916.	15	.	.	Walter Clee [illegible] Llanfair Waterdine
	Carried Forward £	131	12	9	

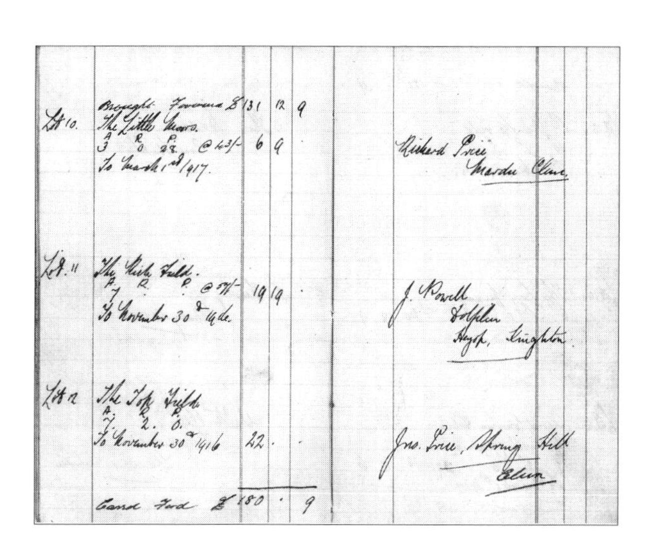

Lot	Field	£	s	d	Tenant
	Brought Forward £	131	12	9	
Lot 10.	The Little Moors. 3 0 28. @ 43/- To March 1st 1917.	6	9		Richard Price Mardu Clun
Lot 11	The [illegible] Field. @ 57/- To November 30th 1916.	19	19	.	J. Powell [illegible] Heyop, Knighton
Lot 12	The Top Field. 7 2 0 To November 30th 1916	22	.	.	Jno. Price, Spring Hill Clun
	Carried Forward £	180	.	9	

Lot	Field	£	s	d	Tenant
	Brought Forward £	180	.	9	
Lot 13	The Wide Top Field 10 1 0 @ November 30th 1916.	23	.	.	Edward Thomas [illegible] Knighton
Lot 14	The Long Meadow. 6 1 0 @ 67/-	20	18	9	Wm Clee [illegible] Beguildy Knighton
Lot 15.	Second Common Field. The [illegible]. 8 0 0 39/- To March 1st 1917.	16	11	6	Jas Edwards [illegible] Beguildy
	Carried Forward £	240	11		

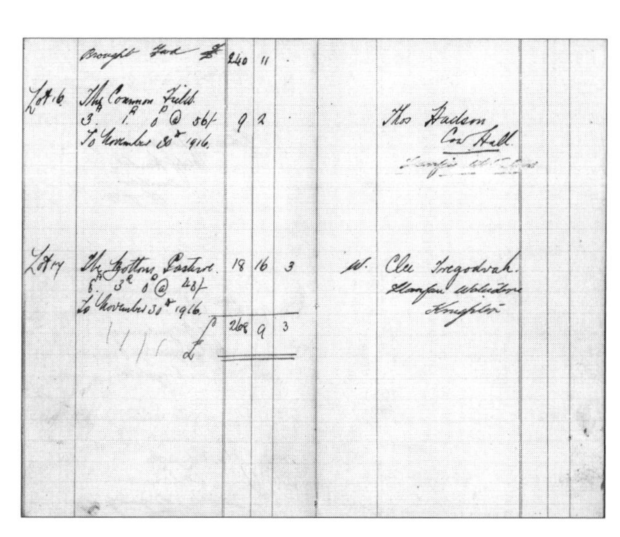

Lot	Field	£	s	d	Tenant
	Brought Forward £	240	11	.	
Lot 16.	The Common Field. 3. 1 0 @ 56/- To November 30th 1916.	9	2		Thos Hudson Cow Hall. Llanfair Waterdine
Lot 17	The Bottom Pasture. 6 3 0 @ 48/- To November 30th 1916.	18	16	3	W. Clee [illegible] Llanfair Waterdine Knighton
	£	268	9	3	

The farm passed into the possession of Mr. A. E. Parker who lived in Newcastle village and he let it for many years. Jack Stephens who had come from Felindre took over the tenancy during the war and bought the farm in 1956 for £3,200. This included Brook Cottage (now Lower Bryn Bedw) and its three acres of land.

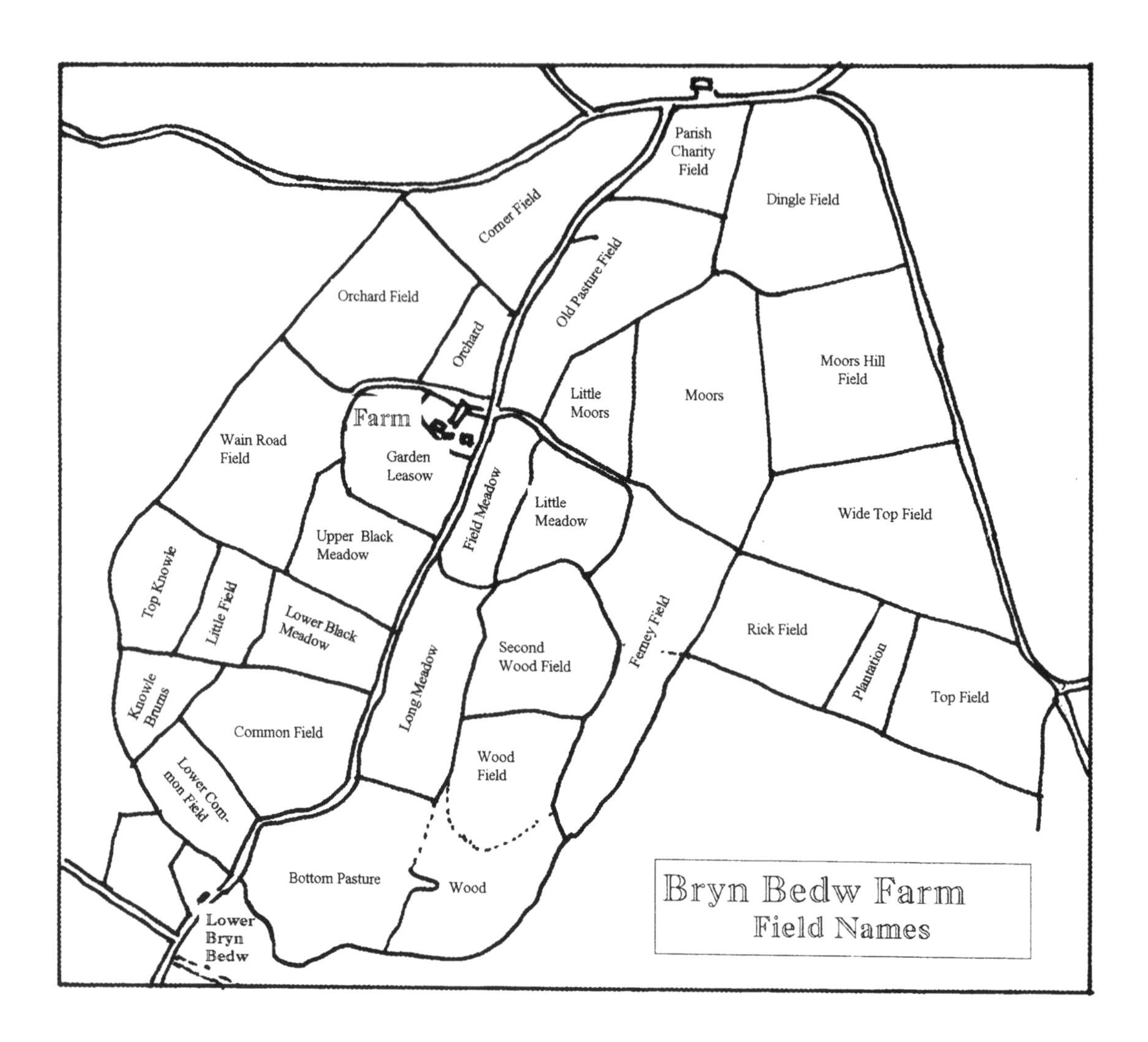

Jack and Edith Stephens farmed until October 1981 when they retired. They always kept Hereford cattle and Kerry sheep. They held a farm sale just as John Hudson had in 1915. The prices cattle, sheep and machinery made at this time can be compared with prices from 1915. The farm was then let for grazing for several years up until 1998 when on the death of Edith it was sold at auction. Unusually the property was purchased by one buyer. Most farms of this size in this area are now broken up and their land shared between larger farms. This has happened to many medium sized farms in the past twenty years. In 1999 excluding Lower Bryn Bedw, but including two of the three acres of cottage land, the farm made £523,000 at auction.

INVENTORY
Mr. J. Stephens, Bryn Bedw, Dutlas, Knighton, Powys.

IMPLEMENTS:

Lot No	Description	VAT	£
1	Drenching Fluid	.30	2.00
2	Formalin	.38	2.50
3	Automatic Drencher	1.65	11.00
4	Battery Charger	1.50	10.00
51	Foot Rot Bath	1.50	10.00
52	2 Galvanised Sheep Troughs	4.50	30.00
53	Ditto	4.65	31.00
54	Ditto		
55	2 Wooden Sheep Troughs	.75	5.00
56	Ditto	1.35	9.00
57	Ditto	1.05	7.00
58	Ditto	1.35	9.00
58A	Ditto	1.35	9.00
58B	Ditto	1.20	8.00
59	Sheep Cratch	8.70	58.00
60	Ditto	8.70	58.00
61	Ditto	5.10	34.00
62	Ditto	6.60	44.00
63	Ditto	5.85	39.00
64	Ditto	5.25	35.00
65	Ditto	5.85	39.00
66	Ditto	5.10	34.00
67	Ditto	3.60	24.00
68	Small Cruch for dehorning Calves	6.90	46.00
69	Kibbler	.90	6.00
70	Fisher Humphries Ridger – 3 row	6.90	46.00
71	Perry Bale Sledge	11.10	74.00
72	Massey Ferguson Muck Spreader	8.10	54.00
73	Massey Ferguson 9 tyre Scaffle	9.15	61.00
74	Star 2-furrow plough	4.80	32.00
75	Yard Scraper	15.30	102.00
76	Pierce Discs	12.00	80.00
77	Spike Harrows	9.60	64.00
78	Hedge Trimmer	15.00	100.00
79	Flat Roll	.15	1.00
80	McConnell Bale Slave	16.80	112.00
81	Exmoor Elevator	38.25	255.00
82	David Thomas Bale Carrier	19.80	132.00
83	Acrobat	5.40	36.00
84	Kuhn 2 row tedder	14.40	96.00
85	Harvest Trailer	7.95	53.00
86	Ford 3000 Tractor with fore end loader Pick-up hitch, KNT 458P	390.00	2,600.00
87	Zetor 3545 4 wheel drive tractor	87.00	580.00
	Total:	£755.78	£5,038.50

SHEEP:

Lot No	Description	£
EWES		
1	10 Ewes, 3 y.o.	390.00
2	10 Ewes, 3 y.o.	390.00
3	12 Ewes, 3 y.o.	408.00
4	11 Ewes, 3 y.o.	385.00
5	10 Ewes, 2 y.o	445.00
6	10 Ewes, 2 y.o.	445.00
7	14 Ewes, 2 y.o.	525.00
YEARLINGS		
8	10 Yearling Ewes	465.00
9	10 Yearling Ewes	470.00
10	10 Yearling Ewes	455.00
11	10 Yearling Ewes	370.00
12	8 Yearling and 2 2 y.o. Ewes	470.00
13	7 Stock Ewes	140.00
EWE LAMBS		
14	10 Ewe Lambs	370.00
15	10 Ewe Lambs	370.00
16	9 Ewe Lambs	274.50
17	10 Ewe Lambs	280.00
18	10 Ewe Lambs	270.00
19	10 Ewe Lambs	305.00
20	11 Ewe Lambs	275.00
WETHER LAMBS		
21	20 Wether Lambs	670.00
22	22 Wether Lambs	693.00
23	21 Wether Lambs	567.00
RAMS		
	1 Ram	25.20
	1 Yearling Ram	65.10
	1 Ram 2 y.o.	33.60
	1 Yearling Ram	44.10
LAMBS		
	6 Lambs	102.00
	1 Ram Lamb	81.90
	1 Ram Lamb	44.10
	1 Ewe Lamb	7.00
	1 Ewe	8.50
		£9,844.00

CATTLE:

Lot No	Description	£
1–2	Hereford Blue Cow (3rd Calver) with her Hereford Blue Heifer Calf (612)	565.00
3–4	Hereford Cow (2nd Calver) (466) with her Hereford Heifer Calf (630)	470.00
5–6	Hereford Cow (2nd Calver) (501) with her Hereford Heifer Calf (614)	555.00
7	Hereford Cow (2nd Calver) (484)	370.00
8	Hereford Bull Calf (629)	212.00
9–10	Hereford Cow (3rd Calver) (494) with Hereford Bull Calf (615)	435.00
11	Hereford Cow (3rd Calver) (406)	332.00
12	Hereford Bull Calf (616)	186.00
13	Hereford Cow (4th Calver) (374)	312.00
14	Hereford Bull Calf (617)	220.00
15-16	Hereford Cow (1st Calver) (523) with her Hereford Bull Calf (618)	458.00
17-19	Hereford Cow (4th Calver) (405) with 2 Hereford Bull Calves (619) and (620)	520.00
20	Hereford Cow (308)	338.00
21	Hereford Bull Calf (613)	226.00
22	Hereford Cow (3rd Calver) (290)	352.00
23	Hereford Heifer Calf (621)	182.00
24	Hereford Grey Cow (449)	365.00
25	Hereford Cross Friesian Heifer Calf (F0712 664)	186.00
26	Hereford Cow (1st Calver) (527)	370.00
27	Hereford Bull Calf (629)	180.00
28–29	Hereford Cow (1st Calver) (572) with Hereford Bull Calf (627)	470.00
30	Hereford Cow (4th Calver) (331)	340.00
31	Hereford Heifer Calf (624)	148.00
32	Hereford Cow (3rd Calver) (469)	398.00
33	Hereford Cross Friesian Heifer Calf (M6147 940)	182.00
34	Hereford Cow (1st Calver) (571)	330.00
35	Hereford Bull Calf (622)	165.00
36	Hereford Cow (1st Calver) (573)	398.00
37	Hereford Bull Calf (631)	196.00
38	Hereford Cow (1st Calver) (517)	380.00
39	Hereford Bull Calf (628)	196.00
40	Hereford Grey Cow (1st Calver) (509)	390.00
41	Hereford Grey Bull Calf (633)	210.00
42	Hereford Cow (3rd Calver) (458)	370.00
43	Hereford Bull Calf (636)	202.00
44	Hereford Cow (3rd Calver) (410)	355.00
45	Hereford Bull Calf (637)	220.00
46	Hereford Cow (3rd Calver) (404)	342.00
47	Hereford Bull Calf (639)	215.00
48	Hereford Grey Cow (1st Calver) (570)	402.00
49	Hereford Grey Heifer Calf (623)	138.00
50	Hereford Cow (1st Calver) (521)	285.00
51	Hereford Heifer Calf (634)	135.00
52	Hereford Cow (2nd Calver)	388.00
53	Hereford Heifer Calf (635)	124.00
54	Hereford Heifer (1st Calver) (626)	345.00
55	NO LOT (out)	
56	Hereford Cow (1st Calver) (511)	370.00
57	Hereford Heifer Calf (632)	142.00
58	Hereford In Calf Heifer (604)	345.00
59	Hereford In Calf Heifer (605)	345.00
60	Hereford In Calf Heifer (610)	345.00
61	Hereford Blue In Calf Heifer (608)	475.00
62	Hereford In Calf Heifer (602)	335.00
63–64	2 Hereford Heifers (63–589, 64–590)	536.00
65–66	2 Hereford Heifers (65–598, 66–603)	544.00
67-68	2 Hereford Heifers (67–596, 68–606)	536.00
69-70	2 Hereford Heifers (69–591, 70–587)	520.00
71-72	2 Hereford Heifers (71–588, 72–592)	480.00
73-74	2 Hereford Heifers (73–595, 74–592)	474.00
75, 76, 77	3 Hereford Heifers (75–597, 76–594, 77–586)	570.00
78	Hereford Bull – 5 y.o. (H4917–1100)	500.00
	Total:	£20,675.00

PRODUCE:

Lot No	Description	£
A	Approximately 550 bales of Hay	410.00
B	Approximately 500 bales of Hay	485.00
C	Approximately 350 bales of Hay	300.00
D	Approximately 430 bales of Hay	362.00
E	Approximately 430 bales of Hay	370.00
		£1,927.00

GRASS KEEP:

Lot No	Description	£
1	26 Acres of Winter Keep	468.00
2	32 Acres of Winter Keep	416.00
3	75 Acres of Winter Keep	1,200.00
4	18 Acres of Winter Keep	306.00
		£2,390.00

Bryn Bedw, Dutlas, Knighton, Powys.

SUMMARY

IMPLEMENTS	£ 5,038.50
V.A.T.	*£755.78*
SHEEP	£ 9,844.00
CATTLE	£20,675.00
PRODUCE	£ 1,927.00
GRASS KEEP	£ 2,390.00
	£39,874.50
V.A.T.	£ 755.78
	£40,630.28

Farm Sale, 1982.

Cattle enter the Sale Ring

Hereford Cattle

Buyers discuss animals

Part Four

Parish Committees
Concerns
Clubs and Societies
Activities Past and Present

The Parish Council

The local Government Act of 1894 led to the setting up of many Parish Councils including Llanfair Waterdine. The first meeting of the council took place on December 7th 1894. The vicar at the time, Rev. C. H. Bowman, became the first Chairman. John Harper in his 'Short History of Llanfair Waterdine' provides a copy of notes from the first minutes.

It will be noted that Edward Gwilt, grandfather of Hazel, John and Trevor, now at Cwm Collo, was on the first council. He then lived at The Bwlch. Also on the council was William Evans, grandfather of Joan Hobby who then lived in the village and Mr. Hatfield the village Headmaster. Richard Jordan was the carpenter who pointed out what an excellent carpenter he was by leaving a piece of wood with a message to this effect at Cwm Cole in 1887. He lived in a cottage at Melin-y-grogue at that time.

4

11.

At the first meeting of the Parish Council, all the members being present and accepting office, it was proposed by Mr. Edwards and seconded by Mr. Jordan and carried unanimously that Rev. C.H. Bowman be Chairman – Rev. C.H. Bowman was appointed Clerk without Salary and Mr. Hatfield was appointed Treasurer – It was ordered that the necessary books and forms be obtained from Mr. Langford. It was decided not to appoint Committees or Trustees of Charities, but for the whole Council to act together in all matters.

Dated Dec: 7. 1894.

John Edwards C H Bowman Chairman
Edward Gwilt
Richard Griffiths
Richard Jordan
William Evans

At the first meeting of the Parish Council all the members being present and accepting office it was proposed by Mr. Edwards and seconded by Mr. Jordan and carried unanimously that Rev. C. H. Bowman be Chairman – Rev. C. H. Bowman was appointed clerk without salary and Mr. Hatfield was appointed Treasurer. It was ordered that the necessary books and forms be obtained from Mr. Langford. It was decided not to appoint committees or trustees of charities but for the whole Council to act together in all matters.

Dated Dec. 7th 1894.

C. H. Bowman.
Chairman.

John Edwards.
Edward Gwilt.
Richard Griffiths.
Richard Jordan.
William Evans.

To record the tasks undertaken by the Parish Council at that time we can do no better than reproduce the work done by Mr. Harper on this subject.

The first Annual Meeting in April 1895, with Rev. Bowman in the Chair, appointed Edward Gwilt and Edward Pryce as Overseers and decided on 1d rate for the School.

In 1895 there was a request to the Postmaster for a delivery to "the upper end of the Parish", and in November 1900 there is a request to the G.P.O. for a Post Office and Telegraph Office in the village. By February 1901 no replies had been received. In 1910 and 1911 there were repeated requests for a Post Office in the village and for a six day delivery. Throughout 1918 there was continuing dissatisfaction with the postal arrangements culminating in August 1919 with a letter from the Postmaster at Llandrindod Wells refusing a Sub-Post Office in the village. However, during the 1920's the village acquired a Post Office, and in 1932 a request was made to Llandrindod Wells to allow the Postmistress to issue licences. Continual efforts for the installation of a telephone bore fruit in 1933 when several agreements were entered into. In January it was agreed to pay £6.10.0 annually for five years to the Chief Constable of Radnorshire to guarantee the installation of a telephone in the village, and £2.5.0 annually for seven years to the Post Office. There followed an Indenture between the Parish Councils of Beguildy and Llanfairwaterdine, and the Postmaster General to extend the Post Office system of telephones to the Post Offices at Felindre, Beguildy, Dutlas and Knucklas in the County of Radnor; and Llanfairwaterdine in the County of Salop; to open and work telephone call offices there, and to connect the offices with the exchange at Knighton or any alternative required by the Postmaster General. The Indenture required a guarantee of minimum receipts of £20 per year or the guarantors to make up the difference by a maximum of £4.10.0. Any excess to be carried forward to the next year. In 1935 we find an Indemnity from The Ministry of Health for payment to Radnor Police Authority to cover the cost incurred in arranging the extension of the telephone to Beguildy Police Station, but some six months later we find the Ministry refusing permission for the final two payments to the Police Authority. In March 1938 there is a further request for a telephone kiosk in the village.

Throughout its history the Parish Council has had continuous problems with the parish roads. In June 1898 a man was appointed to open the old road between Tregodfa and the Pound. By December this work was completed and the Parish Council issued an order on the rates to pay for repairs to Black Spring and the opening of the road. In 1899 the Chairman was directed to write to the District Council regarding the dangerous state of the footbridge at Panpwnton and the general neglect of the roads. In November 1900 the Parish Council complained to the County Council that the District Council had refused to maintain and repair the highway leading from Panpwnton to Knighton, and a requisition was sent to the District Council requesting the roads in Llanfairwaterdine be put in proper order, and that the railed fence from "The Old Shop" to Melinagrog and also by the Mill Pond required immediate attention. By February 1901 no progress had been made. In May 1904 the District Council was asked to take over the road leading from Hurgin Road to the Block Gate. At about the same time the Parish Council received a letter from Lilleshall Parish Council suggesting there should be two lights on all vehicles. The Parish Council were not in favour of this. In 1909 they requested an arch over the watercourse across the road at Melenygrogue, and passed a resolution urging the building of a bridge over the River Teme at Rhunnis. In 1934 the Parish Council sent a request to Radnor District Council for a signpost at Lloyney pointing to Llanfairwaterdine, and also a signpost at the Old Shop for Clun and Newcastle.

The Parish Council annually appointed six Parish Constables up until 1952, and back in 1899 the Council enquired the cost of a Resident Policeman. This turned out to be £84 per annum (the appointment to be made under 3&4 Vic. c.88 S19). The Council agreed the matter stand over for the time being.

Overseers ceased to be appointed after 1926.

In 1933 it was reported that there was no need this year for a Sparrow Club as no damage by House Sparrows had been notified.

In September 1949 there was a discussion in the Parish Council on the possibility of Electrical Supply to the Parish, and under the National Parks and Access to the Countryside Act. 1949 a survey and Schedule of footpaths was undertaken in November and December 1950.

Llanfair Waterdine Parish Councillors and their wives, 1980

Ann Gwilt, Harold Gwilt, Doug Powell, Freda Powell, Fred Beavan, Wilf Gough, Joan Hobby, Jocelyn Williams, Jim Williams, Vera Gough Mig Beavan, Aubrey Clee, Dolly Clee, Bert Hobby

PARISH COUNCIL CLERKS

1894. Rev. C. H. Bowman.
1899. Frank Beavan.
1908. John Charles Evans.
1949. P. E. Hill.
1950. Aubrey Clee.
1985. Norman R. Tillett.
1988. Brian Reason.
1991. Paul Simmons.
1996. Gordon Singleton.

In 1999 the work of the Parish Council continues to be dominated by the state of the roads. A working relationship has developed between the council and the Highways Department at South Shropshire District Council in Ludlow. Mr. Rutherford, the present District Surveyor, now meets council members and actually visits lengths of road under discussion for repair and improvement. Over the past three to four years about £35,000–£40,000 a year has been spent on the Parish roads.

The bridge at the Rhunnis, first requested in 1909, was finally put in place in the early 1960s. The signpost at the Old Shop, requested in 1934, still stands. The electricity supply did not reach the last homes in the Parish until 1982 and footpaths and rights-of-way are still under heated discussion.

The Sparrow Club which was charged with preventing damage by house sparrows is certainly not needed as we reach the end of the century. House sparrows have become quite rare in many places. There are however small flocks at Stoney Pound and at Monaughty Poeth and occasional pairs in other parts of the Parish.

PARISH COUNCIL CHAIRMEN

1894	Rev. C. H. Bowman
1898	F. L. Green
1900	Rev. C. H. Stoker
1901–1909 (Oct)	T. Matkin
1909 (Oct) –1914	Rev. H. E. Mason
1915	T. S. Jones
1926	F. E. Beavan
1928	Richard Swancott
1929	John E. Jarman
1930	F. E. Beavan
1936	Penry Evans
1937	F. E. Beavan
1942	Penry Evans
1954	B. P. Hobby
1955	Penry Evans
1957	E. G. Jones
1966	A. F. Beavan
1991	B. J. Williams

The present Parish Council

Llewellyn Morgan, Gordon Singleton (Clerk), Fred Beavan, Ruby Thomas, Robert Davies, John Williams, Jim Williams (Chairman), Raymond Matthews, Barry Swancott

Llanfair Waterdine Parochial Church Council

The Parochial Church Council (PCC) is required, as stated in the Parochial Church Councils (Powers) Measure 1956, to co-operate with the minister in promoting in the parish the Whole Mission of the Church, pastoral, evangelistic, social and ecumenical.

The PCC consists of a Chairman (current Vicar/Priest in Charge)– Rev. Eileen Lloyd, two Church Wardens – Andrew MacLauchlan and Ruth Davies, two Elected Members of the Deanery Synod – Mary Chapman and Mary Simmons, Vice Chairman – John Williams, Secretary – Mary Morgan, Treasurer – Mary Townshend and elected members, Fred Beavan, Doreen Hart, Joan Hobby, Eva MacLauchlan, Ann Matthews, Freda Powell, Joan Rhodes, Betty Williams and Glenys Williams.

The PCC meets about five or six times a year to discuss a wide range of issues, with a smaller committee within (Standing Committee) meeting as required to discuss more complicated or lengthy issues and reporting back to the PCC.

Members of the PCC arrange rotas for the Cleaning of the Church, Flower Arranging, Sidesmen, Leaders of Intercessions, Readers, Coffee after certain Services, etc. We are fortunate in that we have one service each Sunday, apart from the fifth Sunday in the month when a joint service is held at one of the four churches in our Benefice, namely, Bucknell, Stowe, Chapel Lawn and ourselves. During the year we also have special services such as Christingle, Mothering Sunday, Songs of Praise, Bereavement,. Harvest, Crib when the children of our parish take a very active part.

With the help of the wider community, the PCC hold various fund-raising events annually. These regularly include Coffee Mornings/Evenings, The Wakes, Sponsored Walks, Quizzes, Harvest Supper, Whist Drives, Christmas Fayre and Auction and Concerts. Other events are arranged when extra funds are required for improvement to the Church Building etc. The upkeep and maintenance of the Church Building and Churchyard is a constant source of concern but through the continuing generosity and hard work of our parishioners over the years, much has been achieved as is very evident today. We hope and like to think that our Church is open, friendly and welcoming to everyone who enters.

Ruth Davies.

The Village Hall Committee

The committee was formed when the hall closed as a school and the first meeting took place on 10th August 1960. The committee held a house to house collection which raised over £800 – a great deal of money in 1960! The hall was finally purchased from the Education Authorities in 1963 for the sum of £200. Much money was needed for alterations and a new roof and some Grant Aid was obtained.

The Village Hall Committee and partners at their Christmas Dinner, 1998

Over the years the Village Hall Committee have been responsible for the general upkeep, renovation and repair of the Hall, and for fund raising, letting and cleaning. Many improvements have been made and committee members gave many hours of their time and actual physical

Llanfair Waterdine Village Choir 1969

Bob Heywood, Dennis Evans, D.I. Davies, Fred Roberts, Reg Bufton, DonFelton, Harold Morgan, Llewellyn Morgan, Fred Parry
Ann Davies, Sheila Morgan, Connie Beaumont, Blanche Beaumont, Dolly Bufton, Jocelyn Williams., Dolly Clee, Daphne Felton, E. Palfrey, Betty Brush
Peggy Matthews, Glenys Williams, Betty Williams, Vera Price, Freda Harroway, Mary Davies, Nancy Cummins, Clare Blackshaw, Mrs Blackshaw, Mrs Harding Price

effort to keep the hall going. The hall is now in quite a good state of repair and is in constant use by people from inside and outside the Parish. It is used for Public and Private functions, by many organisations and for meetings and concerts.

The Annual General Meeting takes place in the first week in December and the Hall is a registered charity. For the past two years a small profit has been made from lettings and this seems to prove that the people of Llanfair who gave so generously to that first collection understood that when the village school closed a meeting place for the community is essential.

The Charities

The Llanfair Waterdine Charities were handed over to Trustees from the Guardianship of the Parish Council, Vicar and Church Wardens in 1977.

The actual charities are:

1. The Charity of Priscilla Davies founded from her will dated 16th October 1871. She left £130 to be invested for the poor of the Parish. She wished the benefit to be felt at Christmas. The Vicar, Church Wardens and two trustees used to meet at the School on December 20th and people from local cottages would be there to collect their Christmas Charity money. In more modern times a tradition has grown up that all parishioners over the age of 70 are given a small sum of money at Christmas.

2. The Charity of John Edwards who lived at Brampton Bryan. He left £100 for the benefit of the poor of Llanfair in his will dated November 11th 1856.

3. The Hordy field comprises a three acre field from an inclosure award dated 16th February 1859. This field was intended for the building of a school. The income from letting the grazing is thus spent on the young people of the Parish.

4. Llanfair Hills Gardens Charity is an inclosure dated 1st July 1891 and was meant to provide gardens for the poor and a peat cutting area.

5. Pryce and others consists of three acres of land near Monaughty Poeth and was left to the Parish in a conveyance dated 11th January 1714. The land is let for grazing each year.

6. The Stony Pound Poor Charities is a small patch of land inclosed in July 1891 as an allotment for field gardens for the poor.

7. The Turbary Charity Land for Fuel was inclosed in July 1891 and is again near Stony Pound. Patches of land amount to well over thirty acres.

A new Charity is in the process of being formed. Joan Adams who lives at The Vedw (also the home of Priscilla Davies) has recently offered a field opposite her home for the use of the Parish. This will join those already administered by the Trustees for the benefit of the people of Llanfair Waterdine.

The Trustees are appointed by the Parish Council. There are five nominated Trustees and one co-optative Trustee who should have knowledge of the Parish through either living or working in it.

The first trustees when the charities were taken over from the Parish Council and the Church and came under the control of the Charity Commission in 1977 were:

Fred Beavan – The Graig. Bert Hobby – Melin-y-grogue. Harold Gwilt – Rose Villa. Wilfred Gough – Panpwnton. Doug Powell – The Cwm.

Fred Beavan is the Chairman of the Trustees, the others being:

Giles Swancott – Tregodfa. Robert Davies – Teme Cottage. John Williams – Panpwnton. Jim Williams – Monaughty. The co-opted member is Gordon Singleton – Lower Bryn Bedw.

The charities are carefully administered and the land is managed with conservation and income taken into account.

In 1999 apart from giving £20 to each Parishioner over the age of 70 the charities have been able to give £500 to the Community Taxi Scheme in Knighton so that parishioners in Llanfair who have no transport can use a subsidised taxi service. The rent of the Village Hall for the Youth Club has been paid for the year and the Trustees have agreed to provide a millennium gift for all the children in the parish. If it proves to be a hard winter a grant will be made to the elderly for heating and financial support has been given to the Youth Club. The Charity Commissioners will not allow the Trustees to give money to individuals if their needs are met by normal state benefits. This can cause some difficulties but there are always worthwhile projects needing funds and the Trustees do their best to act constructively.

Agriculture in Llanfair Waterdine

In the Nineteenth Century the main employment in Llanfair Waterdine parish was agriculture. After the First World War (1914–18) the numbers employed began to drop off drastically and the drop accelerated during and after the Second World War (1939–45).

Figures taken from the 1851 Census suggest that there were about 100 general farm labourers plus 2 shepherds, 1 cowman and 1 wagoner, totalling 104 men employed on 48 farms in the parish. By the end of the century general farm labourers numbered 52 but a more professional type of worker was beginning to emerge. The general farm labourer was the unskilled worker, others began to specialise so that there were 8 cowmen, 8 wagoners, 2 shepherds and 4 bailiffs, making a total of 74 workers servicing 45 farms. This coincided with a drop of 128 inhabitants in the parish.

One hundred years later in 1999, due to amalgamation, there are only 18 farms in the parish and only 9 full time farm workers.

Nowadays much of the work is done by contractors: these tasks include shearing, silaging, hedge trimming and ploughing. A great deal of machinery is used so less manual labour is needed.

However, hedge laying and hedge restoration are now being encouraged due to the fact that we live in an environmentally sensitive area. This helps to create some employment.

In 1841 there were 31 housekeepers and house servants and by the end of the century the number had increased to 36. Now there are none.

Robert Davies, Teme Cottage

Hay making at Skyborry

Ted 'the Bwlch' rows up a field of hay

Ted Owens and horse replace a gate post at Cwm Cote

Pigs at Lloyney Mill

Working in the hay field

Struggling to put bales in an old building

Piling up bales

An acrobat

An abandoned plough

A thistle cutter

A saw bench

Stooks of corn

A chaff cutter

A winnower

Gene Davies (right) with Richard Bevan

Typical footwear

Local transport

During the last century there were also a number of self-employed stone masons, carpenters/wheelwrights, blacksmiths, tailors, dressmakers and shoemakers, as well as millers and the occasional mole catcher and roadman. The parish was self-sufficient and somebody could provide almost any service which was needed. In 1999 there are very few work opportunities within the parish for young people. The average age of our inhabitants is now 46 years and we have very few people living here between the ages of 20 and 40 as they have to seek employment elsewhere.

John Williams.

BSE

Bovine Spongiform Encephalitis (BSE) is a disease unique to cattle, which causes a deterioration of the brain tissue in older cows. The physical symptoms of the disease are loss of co-ordination and the eventual death of the animal due to the complete breakdown of the Central Nervous System.

The disease was first recognised in the early 1980's by a vet in Kent. Some time elapsed before the disease had official recognition, and even then there was little understanding of its origin and method of transmission. The disease was largely confined to the dairy herds of the UK, however there were reported outbreaks in Ireland, France and Germany. Further investigation suggested that the high levels of concentrate protein fed to the dairy cattle may be the cause of spread of the disease. This theory was further substantiated where it emerged that the source of raw protein in a number of manufactured feeds was ground up meat and bone meal, which is a by-product from the slaughter of cattle and sheep. This material can only be used after undergoing a process of heat treatment, however it is interesting to note that in 1979 the Government unilaterally reduced the required temperature treatment to below existing levels in the rest of Europe. We can only guess as to whether this single act precipitated the worst outbreak of disease in cattle this century.

Further studies in the late eighties quickly brought to an end the use of bovine material in animal feeds, however the practice still continued in other European countries. All cattle showing any symptoms of the disease were destroyed and the carcasses incinerated to prevent cross contamination of any diseased material into the human food chain. Public concern was only aroused when it emerged that the diseased brain tissue of the BSE cow showed similarities to brain tissue from victims of the human brain disease Cretzfeld Jacobs Disease (CJD). CJD is a disease that is well documented and more typically affecting the older population, so it was met with grave concern that there appeared to be an increase in the number of younger people contracting the disease. It was the emergence of this new variant CJD (nv. CJD) which provided the catalyst to the ensuing media hysteria which proclaimed British Beef as being unsafe to eat. In the absence of any credible scientific evidence to link BSE to nv. CJD it was left to speculation by the less responsible members of the scientific community as to the extent of the likely epidemic which would result in the beef eating population. Eventually the Government's own scientific advisory body (SEAC) succumbed to the media pressure and public disquiet by advising the Government that despite no scientific evidence to link BSE and nv. CJD that is was 'probable' that there was a link.

This plunged the UK cattle industry into almost total disarray with the initial reaction being a total shut down of all outlets for cows and beef animals. European ministers were quick to condemn all forms of beef and beef products of British origin, by implementing a world wide ban on exports of British beef, which resulted in a collapse in beef consumption in the wake of the myriad of scare stories that filled the media. The Government eventually acted to restore confidence by bolstering the regulations on the abattoirs and banning any cattle over the age of thirty months from entering the human food chain. This measure in itself had enormous

PHF1998341CPS1369.dat:122:1

Cattle Id:

UK F9504 00254

British Cattle
Movement Service

Applicant's address:

LE WILLIAMS & SON
MONAUGHTY POETH
KNIGHTON
POWYS
LD7 1TT

This is a Cattle Passport, which should be kept in a safe place. Please sign the first box in the 1st Movement Summary section.

Please detach this cover. If the address shown is incorrect, please complete the back of this page and return this slip to the BCMS Correspondence Address.

UK F9504 00253
Cattle Passport

Eartag

UK F9504 00253

British Cattle
Movement Service

Electronic Id

For future use

Animal Details

Breed: CHAROLAIS X
Sex: MALE
DoB: 30 10 1998

Genetic Dam Id: J2047 993
Issue / Version: 08 12 1998 / 01
Re-Issue / Version:

1ST 26/09/99 35/044/0039

Beef Special Premium Scheme

8 months old: 30 06 1999
21 months old: 30 07 2000

A 'passport' needed by every cow and calf so that its parentage can be traced

financial implications for both the farmer and the tax-payer, since there was insufficient capacity to incinerate these unwanted carcasses, thus requiring a massive cold-storage operation to be put in place. I believe in years to come there will be many questions asked as to the morality behind decisions to destroy in excess of a million perfectly healthy cattle in order to rebuild consumer confidence when half the world's population are regularly facing that other life threatening situation of 'no food' which has been scientifically proven to result in death by starvation.

Beef and sheep production is the primary source of income for all farming businesses on the mid-Wales borders thus the impact of the BSE crisis has been extremely damaging to the prosperity of the whole area. Many of these farmers have never seen a case of BSE and the whole experience has been one where they have often been overlooked in a drama that has been played out somewhere else by people who have little understanding of what effect their actions are having on an individual's livelihood.

Currently in 1999 the ban on British Beef exports has been lifted, however the stringent regulations required to export has meant there is only one abattoir willing to dedicate its capacity to the export trade at present.

To conclude, it is reassuring to note that the much heralded epidemic in cases of nv. CJD did not materialise, and the number of confirmed cases of BSE in cattle has dropped dramatically as predicted. The cause of this terrifying disease has yet to be established, however, there are strong suggestions that the use of organo-phosphate chemicals may be a causal-agent, with the use of meat and meal in the diets being a reason for the rapid spread. Whatever the reasons, the whole episode has been a sad chapter in the history of farming. However, I would hope it has also contributed to developing a food production system in the UK which ensures that in the future the consumer can always expect near perfection with respect to food safety and quality when they ask for British.

Derek Beavan

An ear tag

The Common Agricultural Policy and how it relates to Farming in our area

The Common Agricultural Policy (C.A.P.) is designed to harmonise agricultural support and standards throughout all the countries in the European Union and the ultimate aim is that all farm produce can then be traded equally within the whole group of countries and beyond. This has been the objective for the 25 years or so that we have been members. Due to national governments interference and illegal restrictions "free and equal trade" for all agricultural products has never yet been achieved.

At the time of writing the final draft of the C.A.P. agenda 2000 reforms have yet to be agreed, no specific figures and details are available. However, C.A.P. has a vast effect on the way we farm our land and its broad objectives and influences are worthy of note especially in relation to how they have affected and are likely to affect the type of farming carried out in this area.

Most of the land we farm is designated as 'less favoured area' (LFA) with most being classified as severely disadvantaged due to the height above sea level, the harshness of the climate, the poor natural fertility of the soil and the distance from our markets. The support we get for this is funded partly from Europe and partly from National Government. It is designed not only to compensate farmers for the difficulties mentioned above, but also through doing so to promote a viable and vibrant rural economy in the more remote areas of the country.

The payments under this scheme have, to date, been made on the number of eligible suckler cows and ewes kept on a farm with an enhanced rate being paid for hill breeds of ewe. The importance of these payments to us is considerable but politically the will to fund them is diminishing with the preference being to pay money to farms in areas such as ours for environmental enhancement schemes such as 'The Clun Environmentally Sensitive Area Scheme' which most farms in Llanfair Parish are involved with. These schemes are more acceptable to general tax payers and are not linked in any way to the level of agricultural production on our farms. Under the payment review for H.L.C.A's it seems likely that this will not be linked to production payments and will be paid at an amount relating to the area farmed. It appears that this will favour the larger, more extensively run farms, at the expense of smaller family farms which are most in need of protection. A possible advantage of this method of payment is that it may encourage more farmers to go into more extensive organic production and some may diversify into more unusual livestock enterprises such as keeping deer, goats or even wild boar etc .

The biggest changes to the administration of agricultural support within the C.A.P. have undoubtedly been the imposition of Quotas on suckler cows and ewes and the introduction of the 'Integrated Administration and Control System' (I.A.C.S.). These two changes have had a sinister and unforeseen effect on the way we operate our farms and on our relationship with the Ministry of Agriculture, Fisheries and Food (M.A.F.F.). Quotas were meant to be a mechanism to safeguard the production of given commodities within areas and on farms where they had traditionally been carried out and to allow total production to be limited and kept within financial budgets. The down side for farmers is that it makes it more difficult and costly to change enterprises on a farm to suit perceived opportunities. It also encourages farmers to keep at least the number of cows and sheep for which they hold a quota, previously they may not have considered keeping so many.

The date May 15th 1993 will always be remembered by farmers. It was the final date for submission of our first I.A.C.S. forms. These were very detailed and different from anything we had seen before. We were required by M.A.F.F. to map and record the areas of all our fields and areas on our farms using new field numbers and in hectares, accurate to two decimal places. We also had to measure and calculate the areas of farm roads, feed areas, woodland, buildings, ponds and streams etc. so that the actual forage and arable areas of the fields could be submitted. For the first time the Ministry placed major emphasis on explanatory leaflets, on the media and directly to farmers that they had to fill in their forms correctly or be prosecuted for fraud. This was a huge insult to the vast majority of farmers who have always carried out their business in a quiet and honest way. Sadly this attitude has been continued by the Ministry with many subsequent schemes and regulations, notably the double tagging of calves and the application of passports for cattle.

The I.A.C.S. form which has to be submitted annually is used by the Ministry to calculate the total forage and arable area for each farm which they then use to limit entitlement to subsidy due, to put restrictions on stocking density, which is calculated in relation to the number of suckler cows, ewes and male cattle kept on a farm and claimed premiums on. This explains the continuing high price paid for farm land and the increase in the number of farms let out for annual grass keep. A farmer can claim extensification payments on cows and male cattle while stocking densities are kept within set limits. This looks likely to change with the possible addition of non-premium claiming cattle to the equation for stocking densities and the tightening of the rules on eligible forage areas. These changes will keep land and grass letting at high prices and make it virtually impossible for new entrants to come into farming, unless there is some form of capping of subsidies which seems unlikely under the current proposals.

There are four main areas of support to farms in this area, these are: Arable Area Premium Schemes (AAPS), Suckler Cow Premium Scheme (SCPS), Beef Special Premium Scheme (BSPS) and Sheep Annual Premium Scheme (SAPS). The Arable Area Premium Scheme pays subsidy on an area used by farmers to grow eligible crops, mainly barley. In Llanfair there are two schemes with a simplified scheme for areas under 15 hectares and requiring no set aside being the one applicable to farms in this area. Only land cultivated since 1987 is automatically eligible for payments.

The Suckler Cow Premium Scheme is paid on eligible breeds of suckler cows annually up to Quota levels held and taking account of a six month retention period for the numbers and a reasonable number of calves born to the herd.

The Beef Special Premium Scheme is paid on male cattle either for bulls once in their lives or for steers twice in their lives with a limit of 90 bull and steer first claims and 90 steer second claims per business in any one year. To be eligible the cattle must be kept for a two month retention period per claim.

The Sheep Annual Premium Scheme is paid on ewes kept for lamb production annually up to quota levels held with a 100 day retention period.

This is a brief description of the C.A.P.S. workings and its effects on the type of farming in this area. As ever the problem for us is in the detail, and we now have constantly to update our knowledge of the schemes and fill in countless forms and co-operate with check ups and inspections on our farms. Of course the financial rewards are considerable and sadly, with current world prices for agricultural produce and with the strength of the pound, none of us could make a profit without some form of support.

Andrew Beavan

Genetically Modified Organisms

Genetically Modified Organisms is the term used to describe a wide range of products that have been and are being developed using the technique of inserting part of the genetic code from one species into another target species to pass on a desired characteristic. Some of the objectives of using these techniques includes breeding plants that are resistant to certain herbicides, plants that are resistant to attack by certain pests, plants that will produce medicines or chemicals, plants that have better qualities for the end user, plants that are able to withstand harsher conditions, give improved yields and even a pre-coloured cotton plant. There is much debate about the desirability and safety of these methods of producing new plants with some areas of the world accepting these plants as safe and other areas expressing grave concerns about their safety.

The effects of this technology on the parish of Llanfair Waterdine could be many and varied. In the short term, possible and perceived consumer resistance to Genetically Modified technology could lead to increased livestock feeds cost. In 1998 in the United States alone, approximately 60% of the soybean area and 30% of the maize area was planted with Genetically Modified varieties. Approvals for the commercial production of these protein crops have also been granted in other important crop growing areas such as Brazil, Argentina and Mexico and others, so this may lead to the amount of genetically modified free protein crops available on the world market declining rapidly. As much of the protein used in livestock feeds in this country is imported, a shortage of these Genetically Modified free proteins could lead to a price rise in the cost of Genetically Modified free livestock feeds. If consumer demands lead to the requirement to produce meat that has been fed on foods free of Genetically Modified Organisms, the rise in the price of livestock feed will have major impact in a livestock rearing area like this.

In the longer term, new and different crops may be able to be grown in this area, such as Soybeans, perhaps leading to a reduction in the reliance on imported proteins for livestock feeds. Crops may also be developed for renewable energy production to replace the dwindling supplies of hydrocarbons and produce energy in a more environmentally friendly manner.

Development of consistently higher yielding crop varieties grown in the more favourable area of the World may lead to long term increases and more economic and thus cheaper livestock production in these areas, putting pressure on less favoured areas such as this parish which have few alternatives to livestock production and thereby increasing the possibility of rural depopulation.

Genetically Modified Organisms are controversial developments in plant breeding with many supporters and opponents of the technology, and whatever the result of the debate in this country, this technology looks set to have a major impact in both the short and long term of the parish.

David Morgan

Europe and the Euro

Being a child of the Second World War, I am thankful that the European countries are working together within the European Parliament and that we have the European Central Bank. The welding together of separate countries is welcome but the results seem rather remote from this part of the world. The exception is the Common Agricultural Policy which has, I think, had a profound and beneficial effect on the local farming community over the years.

I anticipate, before long, when I buy a cup of tea that I shall be able to pay for it in Euros rather than pounds.

Esther Cummins

Medical Services for Llanfair Waterdine and Lloyney 1999

Medical services are all based in Knighton where there is a small hospital providing geriatric, maternity and post-operative care but without facilities for emergencies or surgery.

The two G.P. clinics in the town see patients (mostly by appointment) and if necessary refer them to hospitals in Hereford or Shrewsbury for specialist opinion and further afield for certain specialist treatment. There is also a G.P. practice in Clun used by parishioners who live closer to Clun than to Knighton. It is run by Knighton G.P.'s.

A recent welcome improvement to local services has been the monthly visits to the hospital of consultants in geriatrics, obstetrics, gynaecology, ophthalmology and psychology. There is an ambulance available if it is needed and in extreme cases the Air Ambulance can be called. This is maintained by voluntary contributions and has popular local support. A few people choose to pay their doctors privately but most rely on the National Health Service which funds the clinics and hospital.

There is one pharmacy in Knighton which dispenses prescriptions – free for old-age pensioners and children, and at a standard NHS fee for most others. In Clun medicines are dispensed by the G.P. surgery.

Dental treatment and orthodontic services are available in Knighton (both private and NHS) and an optician attends on certain days. There is a busy physiotherapy service based at the hospital which also provides occupational therapy.

Nurses are employed at the G.P. clinics to do blood pressure checks, inoculations etc. Health visitors and district nurses visit patients and the new born at home to carry out recommended and statutory checks on child development – sight and hearing tests etc.

There is also a visiting counsellor for trauma cases and the bereaved, and a visiting community psychiatric nurse. The three yearly Breast Screening Scheme has proved invaluable.

Mary Townshend

Teme Valley Doctor

The last 40 years have seen many changes. Some of them are due to scientific advances such as the discovery of the various antibiotics and new medicines which have been introduced but these, valuable as they have been, apply to the whole country and not just to our area.

In some ways the most important differences have been part of the great social changes which have come about during this time. They are most conveniently grouped under several headings.

The doctor's car is pulled from the mud outside Black Hall, 1930s.

Communications. All over the area there have been vast improvements not only in the public roads but in lanes leading to individual farms and houses. Not many people now have to walk for a mile or more to get to a motorable road. More families have at least one motor vehicle. Forty years ago many were dependent on the weekly bus to town on market day and faced a long tramp home from the bus stop often carrying a heavy load of shopping.

This has meant that doctors are less often faced with the problem of getting medicines to outlying patients. It is now usually possible for these to be fetched by car from the chemists and the doctor does not need to carry such a variety of emergency drugs.

Of late we have been blessed with less severe winters and we have better snow clearance machinery which has been a great relief. Fewer back roads are now liable to blockage by flooding of small streams as most of the worst fords have been bridged.

Ambulances. We now have a proper professionally trained service with suitably equipped vehicles and skilled drivers and attendants. Forty years ago we had only volunteer drivers and sometimes were lucky enough to find a retired nurse as an attendant. In severe cases the doctor often had to go with the patient to Hereford or Shrewsbury. Even now there are problems with terrain. The Air Ambulance cannot always fly at night or in severe weather.

The WI presents a cheque, results of a sponsored walk, to Harold Jones for Knighton Hospital

Mary Morgan (president), Peggy Matthews (treasurer), Harold Jones (vet), Dr Davies

Messages. Many more homes now have a telephone or are within walking distance of one. Previously messages for help could come in a variety of ways. Perhaps a neighbour would see that someone's smoke was not coming from their chimney and start an alert. One place relied on hanging a white cloth over the hedge, daytime only which would mean to their nearest neighbour a mile away that a doctor was needed. Often calls came in late in the day when the husband got home from work and the wife would stay with a sick child while he went to send word. These 'edge of night' calls were common and it was better to be sure early than start an obvious emergency during the night.

Housing. Most of the really bad places are now deserted. The arrival of mains electricity has done, probably, more than anything else. It has brought light, heating, wireless and T.V. The increase in reliable drinking water has done much to reduce gut upsets and made washing, laundering and general cleanliness better, long an uphill struggle. Warmth too has improved. No longer are people dependent on a smoking open fire to combat cold and damp. It has also made domiciliary midwifery less of a potential nightmare. I have vivid memories of difficult forceps deliveries and the consequent stitching up done by the light of a hurricane lamp.

Mental Isolation. Arising out of the arrival of telephones, wireless and television has come the breakdown of mental isolation of people in scattered houses. No longer are people dependent on occasional meetings with their neighbours, chapel or market day contacts and the weekly newspaper for knowledge of the world. They can see for themselves in their own homes.

Dr. Brian Davies

Roads and Communications

The 20th Century has seen the arrival – very late when compared to most of Britain – of the motor car and tractor, the telephone and, last but not least, mains electricity. Behind this last has come radio, television and the instant one way communication of events world wide and beyond.

Railways don't feature much in the Teme Valley above Knucklas. They have changed from steam to diesel power and can still be late. They now carry fewer people and no freight. Sheep and cattle used to walk or could travel by train to market. Now it's lorries for all livestock and all bulk supplies; and the vehicles grow larger ever year, but not the roads which carry them. One thing that has hardly altered at all – we still have "the Post" delivered daily throughout the year: bills have a way of reaching us on time.

The strangest result of all these changes may be seen in the pace of life. People seem to have less time. They are always under some strange sort of pressure. I am sure there are still 24 hours in the day but the advantages of faster travel have been offset by the 'speed of life'! And vehicles crash into each other more frequently than in the past, often with more serious results.

The only railway line in the parish

A steam train leaves Knighton

One most noticeable change is the way that all the improvements in communications mean that there is much less communicating. When neighbours rode by on their ponies or bicycles they could stop for a chat or at least 'pass the time of day' and catch up on the latest gossip. All that has gone. Now we learn only what other important people want to tell us.

Maybe the next century will see us begin to think for ourselves again.

Jim Cummins.

Tourism in Llanfair Waterdine and Lloyney

There were few tourists coming here before the war. There were a few fishermen who came to 'fly fish' for trout in the River Teme.

Offa's Dyke near Spring Hill

After the war tourism gradually increased until today it is regarded as a valuable source of income. There is an excellent Tourist Information Centre in Knighton.

Described as "an environmentally sensitive area of outstanding natural beauty" one can understand any visitor who enjoys the countryside booking up!

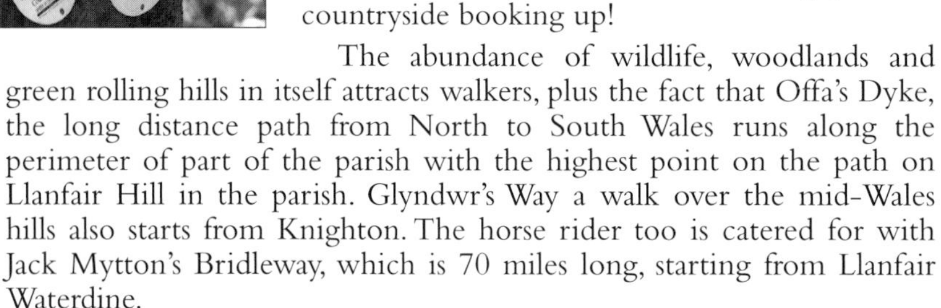

The abundance of wildlife, woodlands and green rolling hills in itself attracts walkers, plus the fact that Offa's Dyke, the long distance path from North to South Wales runs along the perimeter of part of the parish with the highest point on the path on Llanfair Hill in the parish. Glyndwr's Way a walk over the mid-Wales hills also starts from Knighton. The horse rider too is catered for with Jack Mytton's Bridleway, which is 70 miles long, starting from Llanfair Waterdine.

For those who enjoy motoring there are such places as Medieval Ludlow, the Black and White Villages of Herefordshire, the Dams of the Elan Valley, Stokesay and Powys Castles – all with wonderful scenic views en route.

There are several Bed and Breakfast residences locally, some of which do an evening meal and The Mill at Lloyney includes art classes too. For self-catering there are farmhouse apartments and quaint furnished cottages. Camping and caravan sites are also available.

Near the Dyke in winter

Near the Dyke in summer

One realises that for people living in busy towns and cities our quiet valley must be a "blissful retreat". To quote one visitor "Heaven on Earth!" Long may our tourist industry continue to flourish. 1999 prices vary from a couple of pounds to pitch a tent or park a caravan, £15–£20 per night for Bed & Breakfast up to £160–£600 per week to rent a cottage, depending on the number of bedrooms, its position and amenities.

Jocelyn Williams

Our Vicar Writes

Mary Morgan, Eva Maclaughlan and Rev Eileen Lloyd work on the Altar Frontals

One evening in early January, 1995, I was sitting in front of the television watching 'Kavanagh QC'. The plot was beyond me – I couldn't concentrate – I was waiting for the phone to ring. When eventually it did, John Saxbee, the Bishop of Ludlow spoke the words which were to bring about a change in direction for my life. He told me that the parish representatives of Llanfair Waterdine, Stowe, Chapel Lawn and Bucknell had asked him to invite me to be the next Vicar. I confess I burst into tears – it had been a long day, with visits to all the churches, meeting with Church Wardens, a formal interview, worship and an open parish meeting. I was tired, excited and scared – and my answer was a heartfelt 'Yes'. The process of appointing a Vicar to the parishes had been going on for some time, it had been soaked in prayer and there was a sense of God's touch upon it. From then on, things moved quickly and I was licensed to minister in this benefice of four parishes, on 9th March 1995.

News of the appointment created something of a stir. Whilst I had expected some parishioners to feel hurt and rejected by the appointment, I had not anticipated the reaction in the Diocese as a whole. This was the first appointment of a woman to such a parish post. It had been an open process of advertising and interviewing, and this move, which had seemed merely personal, had suddenly taken on a much wider significance, for both men and women. Many, many people were highly delighted, although there were also some who felt the appointment was a political move and they were waiting in the wings for me to fail. At that stage, there were large number of people who had not experienced the ministry of women. So for quite some time weddings, funerals and christenings became occasions for conversations which began, 'Oh, a lady Vicar ... I didn't agree with women priests ... but now ... I've changed my mind'. Of course it is wonderful when people enjoy a service and they begin to sense a greater richness in the Church through having both men and women serving as priests, but it is a heavy burden for the women to carry. If I do something well, then women's ministry goes up in people's estimation, whereas, if I have a bad day, if I make a mistake, then people condemn all women as incompetent. This is inevitable at this stage in the life of the Church, but it is not easy to live with.

Fred Beavan and the Rev Eileen Lloyd

After four and a half years in the parishes, I feel as if I belong. People have been tremendously supportive and accepting of a 'townie'. Although I was born and brought up in Liverpool, I have always appreciated open space – hills and rivers – so in a sense living in this area is something of a coming home. There is a friendliness and trust here which has been lost from many urban areas. The pace of life is slower – perhaps more in accord with the rhythm of the seasons and the evolution of the landscape. I have learned not to expect rapid decisions or action – patience is truly a virtue! Soon after I arrived, John Williams of Panpwnton arranged a 'Meet the Vicar' evening at Everest Hall. It would give folk a chance to get to know me over a cup of coffee and a biscuit, he said. So having had my evening meal, I arrived for the meeting, to find the tables groaning with what looked like a harvest supper – my introduction to Llanfair hospitality.

The four parishes in the benefice are all very different, all special, and I have to share my time between them. Inevitably, that means I cannot always be where I want to be, do what I want to do. Ideally I would like to celebrate the great festivals of Christmas and Easter with each community – but I can't be in two places at once. That is one of the real struggles of rural ministry – one gets to know people, one shares the journey with them – but then there are times when one has to be elsewhere. If I'm missing from a Coffee Morning or a Concert, it could be because I am with a bereaved family in another parish. Rural ministry is always messy, provisional, unfinished – there is never enough of the priest to go around. The days when every parish had a vicar, a man who helped with the harvest and who visited every home regularly are long gone – if they ever existed – and God's church faces a new era, a new challenge.

All in all it is a great privilege to minster here where the church is valued by the whole community and not just those who worship on a Sunday. People allow me to share with them some very deep and personal moments in their lives; they include me in their celebrations and their sorrows; some keep a watchful eye and ensure that I find time to play too! And for that I give thanks. Someone once described a priest as 'A real person; someone who is a visual aid for God' – if I can live that out – with you and for you – then I will be satisfied.

Rev. Eileen Lloyd

The Mothers Union in Llanfair Waterdine

A Mothers Union Branch has existed in Llanfair for many years. It was active between the 1920s to the early 1950s. It was reformed on March 29th 1957. The vicar at the time was Rev. Wynne Jones and his wife Mrs. Wynne Jones was the enrolling member.

Members present at the first meeting were: *Mrs. A. Evans, Mrs. L. Evans, Mrs. Beavan, Mrs. Cummins, Mrs. T. S. Jones, Mrs. Beaumont, Miss Bright, Mrs. C. Williams, Mrs. Gwilt, Mrs. Clee, Mrs. Farmer, Mrs. W. Gough, Mrs. Davies, Mrs. Hammond, Mrs. Marpole, Mrs. I Hughes, Mrs. L. Williams and Mrs. Hobby.*

Business meetings were held in the then school, now Everest Hall. Services were held in church with speakers on various topics and Corporate Communion twice a year. The MU banner made by members hangs in the church. Subscription for the year was 3/6d.

By 1993 membership had dropped to 8 and three of these wished to give up membership. It was agreed that the remaining five members would join the Bucknell branch.

Bucknell and Llanfair Mothers Union has an active membership of eighteen with several others joining in for social and fund raising events. Meetings are held on the first Tuesday of each month, usually in members houses, either in Bucknell or Llanfair. The Mothers Union takes an active interest in village activities and in the church etc. Children's posies on Mothering Sunday were started by the Mothers Union. The Branch holds a fund raising Garden Party annually for charity and also hold a fund raising event in the Autumn for local charities and an overseas charity.

Joan Hobby
Anne Matthews

Youth club

Llanfair Waterdine Youth Club

The club has been running for nearly a year. It was started in November 1998 at a memorable bonfire night following discussion between a group of parents and children living in the parish. Our aim was to create a regular social meeting place for the children in and around Llanfair. We felt that this was long overdue since there are probably more children living in the parish now than for some considerable time. Furthermore, the disparate nature of the parish so that children are often living in rather isolated conditions and the fact that they attend six different schools meant that the need for a focus or venue to bring all these children together was all the more necessary.

The club is run on a totally voluntary basis by the parent leaders Caroline Adams-Evans, Andrew Beavan, Janet Lewis, Kate Martin, David Powell and Debbie Watkins. We meet at the Everest Hall every Wednesday in term time from 7.00 to 8.30 and thanks to Andrew we are also able to make use of the river and Llanavidy for football, rounders, obstacle races and barbecues.

The Club has proved to be a great success with numbers rising steadily from around 20 to a peak of 40 most recently. We are now in the position where we have to put children on a waiting list. The children range in age from 8 to 14 and about 15 live in the parish, the rest coming from Beguildy, Lloyney and Knucklas.

Youth Club
Some of the adults

David Powell, Chairman

Kate Martin, Caroline and a worker at the car wash

Tug O'War, a lot of extra weight!

Mandy Powell cooking with helpers

Youth club

We have been very fortunate in that we have had a great deal of support from the wider community and a grant from the National Lottery so that whereas we started with minimal equipment and resources we had to beg steal or borrow, we now have our own which are housed in the latest addition to the ever expanding village hall... the new shed and our new storage cupboards.

As for activities... we do a lot of sport with the children, Robert Gwilt helps with football and we are now all coming to terms with the rules for badminton, rounders, basketball and indoor hockey. More creative activities include such things as T-shirt painting, cooking or pot designs but our proudest and most visible achievement is the mural in the bar which incorporated all the children's ideas and was painted by them over a number of months while being patiently overseen by Phillipa Boast. Dr. Bliss and Melanie have been brilliant and kindly give up their time to come on a regular basis... getting people to juggle with plastic bags and other spectacular circus skills! Quizzes, a talk by Rosemary Naylor on astronomy including peering down her telescope at Saturn and trips to theatre, football matches and motocross have all happened this year. Often a group of children just like to get together and work out dance routines to the latest music and boogie away on the stage.

Since everyone has been so generous in supporting us we have tried to reciprocate. In the spring we held a car wash for 'Children in Need' and in the summer we held a Coffee Morning up at Llandinshop for the Youth Club and children's charities.

Hopefully the Youth Club will continue to flourish for some considerable time and children will remain a sizeable and vibrant part of the community.

Janet Lewis.

Youth club

Early membership of the WI

Dolly Clee, Mary Beavan, Connie Beaumont, Joan Hobby, Mary Hughes, Dilys Williams, Lilian Evans, Mary Davies, Peggy Mathews

W.I.

Llanfair Waterdine W.I. was formed in December 1926, 20 members were enrolled, with Mrs. Boote the first President. Members walked many miles to attend meetings which were held in the school room on the first Friday of the month at 4.00 p.m., after the children had departed and whilst the room was still warm. Meetings are still held on the first Friday of the month, but at 7.00 p.m. (the time was changed in 1953), and the school

The WI about 1980

Mary Morgan, Mary Davies, Joan Hobby, Ann Harroway, Mary Beavan, Vera Gough, Peggy Matthews

is now Everest Hall, named after Lord Hunt of Llanfair Waterdine, as his family lived in the parish at the time of the conquest of Everest, and Lady Hunt was a W.I. member. Membership is now 30 with Jean Gardner as President, and the majority of members now travel by car.

The format of the meetings has changed very little; business first, then an interesting talk or demonstration, followed by delicious suppers and a good chat. However, the content of the talks and demonstrations has changed over the years; pig curing, pork pie making, etc., having given way to line dancing, microwave cookery, travel talks and slide shows, with I.T. in the future.

Llanfair has always taken part in County events, and has represented the County many times at the Royal Welsh Show, with very good results. County Eisteddfods have also proved very successful; our rounders team won the All Wales Tournament, but unfortunately we don't play rounders now. Under the leadership of Mrs. Freda Harroway we have an enthusiastic Entertainments Group. Many members have served, and still serve on the County Executive and Sub-committees, Miss Grace Barnard and Mrs. Mary Morgan being privileged to serve a three year term as County Chairman.

The WI in 1999

Freda Powell, Iris Leason, Doreen Hart, Chris Austin, Joan Silviter, Ann Harroway, Mary Chapman, Phoebe Bowen, Freda Harroway, Mary Morgan, Rene Gayther, Jean Gardener, Barbara Carter, Winnie Davies, Joan Hobby

Fun, food and friendship are very much in evidence in Llanfair Waterdine, and we are taking a very healthy and lively W.I. into the new Millennium.

Mary Morgan

Bridge

A Contract Bridge Club was started in Llanfair Waterdine in 1996. Monthly meetings were held at the Red Lion Public House. This proved popular and players began to come from as far away as Bucknell and Dolau and the neighbouring valley of Clun. As the numbers increased the frequency of meetings increased and a wider number of venues was established. Now in 1999 the club meets four times a month and in three different places. Regular attendances of six or seven tables are quite normal and over the two and a half years some fifty players have attended the meetings.

Although the club continues to play rubber bridge most of the regulars are able to play hands as though it was duplicate bridge and so it is likely that additional sessions of proper duplicate may be possible in the future.

Due to the success of the club an annual fund raising event for the Samaritans is held in the village hall. This takes the form of a Chicago Bridge Tournament with an excellent supper provided by the ladies of the Samaritans Committee.

Andrew MacLauchlan

Yoga

The Yoga Group started at the Everest Hall in 1995 having first been held at the Community Hall, Knucklas. About 14 people used to attend but there are now 9 or 10 regulars. The Group has had four visits to The Plas Talgarth and all agree that they benefit from Yoga both physically and mentally.

Mary Simmons started the group in 1992 after a conversation with Mary Chapman. At first one or two men occasionally joined in. Sadly they have fallen by the wayside but Mary Chapman has hardly ever missed a week.

Pat Middleton writes – Once a week on a Friday between 10.00a.m. and 11.00 a.m. ladies of various sizes, shapes, age and ability gather together under the guidance of Mary Simmons for a session of Yoga. Yoga has many forms. We concentrate on breathing and gentle but strong exercises and with the help of meditation we try to find the inner self.

Everyone who attends these classes soon feels the benefit. One becomes more supple, the deep breathing cleanses the system and oxygenates the blood. At the end of our exercises we have 10 minutes relaxation. This helps us to find inner peace and so helps us cope with the trials of everyday life. I recommend Yoga to everyone, it can benefit young and old.

Circle Dancing

Circle dancing takes place on the third Monday of each month in The Everest Hall. Mary Simmons takes the classes. The dances come from many different countries, and as the title suggests, are danced in a circle sometimes round a candle. Some of the dances are energetic, others sedate, but all have a charm of their own. The music helps us to interpret the mood of the dance. The evening is an enjoyable social occasion with coffee, tea and biscuits at half time.

Pat Middleton

Darts and Dominoes Teams

The Red Lion, Llanfair Waterdine has fielded at least one Darts Team since the early 1970's. The team originally played in the Knighton League but some 10 years ago a Teme Valley League was formed with teams from each pub in the valley taking part. Matches are played on a 'home and away' basis on Friday nights during the winter months, culminating with Finals night at the end of the season, early March.

Currently two teams are fielded by The Red Lion, with five members per team, made up of John and Julie Bevan, Tom and Christine Jones, Andrew and Anne Beavan, Robert and Anthony Gwilt, Robert Davies and David Powell, drawing on a list of substitutes as required. Each match consists of 5 Singles games, 1 Double and 1 Treble, starting at 401 and a double to get out, with points being scored for a win and thus the League Table is formed, giving a 'Top of the League' winner at the end of the season.

Similarly there has been a Dominoes Team at The Red Lion for over twenty years, also members of the Knighton League. Matches are played on a Wednesday night during the winter months with Finals played at the end of the season. The Red Lion has one team consisting of six members, currently any six of the following players – John Gwilt, Raymond Davies, Brian Hewins, John Morgan, Bernard Dodd, Bert Williams and Robert Davies. Each match consists of 6 Singles and 3 Doubles Games, playing 5's and 3's, 90 holes per game with an exact score required to finish the game.

The Christmas Auction

The Auction is an annual event which raises funds for the Church and on some occasions for the Everest Hall. The evening begins at about 6.00 p.m. when stalls are set up in the Hall to sell produce, jumble, plants, books and cakes. After about an hour the auctioneer takes his place and the auction begins. Most people bring an item or two to be auctioned and then buy items too.

Sheep and live chickens change hands occasionally for quite high prices! (Live animals add to the occasion but one is aware of a slight reaction from members of the Village Hall Committee from whose ranks the hall cleaner will come!)

A Christmas cake, potatoes, fruits and vouchers for free meals usually make the list too along with odds and ends of furniture, the odd exercise bike and lamps and ornaments. The evening sometimes raises temperatures as well as money and at the end a group usually retires to the Red Lion for supper or a reviving drink.

The 'takings' have been over £1,000 for many years now and the actual occasion seems more popular every year.

Ruth Davies

Mike & Liz Lockey, Phillipa Boast and Rosemary Naylor, Mary Comer

Waiting to bid!

Sheep, lamps and wire!

Ruby Thomas and Cicily Tortoriello

The auctioneer, John Williams

Antoinette Lansdale and David Llewellyn

Margaret Swancott waiting to bid?

John Gwilt

Llewelyn Morgan and friend!

Granville and Maureen Bates

Preb. D. Jenkyns dedicates an altar frontal sewn by the team of local women

The Altar Cloths

Female members of the church have met regularly over the past year or so to repair and renovate the altar frontals. These are quite old, probably Victorian and hard worn, or, in some cases, been attacked by mice over the years. Three have been lovingly restored by the ladies whose patience and talent will hopefully be appreciated by future congregations. The fourth (white) one was too badly worn for them to attempt repair. This has been sent to the Hereford Cathedral Broderers for professional repair. Hopefully it will be completed in time for use at Easter 2000.

The colourful church kneelers were woven over the years by members of the church and a variety of other people in celebration of marriages, christenings, in memoriam and by the W.I. and Mothers Union, depicting church festivals and other occasions.

Ruth Davies

The Village Library

The village library started in 1997 when Mary Simmons decided to "thin out" her book collection. She regularly took books in cardboard boxes to the Everest Hall in the boot of her car so that those attending Yoga classes could borrow them. She charged a few pence which was given to Hall funds. The Village Hall Committee managed to get a grant for £300 from the Community Chest charity in Bishop's Castle and Glyn Griffiths built a book cupboard. More people then borrowed books. The National Library Association ran a competition to find self help schemes deserving support. The village library was one of three national finalists and managed to win £1,000. Anne Singleton and Doreen Hart went to London to receive the award from Chris Smith, Minister for the Arts. We were given quite a lot of new books, many of them for children. A tape deck and CD player was purchased using some of the award. This is used by the Circle Dancing Group and the Women's Institute. A Youth Club was formed in late 1998 and in 1999 the National Lottery Small Grants Fund gave a grant to build another storage cupboard for the many children's books now in the Library. The Library continues to be a great success especially with the children.

Llanfair Wakes

The age old custom of Llanfair Wakes was revived in 1952. In the Middle Ages this country fete was an important feature of church and village life. The celebration took the form of a feast day or even a feast week! The date for the event was the Saint's day to whom the church is dedicated – St. Mary.

The Old Wakes began with a morning service in church, the rest of the day was spent in feasting and dancing. It was a traditional celebration carried down through the centuries. Apparently there were stalls throughout the village and cold, thick, rice pudding served with pears was the special food for the occasion. Probably the last person to make the

The skittles. John and Hazel Gwilt

Fancy dress 1999

rice pudding was Mrs. Elizabeth Bowen, Hawthorn Cottage. Her granddaughter, Mrs. Dolly Clee, can remember the enormous earthenware pot in which the pudding was made but she cannot remember the last Wakes which are thought to have taken place around the turn of the century (1900).

Jimmy Rhodes faces the judge!

As a child I remember hearing the legend of the crows in the barn at Skyborry: It went like this:

David Syr Evans was a young lad of about twelve years of age, employed by the farmer at Skyborry to keep the crows off his cornfield while everyone was at the Wakes. David wanted to go to the Wakes too and the Devil, knowing this, offered to guard the crop in return for half of David's soul.

David agreed and happily went off to enjoy himself. The Devil gathered the crows together and shut them up in the old barn opposite Nether Skyborry which still stands today. Soon after this event the boy died and he is supposedly buried half in and half out of Llanfair churchyard because half his soul belonged to the devil. It is said that on rough and stormy nights, when the moon rides high in the sky the ghost of the boy can be seen sitting on the gatepost at Nether Skyborry surrounded by a flock of crows! – So say those with second sight! I have looked for him many times but am still waiting!

The present Wakes was revived on August 15th 1952, the object was to raise money for the church. Giant sized posters were widely displayed advertising this important revival. They were headed by a rhyme.

Llanfair Wakes are famous
Llanfair Wakes are fun
Llanfair Wakes some beating takes
So come and join the fun!

There were many attractions including:

Pedestrian fancy dress, Best Decked tractor and trailer. A Cockerel Race for the ladies (which would be ruled out in this day and age by the RSPCA!). Bowling for the pig, Guessing the weight of the sheep, various stalls. A Country Dance Display by Llanfair Young Farmers. Farmhouse teas etc.

Christine Jones and competitor in the Dog Show

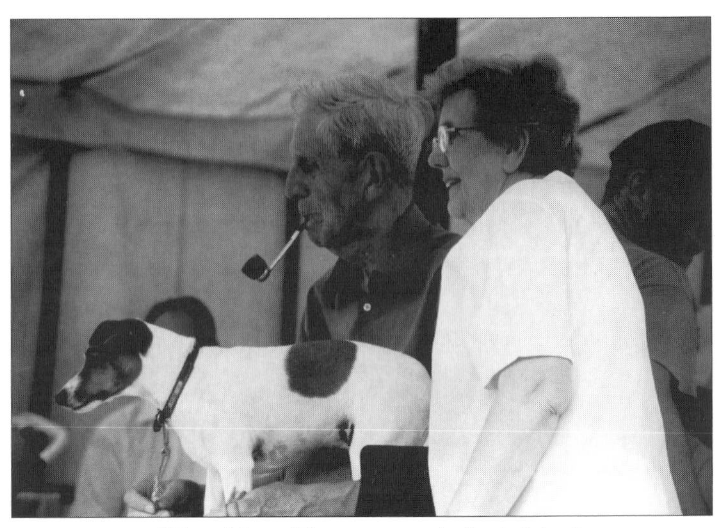
Sid and Joan Thomas – ready for judging!

The day was to conclude with a Gala Dance in the school to replace 'Ye Olde Countrie Dances' which used to be held in the church yard after the original Wakes.

Great preparations were made for the opening. Everyone was busy, organising, making, baking etc. The marquee was set up in the school yard and the village decorated with banners, bunting and flags. The great day dawned – never to be forgotten – spirits were high, but the skies were heavy, black and leaden. The weather forecast was awful – 'a deep depression over the British Isles.' The rain started and went on all day. The Young Farmers' feet squelched as they danced the traditional jigs and reels. Soon the water lapped around the stalls and flowed like a river through the tent. Throughout Britain floods and disasters were reported, the worst being at Lynmouth in Devon where there was serious flooding.

Although the revival of Llanfair Wakes was literally a 'wash out' it was nevertheless the first of many successful 'Wakes' and has gone on ever since as an annual event.

Over the past 47 years the programme has been updated regularly. The Wakes still begins with the fancy dress and there are still stalls in the marquee. Other activities include sports, pony rides, face painting, a dog show, live music, various competitions (we still guess the weight of the sheep), a fish race, a quiz, teas and a barbecue. An added attraction for the youngsters and their parents is the introduction of the school boy football by Robert Gwilt. All these activities take place on Llan-y-vidy field next to the Village Hall.

Jocelyn Williams

Open Gardens

Community spirit thrives in Llanfair Waterdine and whenever funds are needed for any reason the people of the Parish get together and hold Coffee Mornings/Evenings, Whistdrives, Concerts and other events which will raise money.

During 1984 Drs Richard and Mary Townshend held a coffee evening in their garden at Lower Skyborry and raised money for the Children's Society. The evening was most successful and later became an annual event with the garden being open in the afternoon/evening and teas being provided with help from members of the Mother's Union. Other keen gardeners in the parish became involved and when funds were needed for the Shropshire Historic Churches Trust Dr. Townshend co-ordinated the opening of four gardens. The Townshends were joined by Paul and Mary Simmons at Melin-y-Grogue, Liz and Ken Bond at Ladycroft and Granville and Maureen Bates at Lower Graig. A combined entrance free of £2.50p was charged and plants were sold at Ladycroft and there were teas and a Bring and Buy stall at Lower Graig. The ladies of the parish worked hard during the weekend to provide visitors with cream teas and an array of delicious cakes which were thoroughly enjoyed by everyone. The men arranged the car parking and collected the entrance fees. A considerable amount of money was raised and divided between Shropshire Historic Churches Trust and St. Mary's Church. In 1997 the money was given to the Physiotherapy Unit at Knighton Hospital.

Sadly Mr. Paul Simmons and Dr. Townshend died and Mrs. Bond became too ill to maintain her garden. In 1998 everyone got together to open the garden at the Lower Graig to raise money for the Millennium Fund and despite a very wet weekend many visitors turned up and it proved to be a most successful event.

Maureen Bates

The Diners!

A group of women meets at the Red Lion on the last Tuesday evening of every month. We simply have a meal together, a social chat and enjoy each others company.

About twenty women are involved and the average monthly turnout is about ten. Anyone who wants to come along is welcome. We first got together about seven years ago.

All the people who turned up on that first evening still come along regularly unless they've left the area. Most of us would agree that even if we only meet on a monthly basis we could look to each other for help and support in times of need or just ring up for a chat at any time. Women travel from Knighton, Bucknell, Beguildy and Felindre and most of the group have met and got to know somebody they didn't know before, who they can now count as a friend.

Anne Singleton

The Homeguard

In September 1939, when war broke out, the local Defence Volunteers (L.D.V.) was formed. Every able-bodied man was expected to join. They met in various centres to learn what they might have to do if the country was invaded. At that early stage no weapons or uniforms were issued. Very soon however there was the formation of the Homeguard, sometimes referred to as 'Dad's Army'. The Drill Hall in Knighton became the centre for the distribution of uniforms etc. and also the training centre. It had previously been used by the Territorial Army, who had been called up at the commencement of war.

Llanfair Waterdine, Lloyney, Knucklas and Heyope formed number 4 Platoon of A Company of the 1st Battalion of the Radnorshire Rifles (R.R's). The Llanfair Waterdine and Lloyney section met regularly on Sunday mornings in Llanfair school yard. The Knucklas and Heyope Section met in the club room in Knucklas on Sunday afternoon.

Lieutenant Mann and 2nd Lieutenant Fred Beavan were in charge of the platoon, assisted by sergeants Penry Evans, Tom Bright and Harry Evans. There were about forty men altogether.

Quite early in the war there was the fear of sabotage, particularly of the viaduct, Llangunllo tunnel and the aqueduct in Knighton. The railways were very busy at this time carrying steel and coal etc. and these three vulnerable spots had to be patrolled particularly at night. The local responsibility was for the viaduct. Often on Sundays they would have exercises, either defending or attacking any of these danger spots. On one of these occasions the platoon was actively employed at Knucklas when the shopkeeper there produced some rather strong alcohol, which

Knucklas Viaduct guarded by the Home Guard

was very readily accepted on a hot summer's day; the result being an uncontrollable Dad's Army dashing around, not knowing where to go or what to do, but very merry indeed. One or two of the senior NCOs were trying desperately to hide them under hedges, in case a senior officer appeared!

On another occasion when all the windows were blacked out one Lloyney lady was very concerned because her cottage was newly painted white and would be an obvious target for the bombers. She wanted it camouflaged!

Early in the war when a member of the LDW was attending a smart wedding he had a message to say that a parachute was landing on the Beacon. He hastily left the wedding, dashed home, collected his shotgun, and set off up the Beacon, still in his very best wedding attire. The parachute turned out to be a barrage balloon that had come adrift. A plane tried to shoot it down so it developed into quite an exciting incident!

The home guard in fact spent many very uncomfortable nights patrolling and guarding the viaduct. The trains gave a little 'toot' as they went by to try to cheer the men up!

Motor Cycle Club

Interested people got together to form the Knighton Motor Cycle Club. Their first meeting was held on 26th November 1949. Doug Jones from Dutlas took the chair at the first meeting and Mr. Wooding, father of Joan Adams, was President of the Club. Many local people were keen to join because motorbikes were used to travel to and from work. They hoped to be able to spend leisure time enjoying their bikes. Roger Maughfling married Ann Robertson at about this time and they lived in Trebert Cottage near the Graig. Roger was very aware of the perfect landscape for scrambling on the Graig land near his home. In the early 1950s the first scramble was held and over the years it developed into an occasion when top riders from the National Auto Cycle Union competed.

Club members paid an annual subscription of 7s. 6d. when the club was first formed but because of its success this was soon reduced to 5 shillings.

The scrambles were held at the Graig for many years and drew crowds and competitors from all over Britain and abroad.

Margaret Lloyd

Fanny Price

Isy Hughes

Beryl Evans Margaret Swancott Freda Powell

Brenda Ross, Eva MacLauchlan, Mick Richards

John Hunt, Penry Evans and Col Sykes

(Clockwise from right)
Sarah Beavan and father John
Mary Townshend and Jim Cummins
Dana Tortoriello
Alice Beavan takes the sun
Billy and John Riddle and Polly from Belmount

Trevor Gwilt

Charlie Price 'The Cote'

Who's a pretty girl then?

Isy Hughes at The Graig

Harry Davies

David Morgan (Selley Hall),
Simon Williams (Monaughty)

Esther Cummins buys a plant

Betty Goulding at a Bring and Buy

Bethan and Kate Morgan with mother Llinda, Antoinette Lansdall, Anne Smellie, May Ruell, Sylvia Lloyd

Gordon Evans and Ernie Gough

Llewellyn Morgan, Fred Beavan, Jim Williams and John Williams

Fred and friend!

Hats!

Fred Beavan and Keith Tortoriello

Hew Colvin and Andrew Lewis

Tom Evans

Gordon, Matt & Anne Singleton

Jimmy Rhodes

Jim Cummins and grandchild

Part Five

Life at the Lion!
Short Local Poems
Local Legends

Life at The Lion (Timber!)

A new wood burning stove was installed in the pub lounge. Something which was to have far reaching effects; it became a thing which dominated out lives. Wood stoves in the country vie with the fabled Aga for prominence of position in domestic matters. Feeding the wood-gobbling swines becomes an obsession; one is constantly on the lookout for potential fuel sources. It's 'de rigueur' to have a chain saw. I purchased a monster, of which I was devoutly, but secretly, terrified. On one occasion I was persuaded by one of the enterprising locals to fell a large elm tree which lurked below the pub close to the river. He assured me it was stricken with some ghastly disease, and in truth it was already leaning at a strange angle.

The 'crack' was that he would supply the expertise, although the felling was to be a joint exercise. Once dropped he was to saw it into logs, which we would divide between us. It all sounded splendid, it was a doughty tree and promised tons of logs for the winter. I studied the chain saw manual, which helpfully contained some diagrams and pictures of rather oddly proportioned men felling trees. It all seemed pretty straightforward; if you cut the trunk in the right place the tree was sure to fall exactly where you wanted it to. Confident in my new-found knowledge I agreed. First thing the following Saturday morning was designed at 'F' hour.

It was one of those cold damp autumn days, with the mist still hanging about by the river. The bank from which the tree sprouted was steep and slippery underfoot from overnight rain. My fellow lumberjack was a tall rather gaunt fellow, who was a heavy smoker, with an apparently infinite capacity for beer. He was possessed of a rather laconic sense of wit and made his living as a jobbing builder. Our communication on that morning was somewhat stilted due to our both having seriously over imbibed the previous evening. The weekly darts match had been held in the tap room and my builder friend had played with particular skill, resulting in his being bought many pints. I offer no excuse for my own over-indulgence.

Armed with our chain saws, rope and sundry other items of equipment we scrambled down the bank to the base of the tree. It really was a big tree; the worm of misgiving moved in the pit of my delicate stomach. Discussion as to where to make our first incision followed. My disquiet grew as my man with the expertise confided he'd never "dropped such a big 'un." I conceded 'first strike' to him and his well-used saw howled into life. The smell of petrol and the vibrations of his machine set him coughing in a most alarming way; I crabbed my way up the bank out of scything distance and decided I would be best employed in an observer capacity.

Our intrepid woodsman made excellent progress. My confidence returned. The chain saw snarled and growled at varying pitches, sawdust filled the air and gathered in heaps on the muddy ground. When he cut the motor the ensuing silence was uncanny. I hastened down to view his handiwork. He'd certainly done jolly well; a large segment of trunk had been rather neatly removed – I was impressed. We discussed the pros and cons of attached rope, where the next cut should be made, or whether first we should retire to the pub for 'spirited' coffee. Our musings were rudely interrupted by an unearthly groaning and a loud report. Aghast, we glared at one another for a split second then looked up to see the tree slowly revolving above us. It was every man for himself! Squawking like Billy Bunter I darted upstream towards some other trees where I sought refuge (unwisely, I've since been told) in their midst. Peering out I saw that my comrade in arms had, if anything, made a speedier retreat than me; he had scaled the bank and was peeping out from the garage buildings at the side of the pub. I rapidly switched my gaze to the elm which we had been attacking, it seemed to be unmoving and then, without further warning, it crashed down measuring its length, British heavyweight style, down the slope of the bank and almost into the river.

For a few seconds a still hush hung over everything. Tentatively we approached the stump and stared at the fallen tree, its branches spread and broken. "Dropped just where I reckoned," said my friend the builder, in an almost convincing tone. He was lighting a cigarette and I noticed he was having some difficulty in marrying the flame to the tip of his fag. However, I decided not to mention it, in view of my own undignified and breathless retreat. In fact, neither of us ever again referred to our terror stricken reaction caused by the death rattle of the old elm. This is not to say we never mentioned the felling of the 'forest giant' during the course of many drunken evenings over the ensuing years. No, it became part of local folklore, but details of our craven flight we kept to ourselves.

Having left my now ebullient companion to complete the task, I stashed my unsheathed chain saw in the garage and returned indoors. Detecting my reticence my wife immediately began to question me as to the success of my latest venture. I gave her a censored version of events, but she sensed my unease and ever quick to jump to conclusions wanted to know if I had broken the chain saw! Here I'd been, risking my life, and she was concerned about the damned saw! She was now muttering about the amount of liquor I'd consumed the previous evening and trying to relate this to the allegedly broken implement. Women are such strange creatures; I hold them in great affection but am totally unable to understand their reasoning. Like the tree incident I found retreat was the best course of action and elected to take the dogs for a walk. As I wandered down the lane, herding my older dog like a pig to market, I met my old chum the local log merchant driving in his lorry. I flagged him down and there and then ordered logs to tide us over for the rest of the winter. I had learned a salutary lesson; 'every man to his trade' and mine was not lumberjacking!

Mick Richards

Short Local Poems

Mr Harold Pugh lived at Cwm Mawr as a tenant of the Llanfair Hall Estate in the early 1920's. Stanley Hains or Holloway who lived around Melin-y-grogue probably in one of the cottages wrote the following:

T'was on a Summers evening
Both wet and windy too
When me and Ned
Went stacking oats
For Mr. Harold Pugh.
Although the sheaves were many
And though the hours were few
We stuck them very nicely
For Mr. Harold Pugh.

Ron Morris

Rain

Silent and still, our Valley lies;
The pebbled stream, just gently drifting by;
Water, so shallow, and yet so cool and clear,
Reflecting blue, the almost cloudless sky.
This blue we love to see
When harvest time is near,
But when we till the soil,
And sow our Springtime seed,
Rain, above all things
Becomes our greatest need.

In summertime, the Birds and Beasts,
The plants and trees
Browse at peace, in a dappled streamside breeze,
And wait for drizzling dew soaked Rain
To mute the heat hazed scene.
Now those who in loud cities dwell,
Work many hours indoors,
And often long to be
Quiet, in fields and hedgerows,
Wherever people live,
Its often hard to see
That all good things
Upon the earth are free.
So when at last the Rain begins to fall,
A transformation washes over all;
The stream, fast rises –
Water, dark and brown
Races to join the river,
Then onward to the Town.

Amy Johnson 1970

Skyborry

The hills in joy bear down upon this chalice of rich earth
With gentle arms they hold this blessed green and silver land
Enfolding it to keep its riches free for all to see
They seem to say "Look feast your eyes and wonder at the beauty here"
We hold it safe that you may love and take it to yourself.

Below the hills on gentler slopes
The gold and bronze of autumn spread their cloaks
To give you warmth and sweet content
The rustle of the leaves beneath your feet talk of the strength
That is below – of rock and stone and clods of earth.

The very heart of this beloved vale, the silver stream
Shines in the wintry sunshine thin and pale
Rippling with joy, elusive, gay
It swings thro' fields, now broad and strong
Now thin and steely grey.

And we, intruders in this golden land
Ask only that you make us whole
Enrich our lives with your sure strength
Green peace and silver deep.

Christine Harper
when living in Llanfair Waterdine

Local Legends

Jimmy Briggs

Jimmy first came to Llanfair in about 1941. As far as we know he was from Leeds but when he arrived he had been working on the dams in the Elan Valley as a labourer. Everyone believed that he had run away from something but no one was ever to know what it was. He had a great deal of general knowledge, was fanatical about sport, especially boxing, and wrote in beautiful copper plate. He worked as a labourer on local farms and slept under hedges, in farm buildings or in old houses. Llanwoolley was a favoured place in summer as was Coed-y-Hendre Mill. In winter he made for the pigsty at The Runnis.

John Bevan kept a careful eye on him as he got older and for about the last five years of his life arranged for him to live in a residential home in the winter and a caravan at The Runnis in summer. Jimmy died from bronchitis at the age of 84 and is buried in Llanfair churchyard where a simple headstone reminds us all of a gentle man who lived in the parish for over 50 years.

The King of Llanwoolley

Llanwoolley has been the home of many 'characters' over the years. The 'King of Llanwoolley' who probably lived there at about the turn of the century got his title because he behaved as if he was above the law. It is said that he was a big man physically and he 'got away' with things because local people didn't like to annoy him. He kept two donkeys and used them to pick up sacks of swedes from his neighbours fields at night and bundles of hay and oats at harvest time.

Legend has it that he was allowed to take liberties because he had a temper and could bear a grudge. The neighbour who complained feared the loss of a hayrick or barn so decided a few swedes or a few sheaves of corn or the odd rabbit were a small price to pay for a peaceful life.

Giles Swancott

Jonathan Swancott

Big healthy men were unusual rather than the norm at the turn of the century and physical strength was appreciated.

Jonathan Swancott was a larger than life character who with his wife Anne lived at Cwm Collo. They had eleven children. He lived until the age of 82 and saw ten of his children and his wife die many years before him. His son Richard was the only son to live to old age. He bought Tregodfa and was the grandfather of Giles and Ben and their brothers and sisters.

Giles Swancott

Tug O'War

Joe Davies from Stoney Pound was another character and because of his strength and size had a running trial of strength with Walter Richards who lived at The Hordy. They would 'square up to' each other at regular intervals. They decided to settle their physical differences with a regular 'tug o'war' which took place near the Block Gate above Bryn Bedw and caused a great deal of animated discussion among local men in the early 1930s and perhaps the placing of the odd bet!

The Block Gate was a barrier across the lane which led from The Anchor to Selley Cross. It was either erected to collect tolls from people passing from the parishes of Llanfair to Bettws or

The position of 'The Block Gate'

Newcastle or as a barrier to people who might try to steal animals or crops in one parish and carry them to another. Legends extend to tales of highwaymen who owned horses which could jump the barrier. Along with many other areas of Britain local people tried to claim that Dick Turpin came to the area along with his famous horse Black Bess all the way from Yorkshire. The reason for this is probably because local people would enjoy the idea of the rich being held up by robbers who supported the poor and such stories were as popular in Llanfair as anywhere else.

Giles Swancott

Rights of Way

Horses were heroes especially to people who struggled to keep a working horse themselves. A horse which could jump over or remove a barrier would soon have star status!

George Cadwalader who lodged at what is now Lower Bryn Bedw used to take his horses up over the Hergin fields to graze at Stoney Pound. The owner of the Hergin land objected and chained up the gates. No doubt the landowner felt like many local farmers do now as they see people wandering around their fields! Mr. Cadwalader, not to be thwarted, tied his horses to the gates and removed them and their posts. Needless to say his preferred path is now walked as a 'right of way' with signs, gates and stiles erected by the Local Authority.

Giles Swancott

A Secret Message?

Many years ago while digging potatoes in a field near Llanwoolley I found parts of a brightly coloured glass necklace. Recently I met an expert in jewellery who told me that in late Victorian times young men who wanted to communicate romantic messages to girls they liked used to buy such necklaces. The beads were threaded in a certain order and the girl in question could, by knowing the code 'read' her admirer's 'note'.

Although part of my discovery was missing it was 'to Sarah ... from an admirer'. Sarah Price lived at Llanwoolley for many years. She lived with her two single brothers and never married, was the necklace addressed to her? Who sent it? These trinkets had the advantage of being translated by the people who sent and received them without their families or employers knowing the code.

I often wonder if she lost it or threw it away or perhaps the young man in question got cold feet and never sent it.

Anne Singleton

Part Six

Wildlife
Local Vocabulary
1999 Parish Survey
1999 The News

Wildlife

The wildlife of the area is a reason why some people choose to live here. We are extremely lucky to have such a variety of birds, plants and animals.

The children of the parish were given a questionnaire and asked to observe wildlife for a year. This proved to be too long a time span for most people. Rhys Williams from Lloyney did however write an interesting description of the woodpeckers which regularly visit his family garden. At first he saw just one greater spotted but over three years that one has introduced its mate to the garden and now the fledglings also join them. Recently a green woodpecker, although much more shy and difficult to observe, has also joined them.

Simon Haslem from Nottingham is well known to many local people. He first visited Knighton in 1976 and arrived in Llanfair in 1979 hoping to see buzzards. He writes:—

I first heard of Knighton in 1976 when I was told it was an excellent area to watch buzzards. I went there a few times for weekends and discovered Llanfair Waterdine in 1979 when I visited the parish to watch ravens. Since then I have stayed for many weekends, got to know a lot of local people, and observed a great deal of interesting bird life.

Buzzard

Barn Owl

One of the most interesting birds in the area is the raven. I love to watch them. Their pig-like grunts let you know where they are. You can see them in February nest building and also flying upside down which they do in the mating season. Although there are also many carrion crows and magpies in the area there tend to be even more over the border in Powys.

Llanfair is an excellent area to see Common Buzzards and I have actually counted as many as fifteen circling the Red Lion in Llanfair.

Other birds which are quite common locally are:

Great Spotted Woodpeckers, Robins, Redstarts – usually in June, Blackbirds, Pied Flycatchers, Long Tailed Tits, Rooks, Jays, Common Kestrels, Sparrow Hawks, the occasional Tawny Owl and Barn Owl, Pippits, Skylarks, Lapwings, Jackdaws, Housemartins, Swallows, Swifts, Spotted Flycatchers and Yellowhammers.

I still visit the area regularly and hope to do so for some time to come.

Wren

Birds not mentioned by Simon but seen regularly by local people include:

Heron	Whinchat	Pied Wagtail	Blue Tit
Mallard	Tree Sparrow	Chaffinch	Great Tit
Goosander	Wood Pigeon	Goldfinch	Marsh Tit
Red Kite	Collared Dove	Bullfinch	Nuthatch
Grey Partridge	Cuckoo	Redwing	Tree Creeper
Common Pheasant	Kingfisher	Fieldfare	Starling
Moorhen	Green Woodpecker	Songthrush	House Sparrow
Curlew	Lesser Spotted Woodpecker	Goldcrest	Coal Tit
Wren	Grey Wagtail	Willow Tit	Black Cap
Dunnock	Yellow Wagtail		

A Black stork spent 3 weeks here in August 1990 – a 'first-ever record' for both Shropshire and Radnorshire – it was notified by Dr. R. H. Townshend.

Kingfisher

Many parishes, Llanfair Waterdine among them, used to employ a man to kill sparrows. When corn was stored in ricks and in heaps in granaries thousands of sparrows used to descend on farm buildings and do a great deal of damage. In Llanfair parish there are now only two successful flocks of sparrows, one at Stoney Pound and one at Monaughty. There are smaller flocks around other houses and farms.

The Red Kite has been extinct in this area for some years but a feeding programme at Rhayader has encouraged them to breed there in recent years. They are occasionally seen in our valley. Ten were counted early in the summer of 1999 in a high thermal being 'swept along' in the direction of Offa's Dyke from the Quabbs.

Tawny Owl

Buzzards were quite rare when myxomatosis wiped out the rabbit population but they are now highly successful as is the Kestrel and the Sparrowhawk.

Moorhen, Lapwing, Duck, Curlew and Partridge numbers have declined dramatically in recent years. Badgers and foxes take the eggs of all ground nesting birds.

Pheasants spread into new areas from farms where they are reared for shooting.

Barn Owls used to be common but their numbers dropped as there were less hay barns. Several local people have put up nesting boxes and these are highly successful.

Skylark is still successful where there is gorse cover near Offa's Dyke and on The Turbary. Wrens, Song Thrushes and Long Tailed Tits are becoming more successful and Chaffinches, Blackbirds and Magpies are highly successful.

Nature Notes

Visitors often comment on the number of wild flowers which grow in this area. This is probably because there is little use of pesticides and grass verges are cut quite late to allow plants to seed down. I do think hedges are trimmed too early and too often wiping out berries and nuts which would sustain animals and birds in the winter.

Dormouse

Badgers

We have recently noticed that cowslips are making a return and we recently saw an Adders Tongue fern. Fungi are abundant and we have, in the past, identified 36 different species within a kilometre of our home.

We have seen all the mammals on the attached list and also a yellow necked mouse but never a dormouse.

Last year there were very few wasps and we found only one wasps' nest. Glowworms are also decreasing in numbers as are hedgehogs.

Polecats

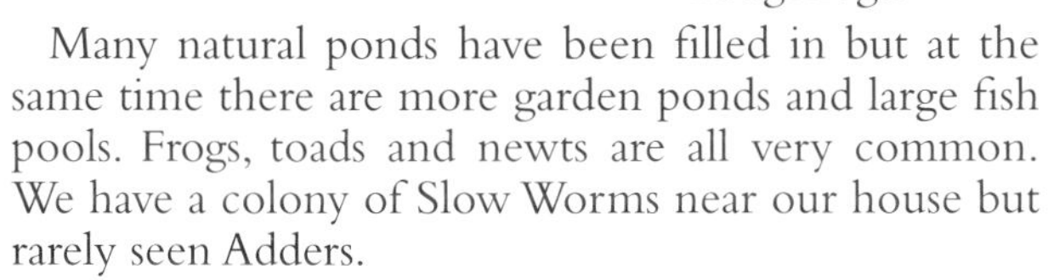

Many natural ponds have been filled in but at the same time there are more garden ponds and large fish pools. Frogs, toads and newts are all very common. We have a colony of Slow Worms near our house but rarely seen Adders.

We are particularly interested in bats and have found pipistrelle, natterers, long eared and Daubentons locally and lesser horseshoe in the next parish.

Birds which are declining nationally are doing quite well locally including: Skylark, Tree Sparrow, Barn Owl, Rook, Linnet, Heron, Kingfisher and Song Thrush. We also see Ravens and Red Kites. We have noticed recently that both Robins and Goldfinches have learned to feed from peanut feeders in the garden as has a woodmouse.

Vera Howard

Foxes

Hare

Butterfly

Comma
Common Blue
Dark Green Fritillary
Dingy Skipper
Gatekeeper
Green-veined White
High Brown Fritillary
Large Skipper
Large White
Meadow Brown
Orange Tip
Painted Lady
Peacock
Pearl-bordered Fritillary
Purple Hairstreak
Red Admiral
Ringlet
Silver-studded Blue
Small Copper
Small Heath
Small Pearl-bordered Fritillary
Small Skipper
Small Tortoiseshell
Small White
Wood White

Moths

Poplar Hawk Moth
Elephant Hawk Moth
Garden Tiger

Insects

Mayfly
Grasshopper
Southern Aeshna Dragonfly
Ruddy Darter
Common Blue Damselfly
Large Red Damselfly
Earwig
Sloe Bug
Pond Skater
Water Boatman
Water Beetle
Common Frog Hopper
Alderfly

Reptiles, Amphibians and Fish

Common Lizard
Slow Worm *becoming rare*
Grass Snake *becoming rare*
Adder
Newt
Common Frog
Common Toad
Eel
Loach
Trout
Bull Head or Millers Thumb

Ches Fly
House Fly
Bluebottle
Yellow Dung Fly
Drone Fly
Crane Fly
May Bug

and many, many others.

Mammals are much more easy to observe and include:

American Mink	Mole
Badger	Natterers Bat
Bank Vole	Noctule
Brown Hare	Otter
Brown Long Eared Bat	
Pipistrelle	
Brown Rat	Polecat
Common Shrew	
Pigmy Shrew	
Daubentons Bat	Rabbit
Field Vole	Stoat
Fox	Water Shrew
Grey Squirrel	Water Vole
Hedgehog	Weasel
House Mouse	Wood Mouse
Lesser Horseshoe Bat	

In recent years the hedgehog has almost disappeared. The badgers have, local people believe, almost wiped them out. The otter and polecat have made a dramatic comeback in recent years.

Local Flora

Bird's-foot trefoil
Black-grass
Vipers Bugloss
Charlock
Common Cow-wheat
Common Poppy
Common Stork's-bill agg.
Dove's-foot Crane's-bill
Fat-hen
Field Pansy
Field Penny-cress
Fool's Parsley
Hedge Mustard
Herb-Robert
Hop Trefoil
Lesser Trefoil
Little Mouse-ear
Scarlet Pimpernel
Shepherd's-purse
Silver Hair-grass
Small Nettle
Smooth Hawk's-beard
Yellow-rattle
Sow Thistle
Foxglove
Common Thistle
Garlic Mustard
Great Mullein
Greater Burdock
Harebell
Hemlock
Hogweed
Lambs Tongue
Nettle-leaved Bellflower
Scabious
Small Teasel
Welted Thistle
Wild Carrot
Red Shank
Cuckooflower
Curled Dock
Devil's-bit Scabious
False Oat-grass
Field Bindweed
Greater Bird's-foot-trefoil
Greater Celandine
Greater Plantain
Greater Stitchwort
Hairy Wood-rush
Hard-fern
Heath Bedstraw
Heath-grass
Hedge Woundwort
Lady's Bedstraw
Lady-fern
Male-fern
Meadow Crane's-bill
Meadow Fescue
Meadow Foxtail
Meadow Thistle
Meadow Vetchling
Mouse-ear-hawkweed
Mugwort
Flowering-rush
Fool's-water-cress
Marsh-marigold
Purple-loosestrife
Water-cress agg.
Woodruff

Barren Strawberry
Betony
Biting Stonecrop
Bloody Crane's-bill
Bog Pimpernel
Broad-leaved Dock
Cock's-foot
Common Bent
Common Bird's-foot-trefoil
Common Comfrey
Common Couch
Common Knapweed
Common Mallow
Common Mouse-ear Chickweed
Common Nettle
Common Ragwort
Common Sorrel
Common Toadflax
Cow Parsley
Creeping Bent
Creeping Soft-grass
Creeping Thistle
Crested Dog's-tail
Kidney Vetch
Mountain Pansy
Oxeye Daisy
Primrose
Rosebay Willowherb
Selfheal
Sneezewort
Sweet Violet
Wild Pansy

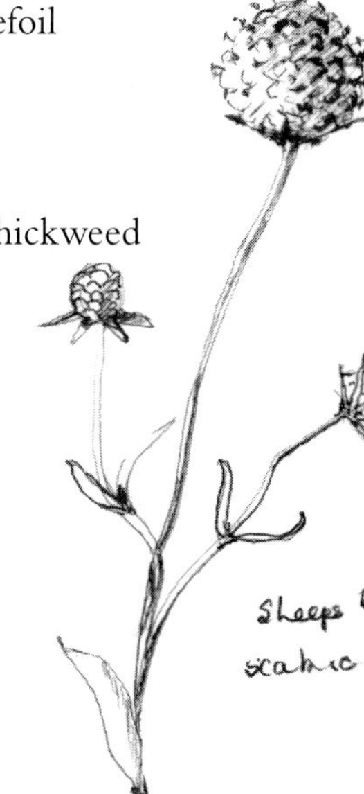

Wild Strawberry
Wood Anemone
Wood Sage
Yarrow
Yellow Archangel
Crab Apple
Elder
Guelder-rose
Hawthorn
Hazel
Holly
Osier
Spindle
Wild Privet
Yew
Common Cottongrass
Common Spike-rush
Wild Teasel
Hedge Bindweed
Honeysuckle
Hop
Ivy
Traveller's-joy
Bluebell
Common Spotted-orchid
Daffodil
Early Marsh-orchid
Enchanter's-nightshade
Field Horsetail
Heath Spotted-orchid
Lily-of-the-valley
Lords-and-Ladies
Meadow Saffron
Moschatel
Ramsons
White Bryony
Yellow Iris
Agrimony
Broad-leaved Willowberb
Bugle
Columbine
Common Dog-violet
Cowslip
Creeping-Jenny
Crosswort
Daisy
Germander Speedwell
Great Willowherb
Greater Spearwort
Ground-ivy
Deadly Nightshade 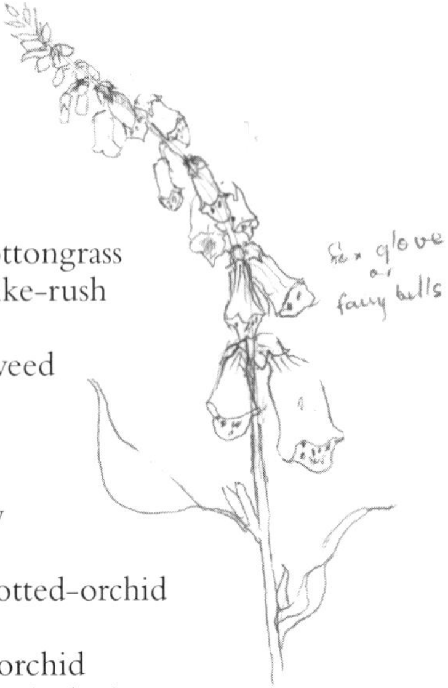 
Dog-rose agg.
Field-rose
Gooseberry
Gorse
Heather
Raspberry
Mountain flax
Alder
Ash
Aspen
Beech
Downy Birch
English Elm
Field Maple
Hornbeam
Pedunculate Oak
Rowan
Silver Birch
Small-leaved Lime
Wild Cherry
Wych Elm
Lambs Tongue
Cow Parsley
Common Rock-rose
Perennial Rye-grass
Quaking-grass
Ragged-Robin
Red Campion
Red Clover
Red Fescue
Rough Meadow-grass
Silverweed
Sweet Vernal-grass
Timothy agg.
Tormentil
Tufted Vetch
Water Mint
White Clover
Wild Thyme
Wood Dock
Wood Spurge
Wormwood
Yorkshire-fog
Zigzag Clover
Bell Heather
Bilberry
Bittersweet
Blackthorn
Bramble agg.
Broom
and many more!

Local Language

With the arrival of T.V. and transport, local language has given way to a national language often incorporating catch phrases from advertisements, songs and comedy shows. Our local vocabulary will gradually disappear. In 1970 the Radnorshire Federation of the W.I. produced a dictionary of local words. We also have phrases and words used in our own parishes. Some of you will recognise them all but some of the younger parishioners may know very few.

A.	affeared	–	afraid
	afore	–	before
	anunt	–	opposite – "The one anunt t'other"
	askel	–	adder, snake
	arm	–	to "arm" someone – to help him along by offering an arm
	anunst	–	up against, next to
	acting a tale	–	telling a story
	all	–	sometimes used as in "They ate the food all"
B.	bitahweddy	–	monotonous, tedious
	breach	–	a breach of folk, a lot of people
	biscake	–	biscuit
	biscaite	–	biscuit
	bullygullion	–	Bullhead, millers thumb (small fish)
	boch	–	to miss a small patch of grass when moving "That meadow is boched terrible"
	burden	–	a bundle (of sticks)
	boosey	–	cattle manger
	boughton	–	"boughton bread" – not home made
	brummock	–	short handled billhook
C.	caedrws	–	shut the door
	cowper	–	coffer or chest
	cag	–	tear "I have cagged my coat on the barbed wire"
	clemmed	–	famished, hungry "I be clemmed"
	chats	–	kindling, dry firewood
	couse	–	to chase or worry "His dog was cousing your sheep"
	cutch	–	1. mound in which potatoes are stored 2. a hare 3. a lie down 4. to cuddle up to
	crousty	–	bad tempered
	come	–	"I don't know what come to him" "I don't know what affected him"
D.	dunning	–	failing, nearly done for
	dytche	–	ditch
	dull	–	silly or stupid act or person
	doubt	–	used "he's gone to town I doubt" meaning "I know he's gone to tow
	dyern	–	eager, determined

Brynorgan

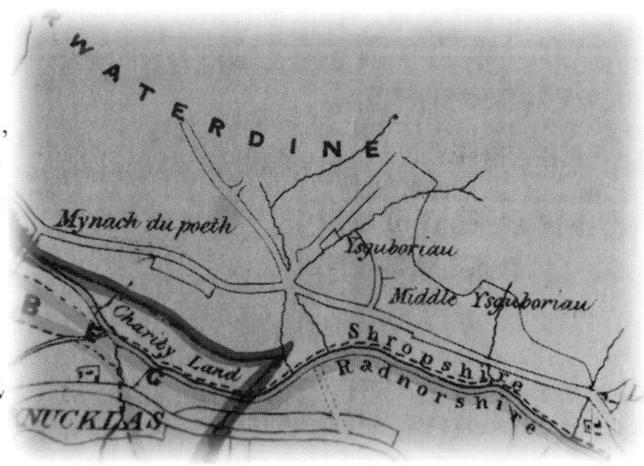

donst – beat "I'll donst thee"
done – "well done you"
dunna – don't
E. ean yean – give birth to
"Evening" – any time after middle of the day
edge of night – near darkness
every bit – ate it up every bit
everyone, every other – picking alternately
F. fled – flew – "The bird fled out and we lost 'un"
"full the house" or "full his hide" – full of himself, above himself, or healthy and fat
fastenment – door or gate fastener
flens – fleas
foul – ugly – "a foul man"
forret – early, forward
figairiment – predicament
fretchet – irritable, bad tempered, upset
feurn – bracken
feg – rough or dead grass
G. glat – a gap in the hedge
gyeland – a slight elevation – "The wheel went over the gyeland"
gambrel – a notched stick used to suspend a carcass
gammey, game – bad-ailing – He's got a gammey leg" or "He's got a game leg"
glemmy – sultry – "It's very glemmy weather"
gull, gullies – gosling
H. hauve – handle – "The axe hauve is broken"
hisht – "hush"
housing time – winter period when cattle are put indoors
hump – to carry
headland or addlands – border of field which is ploughed last of all
heft – I have any heft of those – a large amount or a large quantity
heady – brainy
hognel – stupid, pig headed
heathering – the long sticks used to top a hedge
hespel – to worry – "I won't be hespelled by him any longer"
I. Indisgestion – indigestion
J. Journ, jern, jeurn – energetic, keen, "workish"
jag – small load – "we'll fetch a bit of a jag in now"
K. kaid – bottle fed lamb
kank – a fit of temper "in a bit of a kank"
kilt – female salmon in the close season
kweeke – to squeeze
killsheep – a killsheep dog – a dog that worries sheep
kayle – faint, die – "He was almost kayling off"

L. lumper – young boy or lout
lamp – "I'll lamp him" – to beat
lief – "I would just as lief walk" – prefer to
lowcher – Davey Lowcher – a small worthless fish
linnd – flexible, supple
M. moither – rambling in speech
moithered – confused

middling – not very well
miawkin – a scarecrow
middleday – noon
mixen – dunghill
mutch, mitch – to play truant
moocher – a potato that is left in the ground and comes up in the wrong place next year
mye – hay – or to tread loose hay
mun – man – "How are you mun?"
mag – to worry, to henpeck
mex – clean out the cowshed
munna – mustn't
N. next to next – catch as it comes in turn – every one. every other
noise – keeping a noise – opposite to keeping quiet
nut – small – "That calf is a nut"
nid – wedge of wood
nip – to notch – "You have nipped the axe"
nish – tender, delicate
niscal – smallest pig in a litter or runt
noggin – a can of one or two quarts
O. ongo – going, in working order, fit, running
oont – a mole
oonty tump – mole hill
oas – to try – "The dog would not oas to work"
oolent – owl
orl – alder tree
P. pinsens – pinchers
pitch – steep bit of road
poon, pound – to hit or strike – "I'll poon him"
pikle – pitchfork
pishty – small dog
piert – in good health
piece – field – "tumpy piece"
pirish – being miserable
partly – used as practically – "I was partly there"
plock – a small piece of land

Q. qualm – seizure or a turn – "He had a qualm when he was working"
quench – appetite, thirst, taste – "He's lost his quench for it"
quist – wood pigeon
queeke – to squeeze
quell – to kill – "That goose will quell the gullies"

R. ross – moorland
reasty, raysty – bad, gone off, rancid
reen – open furrow between two patches of ploughed field
romily – rumpled, untidy
raip or hraip – a square piece of wood with a handle attached, used to whet a scythe
rack – a footpath

S. scoot – portion, patch, corner – "He has ploughed a good scoot this morning"
scutch – rubbish off cultivated land – "They are burning scutch"
scud – passing shower
snag – a ledge – "a snag of rock"
sollar – ceiling
soundly – "He gave my car soundly a bang" – a severe bang; "soundly of boozers" – heavy drinkers
sore – sad or bad – "It's a sore nuisance"
shape – "There's no shape on him" – he's not doing well
slike – smooth or slippery or shining
slaunch – slop or spill
squanog – a hare
shunna – shouldn't

T. twarly – troublesome
tidling – lamb fed by hand
trim – to scold
tidy – considerable number or good – "A tidy few was there"
theave – female lamb
three half year old – to describe a young animal that is one and a half years old
trouse – spare hedging material, used for filling "glats" in the hedge

U. urchin – hedgehog

V. very same – the same as

W. warmship – warmth from the fire
welter – "That's a welter" – that's a very fine specimen
woont – mole – woont-catcher
whitty, witty – Mountain Ash

Y. Yarp – to talk in a stupid way

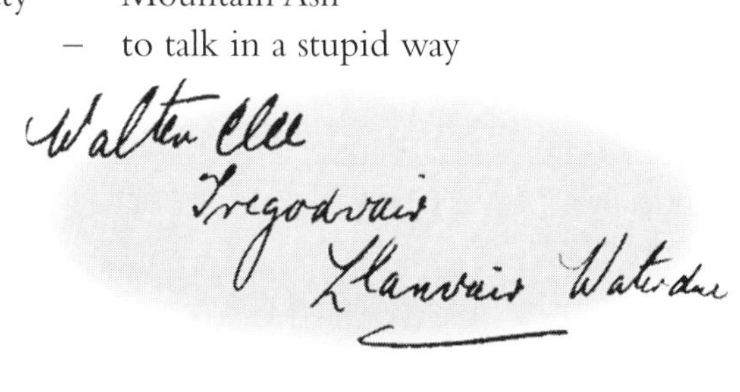

Sayings heard locally and local words.

Well done yon
Tender morning (lovely morning)
He's from off
I didn't know no aim what to say (was at an entire loss)
There's no heed to him (no telling what he is after)
It's summat odd good (very good)
I dunna mean to say no harm (to give offence)
To lap up (to wrap a parcel or fleece)
Yon munna say dunna, that inna right:
You shouldna say shunna, that inna polite.

chimbly – chimney	doost – dust
elder – udder	yow – ewe
in ean – in lamb	fild – field
fizzles – thistles	daince – dance
gorst – gorse	fe-ern – fern
homber – hammer	huck – hook
ornary – ordinary	ship – sheep
sprod – spread	ful – full
bruck – brook	fit – feet
bif – beef	wain – wagon
melk – milk	

I wunna (won't) go to school – you canna (can't) make me
There's tempest about (a storm brewing)
He dunna half pull his chops about – speaks rather well
He lives up ont the top of the town
How wist thee? – How are you?
Lord surry my auld corns be hurting I canno go just none
No place like the butt of your own smoke – no place like home
Do thee give the very top ha penny – for I have pock in hardship – pay the top price because I picked this fruit (for example wimberries) in the rain
Bist 'ee 'ired or bist ee staying on? (are you hired or are you looking for a job)
"How's the old ooman?" – How's the wife
"On less some" – fairly well
"Lord inna her as plain as a gate post/pike staff?" – not very good looking
Going down the street her was bouncing like a ball (jaunty)
Lord surry I feels reel ordinary (poorly, ill)
'Come bye' – get out of the way
Her wunna loose hold on him – she won't let him go
I feels real queer on times – I occasionally feel ill
There was used to be – there once was
How be you this long time? – Not seen you for a long time
He's chawling on a bit o' twist – he's chewing tobacco
She will be here now in a minute

He's as drunk as an old oolent (owl)
Her's pretty big sorted – haughty, proud
Her's gone pretty upperty since her went away from wum – home
Are there erra letters for me? – any
nurran – none
Where did you go last night? (No odds to you – not telling)
Her inna jannocil – straightforward

Local verse about school

Mr. Matkin is a kind old man
He tries to teach us all he can.
Writing, reading, 'rithmatic
He never forgets to use the stick.

When he does he makes us dance
Out of England into France
Out of France and into Spain
Then he brings us back again.

Mr Farmer the Blacksmith and later landlord of The Lloyney Inn then called the Builders Arms was known as Pun iron (pun-hit)

Mr. Hammond the Tailor – Stab rags

Many of these local sayings and words are those remembered by Mona Cadwalader who as Mona Hammond was the daughter of the Tailor at Lloyney.

Eleanor and William Hammond, the tailor ('Stab Rags'). Parents of Mona Cadwalader who lived in Lloyney.

The Llanfair Waterdine Parish Survey January 1999

The Llanfair Waterdine Millennium Committee was set up by the Parish Council in 1997 to consider how to mark the Millennium in the parish.

The Committee is made up of representatives from the Parish Council, the Parochial Church Council, the Everest Hall Committee, the WI, the Over 60s Group, the Children's group, + co-opted members. The Chairman of the Committee is Mrs. Morgan, Selley Hall.

The Committee decided to record in various ways the past, present and future of the parish as seen by the parishioners – a village self-portrait.

The project will include:

an audio tape about farming and our way of life, as it has changed throughout this century.

a village survey, (this questionnaire is a part of that survey).

a collection of present day and archive photographs.

research into Llanfair Waterdine's early history, before 1800.

an exhibition at the Wakes in August 2000.

This questionnaire is an essential part of our village self portrait.

Separately the Over 60s group will be publishing a book.

The Millennium Committee also plans a party and other activities to celebrate the year 2000.

The purposes of this questionnaire are two-fold:

1) To record facts about the parish and the views of the parishioners at the Millennium as a historical archive for future generations.
2) To assess parish needs, and bring forward proposals that may help us continue into the next Millennium as a healthy community.

Most of the questions can be answered simply yes or no, or with a number, or by circling or underlining the relevant answer (i.e. Q. Do you consider yourself *a holiday resident? an incomer? a local? or other description?*). If parts of the form do not apply to you please ignore them.

Hugh Colvin working on the Parish tape

If you want to comment or give details after your basic yes/no/numbers/choices answers *please do so. We welcome your comments.* All sections have a space at the bottom for this purpose, and you are welcome to continue on another sheet or on the blank pages of this questionnaire.

This form is anonymous. We are not asking for your names and addresses.

The survey results will be analysed by Hugh Colvin, (who doesn't know any of your handwriting!) with Andrew Beavan and in due course a summary will be published. When the results have been analysed the forms will be destroyed.

Some sections could lead to you wanting to give answers which would "blow" the anonymity of your answers to the rest of the questionnaire. For instance in the section on Work, you may want to let us know that you want to offer or need childcare, or help with the elderly. In this case please tell Mrs. Morgan or Anne Singleton your personal details, but do not write them on this form. In all cases where you wish to give personal information as a follow-up to answering this questionnaire please contact Mrs. Morgan or Anne Singleton.

Please return this form to Hugh Colvin, or to any member of the Committee, by March 1st 99. An addressed envelope is enclosed.

If you have any queries about this form or you want more copies contact: Hugh Colvin, Mrs. Morgan or Anne Singleton.

The project is supported by grants from Shropshire County Council Arts Services, and from its Economic Development dept., by South Shropshire District Council, Rural Challenge, Leader 2 Clun Valley, Rural Arts in Action, Rural Action on the Environment and the Shropshire Hills and Dales project.

How many parishioners are you speaking for when you fill in this form?

1. over the age of 18 ....

2. under the age of 18 ....

Is only one member of a household filling in this form on behalf of the whole household? ***Yes / No***

Sections:

1. Household details. 2. Work. 3. Housing and public buildings. 4. Transport and Roads. 5. Children up to 11 yrs of age. 6. Young people. 7. Over 60s. 8. For everyone 9. The Countryside. 10. Community, recreation and social life. 11. Everest Hall. 12. Heritage. 13. Local services. 14. Local government. 15. Finally!

1. Household details.

If two or more members of a household are filling in questionnaires please could only one person from each household fill in this particular section.

How many people live in your house? ....

How many Men? .... *How many Women?* .... *How many children?* ....

Please give number of people in your household within each age bracket.

0–5: .... 5–11: .... 11–20: ....21–30: ....31–40: ....

41–50: ....51–60: ....60–70: ....70–80: ....80+: ....

Roughly how long has each member of your household lived in the parish?

.............Years, ...Yrs, ...Yrs, ...Yrs, ...Yrs,

.............Yrs, ...Yrs, ...Yrs, ...Yrs.

How many of the people living in your household were born or raised:

In the parish? .... *Within 20 miles?* .... *Within 50 miles?* .... *Further off?* ....

Do you consider yourself *a holiday resident, an incomer, a local or other description?*

Other Description ....

If your children grew up in the parish, have they moved out of the Parish when grown up?

Yes/No/Both

How many children have stayed in the parish?

How many live *within 20 miles?* .... *within 50?* .... *Further off* ....

If your children are living with you how many are:

at Primary school? .... *Secondary?* .... *College?* .... *or are grown up?* ....

2. Work

Are you *employed / self-employed / retired?*
Other? (Details) ....
If you wish: please tell us the nature of your work (optional answer)
....

Do you work in the parish? *Yes / No*
Do you provide work for other people? *Yes / No*
Would you be interested in starting your own business? *Yes / No*
If so do you know about grants and help which is available? *Yes / No*

What kinds of business do you think are suitable to our parish? (other than farming)
Details ....
....

What services could you offer, either professionally, or as a volunteer to the parish?
Details ....
....

Would you consider offering childcare to others? *Yes / No*
Would you consider offering paid care to an elderly person? *Yes / No*
If you are elderly or housebound would you like to receive help? *Yes / No*

What kind of help is needed?
Details ....
....

Could you provide help of any kind?
Details ....
....

To let us know that you want to offer or need childcare, or help with the elderly, please tell Mrs. Morgan or Anne Singleton your personal details, but do not write them on this form otherwise your anonymity in answering the rest of the questionnaire will be blown! Any comments or suggestions related to this section: (Please continue on another sheet if required)

3. Buildings and Housing

Do you *rent? lease? own your home? or is it a tied cottage?*
Underline or ring your choice

Do you live *with your parents?* or: Do your parents *live with you?*

Is anyone in your household likely to need a house of their own in the next 2–3 years?
Yes / No *Details* ....

Would you prefer this to be in Llanfair parish? Yes / No.

Do you think more houses should be built in the parish? Yes / No.

Of what sort? *Underline or ring your choice(s) and/or give details below.*
Retirement? Starter homes? Housing association? Family? 2 bed? 3 bed? 4 bed? for rent? for owning?
Details ....

....

How many? (over the next 10 years.) ....

Where should any building take place?
In the village centre? near existing farms/ hamlets? Elsewhere?
Underline or ring your choice(s) and/or give details below.
Details ....

....

What other new buildings or alterations to buildings or changes of use do we need – if any? (e.g. Everest Hall extension or flexible internal partitioning, additional uses for the church etc...)
Details ....

....

Near the bus stop at Lloyney

4. Transport and Roads

Does your household have a car? *Yes / No.*
If so how many? ....

If not how do you travel to Knighton?
Underline or ring your choice(s)
Foot? Bicycle? Bus? Rail? Taxi?
Lift from neighbours?

When you go further afield how do you travel? *Underline or ring your choice(s).*
Foot? Bicycle? Your own car? Bus? Rail? Taxi?
Lift from neighbours.

What are your usual destinations other than Knighton? *Underline or ring your choice(s).*
Ludlow? Shrewsbury? Clun/Bishop's Castle? Presteigne/Kington? Newtown/Welshpool?
Builth/Llandrindod Wells? Hereford? Other: ....

If public transport was available would you use it? *Yes / No*
How often? *Daily? Weekly? Occassionally?*
At what time of day? *Depart* .... *Return*..............................

For what purpose would you use public transport if it were available?
School? College? Work? Shopping? Social?

Which of the following would you like to see as public transport?
Dial-a ride? regular Bus service? Neighbours scheme?
(i.e. Ring central ansaphone number to say when you're offering lifts to where and/or to get information on who else might need a lift or be offering a lift.)

Do you feel any of the roads in the parish need repair? *Yes / No*
If so which?
Details ....
....

Is sign posting in the village adequate? *Yes / No*
If No, what needs to be done? (e.g. where is there a particular problem?)
Details ....
....

Do you think there should be a speed limit in the village? *Yes / No*
What should the limit be? .... And where? ....
Details ....
....

Is gritting in winter adequate? *Yes / No*
Should any more of the roads in the village be singled out for gritting or grit piles?
Details ....
....

What other measures could be taken to increase safety on our roads?
Details ....
....

5. Primary school Children

If you have primary school age children how many attend:
Beguildy School? *Newcastle School?* *Knighton School?* *Clun School?* *Other?*
(Optional) Details ....

As the children in the parish attend different schools is it important that they meet socially on a regular basis? *Yes / No*
Do they meet often enough? *Yes / No*
Do you take your children to the special church services? *Yes / No*
Do you take your children to the Everest hall when there is an event suitable for them? *Yes / No*

Please list the good things about bringing up children in the parish.
Underline or ring your choice(s) or please make your own suggestions:
Safe. Relaxed. Unpolluted. Free from urban bad behaviour. Free from commercial pressures. Space. Fresh air. Natural environment. Other.
Details ....
....

Any comments or suggestions:

6. Young People

If there are young people in your household age between 11 and 21 could they answer the following?

What do you think of the social and other facilities on offer in the area (not just in Llanfair) for young people?

Underline or ring your choice(s): Very Good, Good. Adequate, Poor, Very Poor, Non-existent.

Would you like to see more facilities available in the parish? *Yes / No*

What would you suggest? ....

What do you think are the advantages and disadvantages of living where you do?

7. People over 60

The parish has no special facilities for the over 60s. Are you happy with this? *Yes / No*

What facilities would you like to see introduced?

Details ....

....

Transport is often a problem for the elderly. Is this the case for you? *Yes / No*

How can this be overcome?

Details ....

....

Do you use home care/ home help services? *Yes / No*

Are these easy to obtain? *Yes / No*

Are you happy about the emergency services? *Yes / No*

Details ....

....

Are you happy about the Health service provision? (eg Hospitals, the local Doctors Surgery, the Dentist Surgery) *Yes / No*

What is wrong with them?

Details ....

....

Any comments or suggestions?

8. Everyone

What do you think are the advantages and disadvantages of living in Llanfair?

9. The Countryside

For this section only, please say whether you are answering on behalf of a farming household.
Farming / Non-farming

Is the beauty of the landscape in the parish important to you? *Yes / No*

The parish is very rich in wildlife. Are the numbers of wildflowers, birds, animals etc in the parish important to you? *Yes / No*

Was it a good idea that the River Teme was declared an SSSI?
(Site of Special Scientific interest) *Yes / No*

Doe the ESA (Environmental Sensitive Area) scheme make a valuable contribution to keeping our traditional landscape? *Yes / No*

If you "come from off," was the quality of the landscape an important reason for you settling here? *Yes / No*

The ESA scheme and other measures are designed to keep the landscape traditional, some might say to stop the clock. Do you think this is a good idea? *Yes / No*

Do you think farming subsidies give the tax-paying public the right to access to the countryside, or the right to limit what farmers can do on their own land? *Yes / No*

Do townspeople understand the countryside? *Yes / No*

Should fox-hunting with hounds be banned? *Yes / No*

Should badgers be culled? *Yes / No*

Many paths have recently been designated as public footpaths and bridleways and signposted. Is this a good thing? *Yes / No*

Do you use footpaths for work? *Yes / No*

– for recreation? *Yes / No*

Do you use footpaths in other parishes? *Yes / No*

Do you object to potential 4 x 4 leisure use of bridleways? *Yes / No*

Should farmers be subsidised as the conservation guardians/ curators of the countryside? *Yes / No*

Do you think subsidies for food production should be abandoned? *Yes / No*

Many farms in other areas have become rural and part-time retreats for hobby farmers, rich businessmen etc. and some signs of this can already be seen a few miles away around Clun. In other areas food production is no longer as important an activity in the countryside as it was, and farming families have ceased to be the most important group in community life. Is this the future of the area? The Theme valley? a mixture of conservation/tourist minded farms and private mini-estates for ex-townspeople and weekenders?
What is your prediction for the future?

Is the current farming crisis likely to change our way of life? *Yes / No*

How? And what ways forward for farming can you see?

Not all foxes were hunted! 1902

10. Community. Recreation and Social Life

Do you prefer to think of yourself as:

English? Welsh? as (in the nicest possible way!) an incomer? or as "from the Borders"? or another description? Underline or ring your choice or give another description:

....

Do you consider yourself part of Llanfair Waterdine parish? *Yes / No*

The parish population has declined by 60% in the last 100 years. In the absence of a Llanfair school, and with lower church attendance compared to then, is Llanfair the centre for your community life? *Yes / No*

Where else do you look for your community life?

....

How can we reinforce our community life?

....

....

....

Social functions are organised by:

the WI, the church, the Village Hall Committee, the pub, other groups.

Which do you usually attend? *Underline or ring your choice(s) and give further details if you wish:*

....

....

What sporting, arts, cultural, historical, conservation, farming, or other event, meeting, club, class, lecture, entertainment activity would you attend that doesn't exist now?

....

....

Because of our small numbers we cannot support team games like football or cricket. Could you suggest a new sporting activity which might encourage people to get together regularly?

....

Would you be willing to help run an arts, cultural or sporting event, meeting, club, class, league activity. *Yes / No*

If yes what your activity would involve – where, who, how and how many?

....

Why are there so few people in the parish aged between the ages of 20 and 40?

And can anything be done to rectify the situation?

....

....

....

Which types of visitors / visiting activity, if any, should we encourage:
tourism? b&b guests? campers? horse-riders and walkers? or should we: *keep quiet about Llanfair? Underline or ring your choice(s).* And how?

....

Are there any activities we should discourage? *weekenders? campers? caravanners? walkers? horse-riders? motor sports? hunting? shooting? other (describe)*

....

Underline or ring your choice or describe.
How should we discourage these activities?

....

....

....

Should Llanfair go in for a new special event to "raise its profile"? *Yes / No*
If so, what?

....

....

Should Llanfair have any special extra event to bring the community together? *Yes / No*
If so, what?

....

....

Any comments and suggestions

11. Everest Hall and the Church

How often do you visit the hall per year? Underline or ring your choice
Not at all 1–5 times 5–10 times 10–25 times 25–50 times 50 + times

Are you happy with the facilities offered? *Yes / No*

When we last did a questionnaire we asked whether you would be interested in having access to a computer or learning IT skills. If this became available would you be interested? *Yes / No*

What types of use would you want from the computer?
Word processing Accountancy/Book-keeping Internet access E-mail FAX Printing Publishing Photography and Graphics CAD (Architecture/Engineering design packages) Audio and Music processing Video Processing Animation Computer Games Scanner CDROM use CD printing. These are all now affordable but many of these options aren't available at Bishop's Castle or Newcastle. *Underline or ring your choice(s) and give details if you wish:*

....

How often would you use a computer if there was access and training? ....
Does the Hall need an extra room (for computer(s), archives, smaller meetings) *Yes / No*
What improvements or extra facilities would you like to see?
Details ....
....

What events do you attend?
Details ....
....

Have you booked the hall yourself in the last 3 years? *Yes / No*
How often do you visit the church per year? Underline or ring your choice
Not at all 1– 5 times 5–10 times 10–25 times 25–50 times 50 + times
Do you think it will still be in use as a church in 100 years' time?. *Yes / No*
Could the church be used for anything else as well as for services and concerts? *Yes / No*
What? ....
....

Any comments or suggestions

12. Heritage

Which are the buildings in the parish which should be looked after for future generations?
....
....

Which are the other features of the parish (other than buildings) which should be looked after for future generations? *The landscape the woods the Teme archaeological sites Offa's Dyke other. Underline or ring your choice, and/or give details of "other":* ....

Would you be interested in an archive of local historical material stored locally? *Yes / No*
Any comments or suggestions? (cont. on next page)

[12 Heritage continued]

[Any comments or suggestions? (continued)]

13 Local Services:

Do you use *Beguildy Shop/Post Office?* *Yes / No*

Knucklas part-time Post Office *Yes / No*

Do you use the travelling Library *Yes / No*

Do you use the Library in the Village Hall *Yes / No*

Do you know about the Knighton Community car scheme? *Yes / No*

Have you ever used it? *Yes / No*

Do you go to the Cinema? *Yes / No*

Where and how often (per year)? ....

Do you go to: *festivals, concerts, sports events, drama productions, discos, book clubs, adult classes, other. Underline or ring your choice(s) and give details if you wish:* (what? where? and how often?)

....

If we had a recycling scheme would you use it? *Yes / No*

Would you be prepared to take material to a central point? *Yes / No*

Have you needed to contact the police in the last 3 years? *Yes / No*

Were the police's responses to your needs satisfactory? *Yes / No*

What local services do we lack?

Details ....

....

What services need improving and how? (see list at top of this section)

Details ....

....

What services are you satisfied with?

....

Any comments or suggestions?

14. Local Government

Do you know who our Parish councillors are? *Yes / No*
Do you know what the Parish Council's responsibilities, powers and budget are? *Yes / No*
Do you know who our District councillor is? *Yes / No*
Do you know what the District Council's responsibilities, powers and budget are? *Yes / No*
Do you know who our County Councillor is? *Yes / No*
Do you know what the County Council's responsibilities, powers and budget are? *Yes / No*
Would you like your parish, district and county representatives to
come and explain their responsibilities to us? *Yes / No*
Does the Parish Council represent your views and interests? *Yes / No*
If not what should it be doing?
Details ....

....

Are planning controls and procedures adequate? *Yes / No*
Is enough information made available about planning proposals? *Yes / No*
Do you know what the County Structure Plan Revision proposes for Llanfair? *Yes / No*
If not, would you like to know? *Yes / No*
Should there be planning restraints on:
- hedge removal? *Yes / No*
- tree preservation? *Yes / No*
- new farm buildings? *Yes / No*
- large scale forestry? *Yes / No*
- historic buildings, archaeological sites and on landscape? *Yes / No*

Are Local Authorities sufficiently responsive in planning, environmental, schools highways etc, matters? *Yes / No*
If not who should be doing what?
Details ....

Any comments or suggestions?

15. Finally!

Would you like to take part in a debate about some of the issues that have been raised and about some of the facts and views that will come out of this survey, after it has been published? *Yes / No*

Please return this form to Hugh Colvin, by the 1st of March or to a member of the Committee. (Even if you have not completed some sections of the questionnaire)

An addressed envelope is enclosed.

Thank you for your help in filling out this form.
A summary of the results will be published and distributed to each household.

The LlanfairWaterdine Millennium Survey

This survey was carried out during 1999 in order to assess current parish needs, and to record facts about the parish, and the views of the parishioners at this date as a historical record for posterity. Half of Llanfair's 100-odd households replied, representing roughly two-thirds of Llanfair's population. This was a great effort, particularly since it was such a long questionnaire. Thank you. Nobody answered every question in every section, so the results in any particular section do not add up to 100%. Some questions were dropped because of insufficient answers.

A lot of the material we received was in the form of written-in extra comments. Where several write-in comments made roughly the same point we have amalgamated their views.

A few questions / answers are now in different sections from the original questionnaire.

Selected comments are attached to some sections: These have been chosen for their individuality, interest and variety and not because they represent a majority view.

1. Household details. The average parishioner is **46**, and lives in a **2** person household. The balance of men and women is equal. Slightly more of us belong to farming households than non-farming. More than half come "from off." There are few children compared with the national average and the majority belong to incoming families. Very few 20–30 year olds live here.

2. Work. 50 people were self-employed, and **9** were employed. **38** of these worked in the parish. Apart from farming the most suitable businesses for the parish were thought to be small workshop/ home-based, computer, arts/ crafts, light engineering & tourism.

3. Buildings and Housing. 96% owned their own homes. **36%** thought there should be more homes built with **24%** opposed. **34%** favoured any new houses being scattered throughout the parish as against **14%** wanting them in the village centre. Most favoured family & starter homes.

4. Transport. Roads and Road Safety This section produced a lot of write-in comment **94%** of respondents owned their own car, and **2%** did not. **72%** travelled everywhere by car.

The most popular destination outside the area was Ludlow (**70%**).

32% said they would use public transport if available. **52%** wouldn't. **68%** said the roads needed repair. **52%** wanted better gritting. **74%** thought signposting adequate. **44%** wanted a speed limit in the village centre with **32%** opposed. **34%** commented that more drain and gulley clearance would substantially reduce water and frost damage to roads. Many replies deplored the loss of "lengthmen." *Selected comments: Keep potholes – automatically slows down speeds! Less drink to be taken.*

5. Children: 30% replied. There was strong agreement that the children need to meet and that the youth club was answering that need well. Llanfair was seen as a good place to bring up children.

6. Young People: The few replies said they were too far away from friends but they liked the countryside.

7. People over 60: 41 respondents gave their ages as 60 +. **62%** of them were happy with the (lack of) facilities for the elderly in Llanfair and almost all had no problem with transport. Roughly **25%** made comments about poor emergency services reponse times. Most were happy with their doctors, but dentists were criticised. *Selected comment: Emergency services should carry maps; they get lost answering 999 calls.*

8. Everyone: The advantages and disadvantages of living in Llanfair.

Roughly **40%** mentioned the peace, remoteness and beauty of the area and also the community spirit in the parish. The disadvantages of living here centred round isolation (around **12%**) – individual social isolation, physical remoteness from services, and an inward-looking community.

Selected comment: Can't have it both ways! Disadvantages of lack of swift access to medical services and entertainment are consequence of the advantages of living here.

9. The Countryside: This section provoked by far the most comment. **96%** filled it in. Replies were divided between **21 Farming Households** representing **56** people and **27 Non-Farming Households** representing **52** people. The on-farm and the non-farm "votes" were roughly in agreement on almost all issues although non-farm households were generally more heavily in favour of footpaths and on some conservation issues. The two groups disagreed only on fox-hunting and on the effect of the current farming crisis. Amongst the very wide variety of write-in views there were some common themes. There were several suggestions that conservation, and the production/marketting of quality and/or organic food were two potential ways forward for farming: There was also a view that for better or for worse farms would increase in size, and that livestock farming was essential for the preservation of our countryside. There was a strong feeling against the area becoming a part-time retreat for hobby farmers, rich businessmen etc.

90% of all replies valued the beauty of the landscape and the wildlife. **48%** said they came "from off" and that the quality of the landscape had been an important reason for settling here.

92% approved of the ESA scheme as protecting the landscape.

76% approved of the SSSI status of the Teme.

50% did not think farming subsidies gave the tax-paying public the right to access to the countryside, or the right to limit what farmers can do on their own land. **24%** did.

82% thought townspeople did not understand the countryside.

Fox-hunting: Overall: **54%** thought hunting with hounds shouldn't be banned with **30%** opposed.

Farmers voted **8 to 1** for hunting. Non-farmers voted **13 to 11** against.

62% supported the badger cull **18%** opposed it.

68% approved the recent signposting of public footpaths and bridleways, **24%** didn't. Slightly over **50%** used footpaths for recreation. **84%** objected to 4x4 leisure use of green lanes.

62% thought farmers should be subsidised as conservation guardians/curators of the countryside.

50% thought food production subsidies should not be abandoned. 18% disagreed.

36% thought the current farming crisis was likely to change our way of life with **24%** disagreeing. Farmers (**4:1 for**) and non-farmers (**2:1 against**) were at odds on this question.

Selected comment: "Walt Disney has a lot to answer for!"

10. Community. Recreation and Social Life

50% thought of themselves as English, **20%** said "from the borders," **12%** said Welsh, **8%** British, with single households saying European, Anglo-Welsh, half-Welsh and Hybrid.

50% said they were "locals", **24%** said they were "incomers".

Almost everybody felt they belonged to Llanfair. **60%** said it was the centre of their community life, whilst **30%** said it was not the centre of their community life.

40–50% said they attended WI, Church, Everest Hall and Pub events..

40% blamed our population gap – the missing 20–30 yr olds – on the lack of employment. *Selected comment: It's right that they go off & get further education & spread their wings. Some will return.*

Around **one third** of respondents thought various types of holiday visitors should be encouraged whilst another **one third** thought we should keep quiet about Llanfair.

The largest single vote in this section (**40%**) was to discourage visitors involved in motor sports. **60%** with only **6%** opposing were against having an event to raise the profile of Llanfair.

Selected comments: We should not encourage tourists too much or the attractive character of the parish will change. They destroy what they come to see. Townees think the countryside is an empty place, Liberty hall, so they abuse it, but we welcome those who take the trouble to educate themselves about rural life.

11. Everest Hall and the Church:

70% attended Church. **38%** said the church would still be used for worship in 100 years' time with **20%** thinking not. A majority of **34% to 20%** oppose the use of the church for anything else.

86% visited the Everest Hall at least once a year. **56%** are happy with the Hall's facilities. **42%** want an extra room. **18%** don't. **44%** want access to computers. **36%** don't. *Selected comment: Church = Spiritual centre of village, Pub = Body centre, Hall = Mind: adds up to whole people.*

12. Heritage:

The church and the pub were thought the most important buildings in the village to preserve with the Everest Hall a distant third.

75–80% thought the landscape, the woods, the Teme and the Dyke worthy of preservation with **54%** thinking our archaeological sites important. **50%** wanted a local archive.

13. Local Services:

By majorities of about **2 to 1** people DIDN'T use the Beguildy Shop, the Knucklas PO, or the 2 Libraries, or know about the Knighton Community Car Scheme. Only 2 households had ever used the latter. Half of us go to the cinema, half of us don't. **58%** go to concerts. **40%** go to drama, **30%** go to festivals and to adult classes. **28%** go to sports events.

Around **75%** of us would take material to a recycling point in the village if there was one. **24%** of households had had to call the police in the last 3 years, and less than half of them were satisfied with the results. *Selected comment: We should get together to do more for the village ourselves and less through hand-outs.*

14. Local Government

56% of Parish households know who their parish councillors are, **30%** don't. But after that!...

2 out of 3 parishioners do not know what the PC, the District or the County Council's powers, responsiblities and budgets are, and don't know who their District and County councillors are. **56%** would like our representatives to come in person and tell us who they are and what they do. **64%** of us dont know what is in the Llanfair part of the County Structure Plan.

70% – 80% wanted planning controls on hedge removal, tree preservation, large-scale forestry, new farm buildings and on historic buildings, archaeological sites and the landscape, with **6–10%** opposed.

10% were criticial of the PC through write-in comments.

Selected comment: PC should co-opt people who aren't farmers when next there are vacancies.

15.

50% would like to take part in a debate about some of the issues that have been raised and about some of the facts and views that will come out of this survey, after it has been published.

Detailed Results and Comments.

No question was answered by everyone, so no individual answer adds up to 100%.

To work out a rough "vote" on any issue, multiply the number of households voting by 2. (e.g. if 15 households wanted a steam railway service then that's a 30 % vote in favour.)

In the detailed statistics we have given the number of households + the number of people that that represents, so as to give the clearest possible information about your answers. Where only one or two households have taken a particular point of view we've left out the numbers of people represented as this could lead to identification of the households.

Section 1.

Household details. There were **44 men 43 women 21 children**
There were **12** people in **1** person households. **40** people in **20 x 2** person h'holds. **15** people in **5 x 3** person h'holds. **20** people in **5 x 4** person h'holds. **10** people in **2 x 5** person h'holds.

Number of people in the parish within each age bracket.

0–5 **1** *5–11* **12** *11–20* **13** *21–30* **3** *31–40* **14**
41–50 **11** *51–60* **16** *60–70* **20** *70–80* **19** *80+* **2**

The Average Age is **46**.

There are: **85 people** *over 21,* **26 people** *under 21,* **54 people** *under 50,* **57 people** *over 50.*

Roughlv how long has each member of your household lived in the parish?

60+Years **12** *50+Years* **5** *40 Years* **6** *30 Years* **13**
20+Years **5** *10+Years* **20** *0–10 Years* **24**

41 respondents have lived here more than 20 years, **44** less than 20 years.

How many of the people in the parish were born or raised:
in the parish? **41** *within 20 miles?* **9** *within 50?* **4** *further off?* **53**

People born or raised within 20 miles of Llanfair are slighly outnumbered by people "from off."

Children in the parish from families with 1 or more parent raised in the parish: **3 h'holds with 9 children**

Children with parents both of whom come from outside the parish **7 h'holds with 13 children**

How many grown up children have:
Stayed in the parish? **8** *Within 20 miles?* **11** *Within 50?* **8** *Further off* **16**

If your children are living with you how many are?
Pre-school **1** *At Primary school?* **5** *Secondary* **5** *College* **2** *Grown up* **11**

2. Work:

50 respondents are *self-employed* **9** are *employed* **27** are *retired.*
Other answers were *Housewife* **1** *Voluntary Workers* **5** *College* **1**
Do you work in the parish? *Yes* **38** *No* **19**
Do you provide work for other people?
Yes **15 h'hds rep. 26 people** No **10 h'hds rep. 20 people**

What kinds of business do you think are suitable to our parish?(apart from Farming)
Arts and crafts **6 h'hds rep. 16 people**
Computer based **5 h'hds rep. 12 people**
Small w'shops in redundant farm buildings **6 h'hds rep. 11**
Shop/PO **3 h'hds rep. 4.** *with local organic produce,* **2h'hds rep. 3 people**.
Tourism **3 h'hds rep. 6 people**

Home-based **2 h'hds**
Building **2 h'hds 1 h'hd each**
Any that don't cause excess traffic, noise, pollution After school education. Nursery NB Films made here. Outdoor activity holidays, Caravanning, Rural skills training Motocross/grass track Agricultural contracting & mechanical Holidays Recreation

3. Buildings and Housing.

48 h'hds rep. 109 people *own their own home.*
Households with grown up children and parents together. **3h'hd**s
Is anyone in your household likely to need a house of their own in the next 2–3 years?
Yes **1 h'hd** *Would you prefer this to be in Llanfair parish? Yes* **1 h'hd**
Do you think more houses should be built in the parish?
Yes **18 h'hds rep 40 people** *No* **12 h'hds rep 25 people**
Of what sort? *Retirement,* **3 h'hds** *Starter homes,* **11 h'hds rep 26 people**
Housing association, **3h'hds rep 5 people** *Family,* **8 h'hds rep 18 people**
2 bed, **3 h'hds rep 6 people** *3 bed,* **9 h'hds rep 19 people** *4 bed,* **4 h'hds rep 12 people**
Private build **1 h'hd** *for Rent,* **9 h'hds rep 24 people** *for Owning?* **10 h'hds rep 26 people**
Not large executive homes only affordable by wealthy retired people **1 h'hd**
How many? (over the next 10 years)
5–10 **8 h'hds rep 20 people** *10–20* **5 h'hds rep 16 people**
Where should any building take place?
In the village centre? **7 h'hds rep 18 people**
Near existing farms / hamlets; where there have been houses before / on farms in traditional materials/style with original names **17 h'hds rep 42 people**
2 h'hds each *Location is less important than design! and appearance. Some individual ones, no large groups. Comments:* **1 h'hd each** *Small cluster. NO more houses, that's what's special about LLW. Expand the village centre on all sides. Prefer resident home-owners to holiday home-owners. New homes would be for retirees or for those working away since no work in parish. Queried problems of transport, additional traffic and work opportunities if new homes built. Given local job situation adequate houses already on market.*

4. Transport and Roads:

Does your household have a car? *Yes* **47 households**, *No* **1 h'hld**
How many? *1 car,* **25 h'hds** *2 cars,* **19 h'hds** *3 cars,* **2 h'hds** *4 cars* **1 h'hd**
If not how do you travel to Knighton? Taxi / Lift from neighbours **1 h'hld**
When you go further afield how do you travel?
Your own car, **36 h'hds rep. 75 people** *Bus,* **1 H'hld** *Taxi* **2 h'hds**
Rail, **14 h'hds rep. 25 people** *Lift from neighbours.* **2 h'hds**
What are your usual destinations other than Knighton?
Ludlow, **35 h'hds rep. 72 people** *Shrewsbury,* **25 h'hds rep. 53 people**
Clun/Bishop's Castle, **20 h'hds rep. 50 people** *Presteigne/Kington,* **18 h'hds rep. 39 people**
Newtown/Welshpool, **25 h'hds rep. 58 people** *Builth/Llandrindod Wells,* **8 h'hds rep. 19**
Hereford. **29 h'hds rep. 57 people**
If public transport was available would you use it?
Yes **16 h'hds rep. 33 people** *No* **26 h'hds rep. 60 people**
How often? Weekly **3 h'hds rep. 10 people** *Occasionally* **14 h'hds rep. 25 people**
At what time? *Depart. 9 / 9.30 / 10 am* **9 h'hds rep. 16 people**
Return am **2 h'hds rep. 3 people** *3 / 4.30 / 5 / 5.30 pm* **7 h'hds rep. 13 people**
For what purpose would you use public transport if it were available?

School **1 h'hd** *College* **3 h'hds rep. 12 people** *Work* **1 h'hd**
Shopping **17h'hds rep. 36 people** *Social* **11 h'hds rep. 28 people**
Which of the following would you like to see as public transport?
Dial-a ride **7 h'hds rep. 14 people** *Regular Bus service* **8 h'hds rep. 19 people**
Neighbours scheme **14 h'hds rep. 32 people**

Do any village roads need repair Yes **32 h'hds rep. 58 people** *No* **5 h'hds rep. 13 people**
Which: All **6 h'hds rep. 13 people** *Most* **7 h'hds rep. 14 people**
Main rd to village & in village **6 h'hds rep. 9 people** *From the Graig to Selley hall* **2 h'hds**
1 h'hd each *Village to Tregodva, Village to Cwm Collo Near Dutlas, Between Cwm Collo and turn to Blan-y-Drae, School route down Springhill, lethal in frost due to poor drains Cow hall lane.*

Is sign posting adequate? Yes **37 h'hds rep 84 people** *No .* **3 h'hds rep. 8 people**
If No what should be done **1 h'hd each** *Slow signs through village. Sign to Stoneypound/N'castle at T junction at Hergin. Spending on footpaths and signs a waste, no consultation, should be spent on roads. Better signs to Newcastle & Clun. Emergency services and lorries need signs to isolated farms. Keep signs to minimum.*
Do you think there should be a speed limit in the village?
Yes **22 h'hds rep. 48 people** *No.* **16 h'hds rep. 41 people**

What should the limit be? 40mph **1 h'hd** *30mph* **12 h'hds rep. 25 people** *25mph* **1 h'hd**
20mph **6 h'hds rep. 11 people**

And where? The village ie Main rd / Bridge / Vedw / to Church **10 h'hds rep. 23 people**
A Slow Children sign (Black hall to Bridge and church) **2 h'hds** *Don't want speed signs* **1 h'hd**

Is gritting in winter adequate? Yes **14 h'hds rep. 37 people** *No.* **26 h'hds rep. 53 people**
Should any more of the roads in the village be singled out for gritting or grit piles?
More piles for us to use throughout **6 h'hds rep. 14 people.** *Llanfair Village* **4 h'hds rep. 8 people**
All steep pitches along our side of valley **4 h'hds rep. 6** *Nantiago – Vedw turn* **3 h'hds rep. 13 people.**
1 h'hd each *School taxi run to Newcastle between Monaughty and Nantiago. To Melin-y-Grogue and beyond. Lot of mild winters recently; a bad winter would need a lot more grit. Grit should be in bins.*
Comments *Absence of lengthmen leads to flooding and therefore more rapid deterioration of roads (provide local man with local drainage clearance contract spend £1000 now saves £5000 later, and create local work,)* **17 h'hds rep. 38 people**. *More stoned passing places* **3 h'hds rep. 6 people 2 h'hds each** *Drive carefully* **1 h'hd each** *Slow signs on bends. Farmers should clear drains. Less drink to be taken. Teach farmers the highway code. Reminders via newsletter to drivers to watch out for people walking cycling and riding in lanes. No snow clearance. Cycling proficiency lessons for children (?via youth club). Lower hedge heights on bad corners Overhanging trees and hedges need cutting back More lighting. Potholes need dealing with. Keep potholes– automatically slows down speeds! Roads safe here compared to others. Mirrors at Vedw and Teme Cottage turn Sleeping policemen in village and at bad corners No regular maintenance of roads. Roads need cleaning Maintained well but need cleaning Roads should take priority over ft/bridle paths for spending. If public not happy with walk/riding opportunities already they never will be. Use school buses going/returning empty betweeen Knighton/Presteigne Beguildy/Newtown. We can live with a few pot-holes.*

5. Children:

Total No of respondents **7 h'hds rep. 12 children**
How many primary school age children attend
Beguildy School? **7** *Newcastle School?* **4** *Clun School?* **1**
As the children in the parish attend different schools is it important that they meet socially on a regular basis? Yes **13 h'hds rep. 34 people** *No* **1 h'hd**
Do they meet often enough? *Yes* **8 h'hds rep. 21 people** *No* **2 1 h'hd**

Do you take your children to the special church services?
Yes **4 h'hds rep. 15 people** *No* **3 h'hds rep. 8**
Do you take your children to the Everest hall when there is an event suitable for them?
Yes **7 h'hds rep. 19 people** *No* **1 h'hd**
If someone in the parish offered childcare would you use it? *Yes* **3h'hds rep. 12 people**
Would you consider offering childcare to others? *Yes* **2h'hds**
Please list the good things about bringing up children in the parish.
Space. **14 h'hds rep. 40** *Fresh air.* **14 h'hds rep. 40** *Natural environment.* **13 h'hds rep. 39**
Unpolluted. **13 h'hds rep. 38** *Relaxed.* **11 h'hds rep. 35** *Safe.* **10 h'hds rep. 26**
Free of commercial pressures. **11 h'hds rep. 36** *Free from urban bad behaviour* **10 h'hds rep. 34**
Youth club good invention **4 h'hds rep. 11** *and part solves socialisation problem* **1 h'hd**
Country upbringing teaches a sense of responsibility **2 h'hds. I h'hd each** *Great place to bring up kid*
Safe except for some fast traffic. *Art/craft sessions on Sat ams are good*

6. Young People:

What do you think of'the social and other facilities on offer in the area (not just in Llanfair) for young people? *Good. /Adequate,* **1** *Poor,* **3 h'hds rep. 9** *Non-existent* **1 hh'd**
Would you like to see more facilities available in the parish? Yes **3 h'hds rep. 5** No **2 h'hds**
Advantages of living here **2 h'hds each**. *Low noise Not many houses Clean air*
1 h'hd each *Less pollution. More space. Nature Walks. Views. No ugly council-house estate. Plenty to do.*
Disadvantages: **2 h'hds** *Friends too far apart* **I h'hd each** *Not enough facilities Poor transport*

7. People over 60:

41 respondents (out of 115) gave their ages as over 60
There are no special facilities for the over 60s. Are you happy with this?
Yes **18 h'hds rep. 26** *No* **1 h'hd**
What facilities would you like to see introduced?
1 h'hd each *A social club. Discussion groups (with speakers)*
Is Transport a problem for you? *Yes* **2 h'hds** *No* **23 h'hds rep. 42**
If you are elderly or housebound would you like to receive help?
Yes **4h'hds rep. 5 people** *No* **8 h'hds rep. 15 people**
What kind of help is needed? *Gardening* **3h'hds rep. 3 people** *Housework* **1 h'hd**
Do you use home care/ home help services? *Yes* **1 h'hd** *No* **19 h'hds rep. 34**
Are these easy to obtain? *Yes* **3 h'hds rep. 4** *No* **5. h'hds rep. 9**
Are you happy about the emergency services? *Yes* **5 h'hds rep. 10** *No* **7 h'hds rep. 14**
Are you happy about the Health service provision? (e.g. Hospitals. the local Doctors Surgery. the Dentist Surgery) *Yes* **19 h'hds rep. 32** *No* **1 h'hd**, *Yes to doctors, No to dentists* **1 h'hd**
Any comments or suggestions? Dental emergency took 4 days More dentists needed/ NHS dentist only available on one day per week. **4 h'hds rep. 8** *Should be more cross-border co-operation on emergency services. Services should come from Knighton. Slow (lost)ambulances* **6 h'hds rep. 12** *Slow (lost)police* **3 h'hds rep. 6. 1 h'hd each**: *Daily provision for elderly in home is poor. Home help and health services difficult to get due to distance. NHS Waiting lists too long. No food delivery service (There is – Halls. Ed.)*

8. Everyone:

What do you think are the advantages and disadvantages of living in Llanfair?

Advantages: *Beautiful countryside* **22 h'hds rep. 47**
Remoteness/privacy Peaceful/ Quiet **21 h'hds rep. 46**
Community spirit. Nice people **17 h'hds rep. 36**
Crime rate low **3 h'hds rep. 6** *Good walking* **3 h'hds rep. 8**
2 h'hds each *Good Pub. Lucky. No disadvantages. Able to see stars. Thank goodness no street lights. Few trippers.* **1 h'hd each** *Not in a national park thank goodness. Clean air. Wildlife. Lack of built-up areas. Tuffins. Lack of traffic. Good doctors at Clun Excellent school at N'castle. Easy get to coast. Not too far to Birmingham. Plenty of cultural activities and services available in nearby towns (Presteigne/Ludlow.)*
Middling: 2 h'hds each. *Can't have it both ways! Disadvantages of lack of swift access to medical services and entertainment are consequence of the advantages.* **1 h'hd each** *Small community has both advantages and disadvantages. Constantly worried area will change for worse.*

Disadvantages: 6 h'hds rep. 10: *Widely dispersed and inward looking community. It takes a long time to feel welcome and to find out what is going on. Lack of social events. Lack of young people and isolation. Underpopulated esp young people leads to less community life eg at Red Lion.*
2 h'hds each *No school. High council tax, low return in services (as against Radnorshire)* **I h'hd each** *Poor emergency services particularly due to border. Distance from hospitals. No shop or jobs. Long way to services. Forgotten by County tucked away out of sight. Poor support for new businesses and building from centralising and economising LAs. Powys and Teme valley address means in some ways we'd be better off in Powys. Poor transport. Difficult without car. Cost of petrol Economic reliance on I industry No jobs outside farming Not enough children Too few tourists Mobile phones don't work.*

9. The Countryside:

This section provoked the most comments and 96% of respondents filled it in. 21 Farming H'holds representing 56 people, & 27 Non-farming H'holds representing 52 people replied.

Is the beauty of the landscape in the parish important to you?
Farm *Yes* **19 h'hds rep 52** *No* **0** **Non-farm** *Yes* **26 h'hds rep 50** *No* **0**
Overall: *Yes* **45 h'hds rep 102** *No* **0**

The parish is very rich in wildlife Are the wildflowers, birds. animals etc in the parish important to you?
Farm *Yes* **19 h'hds rep 52** *No* **0** **Non-farm** *Yes* **26 h'hds rep 50** *No* **0**
Overall: *Yes* **45 h'hds rep 102** *No* **0**

Was it a good idea that the River Teme was declared an SSSI?
Farm *Yes* **13 h'hds rep 36** *No* **5 h'hds rep 13** **Non-farm** *Yes* **25 h'hds rep 48** *No* **0**
Overall: *Yes* **38 h'hds rep 84** *No* **5 h'hds rep 13**
Comments: **Farm** *Too many restrictions involved in Teme SSSI inc 10 m strip on banks.*

Does the ESA (Environmental Sensitive Area' scheme make a valuable contribution to keeping our traditional landscape?
Farm *Yes* **19 h'hds rep 58** *No* **0** **Non-farm** *Yes* **27 h'hds rep 47** *No* **1 h'hd**
Overall: *Yes* **46 h'hds rep 100** *No* **1 h'hd**
Comments **Farm** *Case for ESA keeping the landscape traditional not proven.*

If you come "from off," was the quality of the landscape an important reason for you settling here?
Farm *Yes* **3 h'hds** *No* **1 h'hd** **Non-farm** *Yes* **21 h'hds rep 38** *No* **0**
Overall: *Yes* **24 h'hds rep c.46** *No* **1h'hd**

The ESA scheme and other measures are designed to keep the landscape traditional, some might say to stop the clock. Do you think this is a good idea?
Farm Yes **17 h'hds rep 41** No **2 h'hds** **Non-farm** Yes **19 h'hds rep 36** No **1 h'hd**
Overall: Yes **36 h'hds rep 77** No **3h'hds**

Do you think farming subsidies give the tax-paying public the right to access to the countryside or the right to limit what farmers can do on their own land?
Farm *Yes* **5 h'hds rep 14** *No* **13 h'hds rep 33**
Non-farm *Yes* **7 h'hds rep 17** *No* **12 h'hds rep 20** **Overall:** *Yes* **12 h'hds rep 31** *No* **25 h'hds rep 53**
Comments **Non-farm** *To some extent* **2 h'hds** *Right to access yes, to limit farmers actions no* **1 h**

Do townspeople understand the countryside?
Farm *Yes* **1 h'hd** *No* **24 h'hds rep 62**
Non-farm *Yes* **7 h'hds rep 16** *No* **17 h'hds rep 32**
Overall: *Yes* **8 h'hds rep c.19** *No* **41 h'hds rep 94**
Comments. **Non-farm:** *Disney has a lot to answer for!* **1 h'hd**

Do Countrypeople understand the town?
No **2 h'hds**

Should fox-hunting with hounds be banned?
Farm *Yes* **2 h'hds** *No* **16 h'hds rep 44**
Non-farm *Yes* **13 h'hds rep 11** *No* **11 h'hds rep 19**
Overall: *Yes* **15 h'hds rep c.16** *No* **27h'hd 63**
Comments **Farm** *Hunting with horse/hounds gives countryside a bad image*
Non-farm *Ban shooting of foxes, it's overkill, we are overrun with rabbits. Prefer to see foxes culled humanely Dislike fox hunting but shouldn't be legally banned.*

Should (some) badgers be culled?
Farm *Yes* **16 h'hds rep 37** *No* **3 h'hds rep 12**
Non-farm *Yes* **15 h'hds rep 25** *No* **6 h'hds rep .15**
Overall: *Yes* **31 h'hds rep 62** *No* **9 h'hds rep. 27**

Many paths have recently been designated as public footpaths and bridleways and signposted. Is this a good thing?
Farm Yes **12 h'hds rep 33.** No **7 h'hds rep 15**
Non-farm Yes **17 h'hds rep 35** No **5 h'hds rep 7**
Overall: Yes **29 h'hds rep 68** No **12 h'hds rep. 22**
Farm: *Only some footpath signs are a good idea. Some footpath marking good, some totally unnecessary*

Do you use footpaths for work?
Farm *Yes* **4 h'hds rep 7** *No* **14 h'hds rep 40**
Non-farm *Yes* **2 h'hds** *No* **14 h'hds rep 29**
Overall: *Yes* **6 h'hds rep c.12** *No* **28 rep 69**

Do you use footpaths for recreation?
Farm *Yes* **7 h'hds rep 20** *No* **11 h'hds rep 25**
Non-farm *Yes* **21 h'hds rep 40** *No* **4 h'hds rep 7**
Overall: *Yes* **28 h'hds rep 60** *No* **15 h'hds rep 32**

Do you use footpaths in other parishes?
Farm *Yes* **7 h'hds rep 22** *No* **10 h'hds rep 25**
Non-farm *Yes* **18 h'hds rep 35** *No* **6 h'hds rep 12**
Overall: *Yes* **25 h'hds rep 57** *No* **26 h'hds rep 37**

Do you obiect to 4x4 leisure use of bridleways?
Farm *Yes* **20 h'hlds rep' 54 people** *No* **0**
Non-farm *Yes* **22 h'hld rep' 41 people** *No* **3 h'hld rep' 8**

Should farmers be subsidised as the conservation guardians/ curators of the countryside?
Farm *Yes* **15 h'hds rep 42** *No* **0**
Non-farm *Yes* **16 h'hds 26** *No* **5 h'hds rep 12**
Overall: *Yes* **31 h'hds rep 68** *No* **5 h'hds rep 12**

Should production subsidies be abandoned?
Farm *Yes* **4 h'hds rep 12** *No* **14 h'hds rep 36**
Non-farm *Yes* **6 h'hds rep 16** *No* **11 h'hds rep 19**
Overall: *Yes* **9 h'hds rep 28** *No* **25 h'hds rep 55**

Many farms in other areas have become rural and part-time retreats for hobby farmers, rich businessmen etc. and some signs of this can already been seen a few miles away around Clun. In other areas food production is no longer as important an activity in the countryside as it was, and farming families have ceased to be the most important group in community life. Is this the future of the area? The Theme valley? a mixture of conservation/tourist-minded farms and private mini-estates for ex-townspeople and weekenders? What is your prediction for the future?
On Farm I h'hd each *Am one! Sorry! (ie weekend hobby farmer on private mini-estate) This is what's happenning – too many non-/part-time residents (encourages crime). Hate idea of Theme valley. Overall a bleak future. Hope it stays the same. May have to scale down farming. The social mix of incomers with new ideas and interests with original farming community great for community May have to farm tourists. May have to return to basic farming i.e. organic. Over 20 farms have been lost to the parish in the last 25–30 years. Farmers may have to get 2nd job.*
Non-farm 2 h'hds *Don't like the above. The above is HELL!!* **1 h'hd each** *Wean farmers off production subsidies with appropriate support. Dread changes as above (esp. as resulting from surveys of this type!) No remarkable change in view except bigger farms I've seen it elsewhere and dislike all the implications of prettified urban dreams out of magazines eroding the real country way of life.*

Is the current farming crisis likely to change our way of life?
Farm *Yes* **13 h'hds rep. 31** *No* **3 h'hds rep. 8**
Non-farm *Yes* **5 h'hds rep. 11** *No* **9 h'hds rep. 18**
Overall: *Yes* **18 h'hds rep 42** *No* **12 h'hds rep 26**

How? And what ways forward for farming can you see? Any comments or suggestions?
Farm: I h'hd each *Farmers not so keen to pass farms on to sons/daughters so generations/traditions of farmers will be lost. Sadly most youngsters leave. Special skills (shearing, hedging, walling, stock) will fade.*
Hope Livestock farming can continue/prosper, so c'side doesn't deteriorate as in 30s. If livestock farming disappears the countryside will just become an untidy overgrown jungle. Livestock farmers need to continue grazing to keep countryside as conservationists want it (unfortunately). Subsidies will transfer to environmental payments & organic farming may be way forward. Farms should seek niche markets/ go organic/ follow consumers' demands. Production subsidies should stay for LFAs provided it doesnt lead to overstocking. Large farms will extensify to cut fixed costs, this will cut employment and investment; this will be bad for employment and local business. Small farms need to diversify. The future is unpredicatable given gov't attitude to agriculture. Continue as now.
Non-farm: I h'hd each *Here subsidised conservation is the most likely way forward, compensating farmers for loss of income from food production, but keeping farms in traditional hands. They could look at better marketing of quality/organic produce. Closer relation to govt agencies and much more conservation work. Farmers should be subsidised as curators of c'side as long as they are aware of their responsibilities Linkage to subsidies –Should be right to roam on moorland, not on crop fields, and farmers should not be allowed to do just anything eg battery farms where none before, new uses for buildings or fields.*
Farm land belongs to farmers, is not a playground for outsiders, less intensive production + conservation is way forward, tourism should be a farming by-product not an end in itself. Manage land for conservation. Townee money useful, rural areas are there for the greater good but not so townees can yomp all over it!
2 h'hds each *Sadly farms will get bigger and houses will be sold without land. More support for conservation. Keep farms in traditional hands. Land must continue to be a working farm area.*
1 h'hd each *Danger that the real experience of the c'side will be replaced by townees fantasies of a romantic countryside full of peasants, endangered species and cuddly farm animals. Disney has a lot to answer for! Farmers should be more self-sufficient, agriculture more mixed and diverse, more in tune with c'side – recently not the case – not their fault, lesson has cost us all.*

Should be less support for production, unless quality/organic. Form local quality meat co-op and grab a share of chattering classes market. Improve quality of stock and produce. Diversify into niche(eg organic) markets and local marketing co-ops (Teme valley lamb)
3 h'hds *Buy British! Import less food. Brits and Brit institutions (army) eat British.*
2 h'hds each *Supermarkets have something to answer for. Farming is cyclical.* **I h'hd each** *Farming needs good support since it is centre of local way of life, otherwise becomes a stagnant retirement/holiday/tourist zone devoid of life. Downturn affects local economy and services. Scientists are to blame for food-scaring off consumers. Shoot the scientists. Start farming tourists; they can bring in far more money than sheep or cattle. Encourage farmers to farm walkers and caravanners by discreet small developments inc toilets* **3 h'hds** *Tourism not the answer. Don't want tourism developed.* **1 h'hd each** *People need to be encouraged to close gates and take rubbish home. Farmers should remove plastic waste from their fields, why not dark green sileage bags instead of white black and pea green. Pessimistic. Out of our hands. Govt decisions ratified by referenda.*

10. Community. Recreation and Social Life:

Nationality: Do you prefer to think of yourself as:
English **25 h'hd rep 50** *"from the Borders/Marches"* **10 h'hd rep 25** *Welsh* **6 h'hd rep 13** *British* **4 h'hd rep 8**. **1 h'hd each** *Anglo-Welsh. Hybrids. European. Half-Welsh and proud of it.*

Identity: Do you prefer to think of yourself as:
A local **25 h'hd rep 68** *an incomer* **12 h'hd rep 22** *resident* **5h'hd rep. 8** *Resident ratepayer* **2 h'hds** **1 h'hd each** *Holiday resident. Retired pensioners. Second home owner. A long term incomer. An incomer who has been made to feel a local. Welcomed. A Stayput.*

Do you consider yourself part of Llanfair Waterdine parish?
Yes **41 h'hd rep 87** *Partly* **1 h'hd** *No.* **3 h'hd rep 13**

The parish population has declined by 60% in the last 100 years. In the absence of a Llanfair school, and with lower church attendance compared to then, is Llanfair the centre for your community life?
Yes **30 h'hd rep 57** *(inc 2 families with children)* *No* **15 h'hd rep 45** *(inc 6 families with children)*

Where else do you look for your community life?
Knighton **11 h'hd rep 29** *Newcastle* **4 h'hd rep 13** *Clun* **3 h'hd rep 9** *Presteigne* **3 h'hd rep 5**
Newtown **2 h'hd** **1 h'hd each:** *Bishop's Castle, Bettws, Beguildy/Felindre, Knucklas garden club Radnorshire through YFC, Birmingham.*

How can we reinforce our community life?:
Pub needs to be more welcoming and we need to make better use of it **8 h'hds rep 14**
Through creating supporting village events **4 h'hd rep 13** *We already have a good community life.* **3 h'hds** **2 h'hds each** *Young blood must be prepared to /or be allowed to take over from the geriatrics. Welcome newcomers. Should be more welcoming to newcomers with new skills and get them and locals working together. Youth Club is a giant step. Community Life is improving with more families using church/Youth Club* **I h'hd each**. *Extend Hall. More publicity for events. More transport needed for people to get to events. Community life grows naturally from within community.*

Which do you usually attend?
Social functions organised by: *WI* **15 h'hd rep 26** *Church* **23 h'hd rep 43** *Everest Hall* **9 h'hd rep 38** *The pub* **20 h'hd rep 42**

What sporting, arts, cultural, historical, conservation, farming or other event, meeting, club, class, lecture, entertainment activity would you attend that doesn't exist now?
Film/talk on (HofW) railway lines, Elan valley dams, specialist talks, with celebrities **3 h'hd rep 6**
2 h'hds each *Dances. Film club.* **I h'hd each** *Folk music Music evenings Local history Crafts Community Music Old time dancing Poetry reading Travelling theatre Net ball Badminton Moto cross/grass track Basketmaking Farming Gardening Natural History and rambling Try anything.*

Because of our small numbers we cannot support team games like football or cricket. Could you suggest a new sporting activity which might encourage people to get together regularly?
Ping pong **5 h'hd rep 10** *Indoor/ 9-pin bowling* **3 h'hds rep 6** *Walking group* **2 h'hds, I h'hd each** *Backgammom. Badminton in hall. Mah Jong. Model car racing club Go-kart track*

Why are there so few people in the parish aged between the ages of 20 and 40?
No work opportunities **20 h'hds rep 46** *(p'ticly for women)* **1 h'hd**, *(under this govt.)* **1 h'hd,** *Housing too costly/Build reasonably priced houses* **7 h'hds rep 18**
2 h'hds each *Poor pay. It's right that over 18s get further ed. and spread wings, some will return.*
1 h'hd each *They move away to train, get better jobs, and then marry. Lack of social life Wealthy incomers price houses out of reach of locals, Council tax too high. Poor transport Too late to rectify! Machinery replaced humans on farms. Natural fluctuation Farms getting larger, no local industry, more retirement situation worsens. Doesn't matter*

Can anything be done to rectify the situation?
Diversify away from farming **2 h'hds I h'hd each** *Encourage small w'shops. Why should we have to have everything for everybody, everywhere? Let people choose, [young people] perhaps town life suits them until they are older! Encourage tourism.*

Which types of visitors/ visiting activity, if any, should we encourage?
Walkers **17 h'hds rep 43** *Campers* **17 h'hds rep 43** *B&b guests* **16 h'hds rep 42**
Tourism **12 h'hds rep 29** *Horse-riders* **9h'hds rep 25** *Keep quiet about Llanfair?* **17 h'hds rep 36**

Are there any activities we should discourage?
Motor sports **20 h'hds rep.41** *Caravanners* **10 h'hds rep 19** *Shooting* **8 h'hds rep 14**. *Hunting* **6 h'hds rep 10** *Campers* **5 h'hds rep 10 2h'hds each** *Horseriders, Weekenders, Walkers* **1 h'hd**

How should we encourage or discourage these activities?
More publicity **4 h'hd rep 11 2 h'hds each** *People who want to come will come. We should not encourage too much or the attractive character of the parish will change. Not too many.*
I h'hd each *Shout about Llanfair to stop it dying Present advertising sufficient – don't spoil the Dyke like the Lake district. If we have too many tourists they'll destroy what they come to see. Discourage day-trippers, go for posh people who appreciate area. Issue guide to countryside rules b&bs etc. Make welcome, and encourage holiday familes to blend in and return annually. Townees think the countryside is an empty place, liberty hall, so they abuse it. Educate them… we'll be nice to you if you take trouble to educate selves about rural life. Educate visitors that countryside is a workplace. Should be more consultation. Farmers say no to land use. Don't accommodate them. The roads are inadequate for them. Should encourage people who will shoot rabbits, crows, rooks and magpies. Discourage shooters, motorsports and caravanners because they put off those we want to attract and damage the environment.*

Should Llanfair go in for a new special event to "raise its profile"?
No **30 h'hds rep 71** *Yes* **3 h'hds rep 5**
Should there be extra event to bring the community together?
Yes **11 h'hds rep 25** *No* **13 h'hds rep 33**

If so what?
2 h'hds each. *Annual Fireworks party Film Club,* **1 h'hd each** *Drinks, Party/ceilidh, Ploughing match. Beating the bounds Pub dressing Community Xmas party Joint clearing up Youth club Run paper/card processing recycling. Major rural festival. Arts Crafts expo. Everest day Community music or play/show to attract and involve all ages/walks of life*

Any comments or suggestions.
1 h'hd *Llanfair should expand or it will fade away. It should create a niche for itself with folk culture rural crafts, downhill cycle track.*

11. Everest Hall and the Church

How often do you visit the hall per year?
Total **43 h'hds rep 91**
Not at all, **5 h'hds rep 17** *1– 5 times,* **18 h'hds rep 37** *5–10,* **2 h'hds rep 4** *10–25,* **7 h'hds rep 18**
25–50, **7 h'hds rep 12** *50 +,* **9 h'hds rep 20**

Are you happy with the facilities currently offered?
Yes **28 h'hds rep 63** *No* **4 h'hds rep 10**

When we last did a questionnaire we asked whether you would be interested in having access to a computer or learning IT skills. If this became available would you be interested?
Yes **22 h'hds rep 51** No **18 h'hds rep 41**

What types of use would you want from the computer?
Word processing **13 h'hds rep 27** *Printing* **11 h'hds rep 24** *Internet access* **8 h'hds rep 21**
Accountancy/Book-keeping **7 h'hds rep 16** *Publishing* **6 h'hds rep 15** *E-mail* **5 h'hds rep 13**
Audio and Music processing **5 h'hds rep 14** *Photography and Graphics* **5 h'hds rep 12**
Fax, **4 h'hds rep 12** *CAD* **3 h'hds rep 9** *Animation* **3 h'hds rep 9** *CD printing, Computer Games, Scanner* **2 h'hds each** *Video Processing, Laminator CDROM use* **1 h'hd**
Ring binder machine **1 h'hd**

How often would you use a computer if there was access and training?
For training **2 h'hds** *weekly* **4 h'hds rep 8** *monthly* **3 h'hd** *Occassionally* **1 h'hd**

What other new buildings or alterations to buildings or changes of use do we need – if any?
Small lockable extension to hall for meetings/storage/archive **15 h'hds rep 36 people**. *None* **2 h'hds**

Does the Hall need an extra room (for computer(s), storage, archives, smaller meetings)?
Yes **21 h'hds rep 48** *No* **9 h'hds rep 25** *Flexible internal partition as at Chapel lawn* **2 h'hds**

What improvements or extra facilities would you like to see?
2 h'hds each *None More storage More heating Storage for chidrens' books and cds*
1 h'hd each *Better bar. For archives. Kitchen redesign. Kitchen floor replaced. Better decoration. Carpet in bar area. Scrap the metal chairs, get better ones.*

Have you booked the hall yourself in the last 3 years?
Yes **11 h'hds**

Church

How often do you visit the church per year?
Total: **35 h'hds rep 75** *Not at all* **6 h'hds rep 17** *1–5 times* **13 h'hds rep 32** *5–10* **2 h'hds rep 4** *10–25* **10 h'hds rep 22** *25–50* **7 h'hds rep 12** *50+* **3 h'hds**

Do you think it will still be in use as a church in 100 years time?.
Yes **19 h'hds rep 42** *No* **10 h'hds rep 24**

Could the church be used for anything else?
Yes **10 h'hds rep 21** *No* **17 h'hds rep 46**
If so what? **2 h'hds** *Meetings, Exhibitions, Music* **1 h'hd** *Music lessons, Poetry Lectures, Photography*

What improvements could you suggest?
Adapt area of church for social activity inc toilet **4 h'hds rep 8** **1 h'hd each** *Church washing-up facilities. Sheep in churchyard. Gypsy's grave needs clearing up. Everest Hall more appropriate than church for most events.*

Any comments or suggestions:
1 h'hd each *Church –Spiritual centre of village, Pub – Body centre, Hall – Mind: adds up to whole people! Change internal design of hall for PO/Info centre and so different activities can co-exist and for cosier small meetings. Must support both buildings. Don't extend hall – increases costs.*

12. Heritage:

Which are the buildings in the parish which should be looked after for future generations?
Church **23 h'hds rep 58** *Pub* **22 h'hds rep 44** *Hall* **13 h'hds rep 32** *Old houses* **11 h'hds rep 21** *Some Barns* **7 h'hds rep 15** *Bridges* **3 h'hds rep 6** *Nantiago* **2 h'hds** *All pre 1900 buildings* **1 h'hd**

Which are the other features of the parish which should be looked after for future generations?
Offa's Dyke **40 h'hds rep 89** *The woods* **41 h'hds rep 87** *The landscape* **38 h'hds rep 87** *The Teme* **36 h'hds rep 77** *Archaeological sites* **27 h'hds rep 64** *Hedges, Lanes* **2 h'hds**

Would you be interested in an local historical archive stored locally?
Yes **25 h'hds rep 55** *No* **2 h'hds**

Any comments or suggestions?
1 h'hd each *Fund farmers to maintain and rent/sell redundant houses, Museum of rural life? Keep signs and labels to minimum.*

13. Local Services:

Do you use Beguildy Shop/PostOffice? *Yes* **14 h'hds rep 33** *No* **30 h'hds rep 66**
Knucklas Part-time Post Office? *Yes* **4 h'hds rep 6** *No* **38 h'hds rep 90**
Do you use the travelling Library? *Yes* **11 h'hds rep 22** *No* **29 h'hds rep 71**
Do you use the Library in the Village Hall? *Yes* **14 h'hds rep 30** *No* **32 h'hds rep 74**
Do you know about the Knighton Community car scheme?
Yes **15 h'hds rep 27** *No* **31 h'hds rep 76**
Have you ever used it? *Yes* **2 h'hds** *No* **42 h'hds rep 92**

Do you go to the Cinema? *Yes* **15 h'hds rep 50** *No* **17 h'hds rep 37**
Where? *Ludlow* **11 h'hds rep 22** *Newtown* **6 h'hds rep 18** *Telford* **4 h'hds rep 14**
Shrewsbury **3 h'hds rep 12** *Presteigne* **2 h'hds rep 6** *elsewhere* **4 h'hds rep 9**
How often (per year)
1–5x **6 h'hds rep 12** *5–10* **8 h'hds rep 26** *10x* **3 h'hds rep 8**, *20x* **3 h'hds rep 7**

Do you go to?
Concerts **29 h'hds rep 64**. *Drama productions* **21 h'hds rep 45** *Festivals* **15 h'hds rep 29**
Adult Classes **15 h'hds rep 31**. *Sports events* **14 h'hds rep 38**. *Discos* **3 h'hds rep 6**.
1 h'hd each *Book clubs, Arts/Craft shows.*
At *Newtown* **7 h'hds rep 19** *Ludlow* **7 h'hds rep 19** *Knighton* **3 h'hds rep 7**
Presteigne **3 h'hds rep 4** *London* **2 h'hds rep 4** *Birmingham, Wolverhampton, Telford, Hay, Bleddfa, Bishop's Castle* **1 h'hd each**

If we had a recycling scheme would you use it? *Yes* **37 h'hds rep 77** *No* **5 h'hds rep 17**
Would you take material to a central point? *Yes* **39 h'hds rep 84** *No* **3 h'hds rep 8**
Comment *No to both. There's already a recycling scheme in Knighton which we use.* **2 h'hds**

Have you needed to contact the police in the last 3 years?
Yes **12 h'hds rep 33** *No* **28 h'hds rep 61**
Were the police's responses to your needs satisfactory?
Yes **5 h'hds rep 15** *No* **7 h'hds rep 22**

What local services do we lack?
Post Office/Shop **4 h'hds rep 8** *Restaurant,* *What Police?* *Shop deliveries in Winter* *Dentists* *School* *Mobile Phones* **1 h'hd each**

What services need improving and how?
Road sweeping/drain maintenance **4 h'hds rep 7.**
2 h'hds each *Care of elderly in own homes. Emergency services should come from Knighton.*
1 h'hd each *Recycling – collection of sorted waste. Emergency services. Weekly Library Bus visits. Gritting. Playgroup. Teenagers services. More action by PC and DC might help.*
Lights at Selley Cross-Little Selley Too far to post box More NHS
What services are you satisfied with?
Refuse, **8 h'hds rep 13** *Local doctors* **4 h'hds rep 8** *Post,* **3 h'hds**
2 h'hds each *School bus Travelling Lbry Village library Local hospices*
1 h'hd each *Local cottage hospitals excellent. Police. Most Services. Roads. Milk*
Would you consider offering paid care to an elderly person?
Yes **4h'hds rep. 8 people**

Any comments or suggestions:
1 h'hd each *Must keep pub, get more community involvement.*
If people want more services these have to be paid for and rates are high enough already.
As we're off the beaten track we need to do it ourselves particularly active pensioners eg chyard grass cutting was a very good communal event inc use of pub. Need P.0./shop P.O. but impractical to get it back. Police are a waste of time, uninterested in thefts, only interested in harrassing rural drivers who've had 2 pints. We should get together to do more physically for the village and less through hand-outs e.g. by building churchyard wall, hall extension ourselves. Hospitals good but very far away.

14. Local Government:

Do you know who Parish councillors are?
Yes **28 h'hds rep 58** *Some* **3 h'hds rep 5** *No* **15 h'hds rep 42**
Do you know what the Parish Council's responsibilities, powers and budget are?
Yes **16 h'hds rep 35** *No* **27 h'hds rep 66**
Do you know who our District councillor is?
Yes **17 h'hds rep 39** *No* **25 h'hds rep 60**
Do you know what the District Council's responsibilities, powers and budget are?
Yes **16 h'hds rep 38** *No* **24 h'hds rep 58**
Do you know who our County Councillor is?
Yes **13 h'hds rep 31** *No* **31 h'hds rep 80**
Do you know what the County Council's responsibilities, powers and budget are?
Yes **17 h'hds rep 40** *No* **24 h'hds rep 56**
Would you like your parish, district and county representatives to come and explain their responsibilities to us?
Yes **28 h'hds rep 61** *No* **10 h'hds rep 30**

Does the Parish Council represent your views and interests?

Yes **18 h'hds rep 41** *No* **7 h'hds rep 14**

If not what should the PC be doing? Comments on the PC.

3 h'hds: *PC never communicates on a feedback loop. It should publish its decisions on the noticeboard and via the newsletter.*

1 h'hd each: *PC represents our views maybe but doesn't enforce them. PC isn't nearly forceful enough to the DC on planning matters. PC should be keeping village tidy and attractive. PC should also ensure that all neighbours to planning applications know what's going on. PC should be pushing for more development, for diversification of economy, and encouraging tourism. PC biassed towards existing farming community and is not forward thinking. We don't want to see a divisive and costly election, but the PC should co-opt at least one or two people who aren't farmers when next there are vacancies. An exclusively farming PC isn't representative, and misses out on skills and knowledge of non-farmers.*

Are planning controls and procedures adequate?

Yes **17 h'hds rep 42** *No.* **10 h'hds rep 28**

Comments **1 h'hd each** *A bit changeable. Not tight enough. Should be more lenient/open*

Is enough information made available about planning proposals?

Yes **16 h'hds rep 38** *No* **14 h'hds rep 41**

Do you know what the County Structure Plan Revision proposes for Llanfair?

Yes **5 h'hds rep 10** *No* **32 h'hds rep 74**

If not. would you like to know?

Yes **18 h'hds rep 59** *No* **5 h'hds rep 15**

Should there be planning restraints on:

Hedge removal, *Yes* **39 h'hds rep 85** *No.* **5 h'hds rep 18**

Tree preservation, *Yes* **37 h'hds rep 81** *No* **4 h'hds rep 16**

Large scale forestry *Yes* **36 h'hds rep 81** *No* **3 h'hds rep 11**

Historic buildings, archaeological sites and on landscape?

Yes **35 h'hds rep 84** *No* **3 h'hds rep 8**

New farm buildings *Yes* **35 h'hds rep 80** *No* **4 h'hds rep 12**

Are Local Authorities sufficiently responsive in planning, environmental, schools, highways etc. matters?

Yes **8 h'hds rep 24** *No* **13 h'hds rep 33**

If not who should be doing what? Any comments?

2 h'hds *Mystifying planning decisions. LAs should take more notice of PC and locals.*

1 h'hd each *LAs don't have enough powers to deal with bad situations or stop loopholes being abused. Don't need any more bureaucrats, less red tape please. Trees and hedges must be farmed correctly so as to ensure future. Ugly buildings are permitted. LAs override local views. LAs centralise to keep costs down and don't act in our interests. Village losing its uniqueness, too many metal signs, dislike picnic spot in hall car park, & rubbish.*

Would you like to take part in a debate about some of the issues that have been raised and about some of the facts and views that will come out of this survey. after it has been published?

Yes **25 h'hds rep 53** (50%) *No* **11 h'hds rep 32** (22%)

Llanfair Waterdine THE NEWS Issue No. 6 February 1999

Lord Hunt.

Since our last Newsletter we have received the sad news of the death of John Hunt. Many of you wrote letters to Joy and her family and she has asked for the following to be included in this news sheet.

To all our friends in Llanfair. Forgive me for not writing separately to each one of you, but I have read all your wonderful letters with gratitude. Llanfair has always been such a special place for us both – and your friendship meant a great deal to John. We have had endless happy memories of times spent with you all – and of walking over his beloved hills. Thank you for being so good to us.

Joy.

There will be a service of Thanksgiving for John's life in Church on Saturday 13th February at 3.00pm when everyone will be most welcome.

Update

The Christmas auction on 12th December was highly successful and raised £1,518.35p for Church restoration funds. This is the highest total ever.

The Children's party at Lloyney on 13th December attracted over 50 children. Father Christmas was quite exhausted! The adults also had an entertaining evening helped by some extra voices and musicians from Felindre. On 18th December the carol service in church was well attended and Knighton Town Silver Band were again most welcome visitors. They accompanied the singing and gave an extra dimension to the occasion. Everyone appreciated their presence and £173 was raised through the collection for the Samaritans.

The new Youth Club which meets each Wednesday at 7.00pm at the Everest Hall is regularly attended by almost 30 children. Their open evening in December was an occasion enjoyed by them and by the many adults who turned up. Much needed funds were raised through a raffle.

Parish Survey (Llanfair)

As you will know already we have been given funds from several organisations to help us commemorate the millennium. One of the conditions for some of this funding is that we do a Parish Survey. This is needed so that future plans can be made by Local Government and other agencies. Every household in Llanfair will receive a questionnaire with this newsletter. Will you please fill it in to the best of your ability and return it in the stamped addressed envelope as soon as you can. Please have them in by the 1st March at the latest. If you need help or extra copies ring or get in touch with Mary Morgan or Anne Singleton. The results of this survey will really help future plans for us all so please do your best.

Church Services

14th March Mother's Day family service 11.00am.

2nd April Good Friday. 2.00pm The Last Hour.

Easter Sunday Communion 11.00am.

Forward planning:

31st May Bank Holiday coffee morning. Venue to be announced.

WI

Carol singing raised over £200 for the first time. The WI Christmas entertainment was enjoyed by all those who attended. The mince pies and punch were delicious.

5th February talk on Llanberris Mountain Rescue Team – Major Maslem-Jones.

5th March 40 years in Education – Mr Myhill.

2nd April A Saudi Experience – Miss Ann Rogers

7th May Gardening – Mrs Polly Smith.

On 19th February there will be a "taster evening" in Line Dancing in the Everest Hall 7.30pm to 9.30pm. Come along and give it a try!

Forward planning. County Show Community Centre Knighton at 2.30pm on 8 May.

Youth Club

Sunday 31 January at 2.30pm. A Treasure Hunt will be held, starting from the Everest Hall. Entry fee £3 per car. The afternoon will end at the Lloyney Inn. Please support us!

Chernobyl Children.

It is the time of year when the organisers have to start planning for the Chernobyl children's visit in July and August. They stay for one month. Our main problem, apart from raising the necessary funds, is finding suitable host parents to care for the youngsters. If anyone feels they could take on this very rewarding commitment we would be happy to hear from you. If anyone could be a standby parent in an emergency or support us in any other way we would also like to hear from you. There will be a get together in the Spring for anyone who is interested. For further details please ring Dorothy Bebbington.

Book Group

Joan, Mary, Jocelyn and Anne have now collected most of your contributions to our Community book. If you haven't "given it in" yet please do it now! It will be less for us to panic about. The material we have had up to now has been varied and interesting. Thank you all.

Whist Drive

There will be a Poultry Whist Drive in the Everest Hall on 16 February at 8.00pm all welcome.

Bridge

The Bridge group continues to meet at the usual venues.

Millennium Clock

The larger clock face is now in place on the Hall. We need to decide whether to have the smaller one, or the one which is in place now and if this is the right position. If you have a view please tell any member of the Millennium Committee or ring John Gwilt.

Parochial Church Council

The PCC often wishes to give funds to charity. Fred and Mig Beavan will hold a coffee evening to raise funds for these charities. 25 February 7.00pm to 9.00pm at The Graig. Table Tennis competition and a Bring and Buy stall and Raffle. Please support this if you can!

Lloyney

The 'Brighten Up Lloyney' group meets at the Lloyney Inn on the first Tuesday of every month at about 8.00pm. Everyone is welcome. The group are holding a Social event at the Lloyney Inn either late in February or early in March. Look out for posters! This will be an exciting evening, when racing films will be shown by Knighton Rotary Club.

Red Lion

Sunday lunch continues on the first Sunday of each month.

Quiz

Saturday 27 February Everest Hall at 7.30pm. Before the lambing! John Peregrine has again agreed to be the questionmaster. Bring your friends and "refreshments"!

Music

If anyone can play a musical instrument and is interested in "making music" will they get in touch with Mig Beavan. All ages and all standards are welcome. Let's see what we can do!

The next edition will be in May. – Anne.

Alice Beavan, Michelle Martin and friends 'help' clear the churchyard

Llanfair Waterdine
THE NEWS
Issue No. 7 May 1999

Lord Hunt

Many people attended the Thanksgiving Service for John's life on February 13th. The order of service was recorded and is on sale at £4.99p. If you would like a tape please get in touch with Ruth Davies as soon as possible. The collection at the Service was in aid of the Youth Club and amounted to almosi £250. John's attractive banner which his family gave to our parish will soon be hanging in church.

Update

Lloyney Social Evening. Owing to the numbers wishing to attend the Lloyney Community Group Social and Race Evening in March, it was held at the Everest Hall. Over £500 was raised for the benefit of the children from Chernobyl and will go towards sponsoring two of the children visiting in the summer.

Whist Drive. The February whist drive made £35 for village hall funds and proved to be an entertaining evening for all those who took part.

Parochial Church Council. The PCC coffee evening held at the Graig was a huge success both socially and financially. It raised £212 for the PCC charity fund. The table tennis champion was John Williams. Fred and Jim Rhodes put up a good show in the veterans class! Thanks are due to Fred and Mig.

Quiz. This was again enjoyed by those who took part and made a profit of £100 for hall funds. This was the best turnout yet with 14 teams taking part. The Autumn quiz with the same format will be in early October.

Parish Survey (Llanfair)

All of you will have received the Survey with the last "News." Many of you were most efficient and returned it promptly. A few still haven't got around to it. If you're one of the latter, please send it in as the results may help shape our parish in the future.

WI

June 4th. Flower arranging Mrs Jean Price. July 2nd. Cookery demonstration – J Pugh. July 19th – 22nd. Royal Welsh Show. On July 16th the WI are organising another line dancing evening in the Everest Hall after the success of their taster evening in February. This time the proceeds will be given towards the visit ol the Chernobyl children.

Youth Club

The Treasure Hunt held in January was a great success although the weather was rather cold and bleak.

The Club has a good turnout every Wednesday at 7.00pm. Members have been to a football match at Shrewsbury and to the Theatre and have many projects planned for the summer. The Club has been awarded £4570 from the Lotteries Small Grants Fund. This money will be used to buy display screens, storage facilities, books and sports equipment much of which will benefit both the Youth Club and users of the Village Hall.

June 19th Coffee Morning in aid of the Youth Club at Llandinshop from 10.00am to 12.30pm. Come along and support our own children and the NSPCC. Admission 50p. There will be games, produce and plant stalls and a raffle, something for everybody! Tickets or information from Caroline Adams, Andrew Beavan, or any youth club committee member.

Chernobyl Children

Lloyney Community Group are organising family walks with social occasions around Lloyney and Llanfair. Everyone is welcome. Please look out for notices.

The Lanterns Cafe in Knighton has a display of paintings by local children and hopes to collect money for the Chernobyl children's visit.

Party. July 23rd. The Chernobyl children will again visit Lloyney, the event will be similar to last year and will take place by the river if the weather is fine. Would people with children and picnics pleace turn up from about 11.00 am onwards. Last year this occasion was enjoyed by the children from Chernobyl their host families and a large group of local people. It is hoped that the same format can be followed with an even bigger welcome and lots of fun and games and food for everyone. Please ring Wendy or Dorothy Bebbington if you wish to help in any way.

Church

May 31st. 10.30am. Bank Holiday **Coffee Morning** at The Coach House with kind permission from Jimmy and Joan. Proceeds to Church funds.

June 10th. **Coffee Evening** at Herb Cottage 7.00pm. tickets £2 proceeds to Church Restoration fund.

Matins. The second Sunday of each month at 9.30am.

Songs of Praise June 27th at 6.30pm in Church. Please let Eileen, Ruth or Andrew know if you have a favourite hymn you would like sung on this occasion.

Saturday July 17th. **Sponsored Walk** and picnic in aid of Church Restoration funds. Meet at Everest Hall 10.30am. Details and sponsor forms available nearer the time.

Churchyard Wall. Work is due to start on the Churchyard wall at the beginning of June.

Wakes. Advance notice Sat August 14th.

Book Group

Material has continued to come in from Llanfair and even from some people who left the area many years ago. We would welcome more material from Lloyney. If you have a contribution please let Jocelyn, Mary, Joan or Anne have it as soon as possible as we are beginning to work to quite serious deadlines.

Millennium Group

Plans are going ahead for the Millennium celebrations. The flagpole has been purchased and the clock for the outside wall of the Everest Hall will be ordered soon. The children of Llanfair are being asked to design a parish flag and will meet in the Everest Hall at 10.00am on Saturday May

29th and Saturday June 12th to paint their designs. The winning design will be made up and will fly from the flagpole on special occasions.

The Parish New Year's Eve Party was discussed and it was suggested that entertainments be available for all the family. Parents will want to attend with their children so that they can be part of the festivities on such an historic occasion.

Parish Council

The Annual Parish Meeting was held on April 20th but was poorly attended. It was agreed that the Green Triangle (Field Garden) be prepared for planting in the Autumn. Andrew Beavan and Llewellyn Morgan agreed to clear the site as some fly tipping has recently taken place. Eleven people have so far paid for their family trees. It is hoped that a final collection will be made in the Autumn.

After between 50 and 60 years as a Parish, District and County Councillor Fred Beavan has decided to retire from the Council. Jim Williams chairman of the Parish Council and Michael Reynolds District Councillor expressed their thanks and gratitude for the effort Fred has put in on our behalf over the years and for the help he has given them personally. Fred must be aware that when there are local problems or complicated queries people will still simply "Ask Fred!". Robert Davies will become the new parish councillor and everyone will hope he will find it an interesting experience and will be a councillor for many years.

Quiz and Bingo

Wednesday June 2nd. 7.30pm. Everest Hall. A Bingo and Picture Quiz evening will be held for families and anyone else who wants to take part in a light hearted evening. Proceeds will be towards the Youth Club and Everest Hall funds. There will be many prizes and a raffle.

Stow Church Funds

Saturday May 22nd. Everest Hall a Quiz at 7.30pm. John Peregrine will be questionmaster, when funds will be raised for our neighbouring parish. All are welcome. Refreshments available entry £5 per team.

Left at The Graig: a TORCH.

The next edition will be in August. – Anne

Llanfair Waterdine THE NEWS Issue No. 8 August 1999

Update

Several fund-raising events have been held since the last "News". On May 31st Jim and Joan Rhodes' Coffee morning and Bring and Buy at The Coach House, in aid of Church funds raised £320. A fortnight later Brenda Ross held a Coffee Evening at Herb Cottage which raised over £100 also for Church funds. On July 16th Line Dancing was held in Everest Hall which raised £43 towards expenses for the visit of the children from Chernobyl. The Christian Aid collection in Llanfair raised £179.30.

On July 17th a group met at the Everest Hall for a sponsored walk along the Dyke. The weather was perfect and a picnic was held en route. The walkers are still collecting from their sponsors but the money will be given to the Church restoration funds. The churchyard wall has come along wonderfully. Further fund raising efforts will however be needed.

Wakes

The Wakes will take place on Saturday August 14th. All the usual attractions will be in place, with a chance for the children to win prizes for their fancy dress and in various sports and games. The football competition will again be a major attraction and teas will be available in the Hall. Produce and bric-a-brac will be welcome. There will be a Barbecue in the evening and of course the usual dogshow and pony rides.

Mig Beaven has produced her usual quiz in aid of Wakes funds. This year the topic is the weather. Sheets are available from many sources including Mig herself, The Red Lion and members of the PCC, 50p each.

WI

Look out for WI stand at Knighton Show where the exhibition will be entitled The Heart of Wales.

September 3rd a talk and video about the Samaritans.

October 1st Shirley Moorhouse, Beadcraft.

November 5th Carwen Maggs, Life on the Ocean Waves.

Youth Club

A Bingo evening and Quiz held on June 2nd was enjoyed by those who attended and raised about £70 for Youth Club Funds. On June 19th a coffee morning with stalls and games – many of them manned by Youth Club members – was held at Llandinshop. Just over £100 was raised to be shared between the Youth Club and the NSPCC.

Chernobyl Children

The children came to Lloyney on July 23rd. The event began at about 3.00pm this year and went on well into the evening. Many local people turned up either to entertain the children, to bring provisions or to join in the events and made it a community effort. Everyone agreed that it was a thoroughly enjoyable and worthwhile event. The weather was perfect and everyone had a happy and memorable afternoon, including the visitors from Belarus.

Church

Songs of Praise

Was held in church on June 27th and was much enjoyed by all those who attended.

August 29th a joint service for all the parishes will be held at Llanfair at 11.00am.

Friday October 22nd Harvest Service at 7.00pm followed by supper in the Everest Hall.

Forward planning. Whist Drive November 29th Everest Hall. The time to be announced.

Grasscutting. Once again many people responded magnificently to the request for help in the churchyard. Two evenings of hard work have transformed the overgrown mass into something resembling our churchyard again. Our grateful thanks to everyone for their help.

The Churchwardens.

Book Group

A printer has been selected and we have begun to send in material.

Millennium Group

The new flagpole and flags have been organised by committee member John Williams and will hopefully fly for the Wakes. The clock has arrived and the committee and John Gwilt also hope to have it in place for the Wakes. The New Years Eve Party was discussed and a working group is being formed to begin planning an Exhibition and Flower Festival to take place on the weekend of the Wakes in 2000.

If anyone has any interesting old tools, clothes, toys or photographs they are prepared to lend will they let Phillipa Boast or Mary Morgan know. Hugh reported that he is busy correlating the results of the questionnaire which was returned by households covering two thirds of the parish population. (An excellent return, thank you.) A copy of the results will be sent to each household with the next newsletter. Patricia Appleton-Fox has been busy researching the history of the parish and we hope to be able to include a summary of her work with the next "News" too.

Parish Council

The first meeting of the Parish Council since the local elections took place in July. No election was held in Llanfair as no-one opposed existing members. Robert Davies was elected unopposed to replace Fred Beavan who retired from the Council. Councillors are now Jim Williams (Chairman), John Williams (vice chairman), Robert Davies, Raymond Matthews, Llewellyn Morgan, Ruby Thomas and Barry Swancott. The clerk is Gordon Singleton. The local District Councillor is Michael Reynolds and our County Councillor Nigel Hartin. A site meeting was held with the Divisional Surveyor where both sides aired their concerns about road safety and road repairs.

Quiz

The next quiz will be at the Everest Hall on Saturday October 2nd at 7.30pm. The usual format. Please come along and bring a few new Quizzers and your own refreshments. Proceeds to the Village Hall.

A New Charity

Some of you will already have heard that Joan Adams has decided to give her corner field opposite The Vedw to the Parish Charities. This is very generous of Joan and will mean that the field will remain as it is, free from building. The legal documents are in the process of being drawn up and The Joan Adams Charity will join the existing charities for the benefit of future generations.

The Parish Charities

The Trustees met early in July. It was agreed that £500 be given to Knighton Community Support Group taxi scheme to enable those who live in the parish and have to rely on public transport to use the subsidised taxi service when they need it. £50 was given towards the Chernobyl children's party and trustees agreed to offer financial support to a gift for the children of the parish for the millennium celebrations. The rent for the Youth Club to the Everest Hall was also paid to the end of the year.

Music and Poetry for a Summer Evening

On August 29th at 7.30pm in The Everest Hall with Judith and Michael Brennan and friends. Tickets £5 from Mary Simmons, proceeds for church restoration funds. Everyone welcome.

Chicago Bridge Evening

A bridge evening with supper will be held on Wednesday October 6th in the Everest Hall at 6.00pm in aid of the Samaritans. Information and tickets can be obtained from Eva MacLauchlan.

Fish Race and Coffee Evening

Maureen and Granville Bates will hold The Fish Race at The Lower Graig on Sunday September 5th at 6.00pm. Proceeds for the Wakes funds. Everyone welcome.

Next Edition November – Anne.

Llanfair Waterdine
THE NEWS
Issue No. 9 November 1999

Millennium Party

Please take a look at the attached invitation, and if you think you and your family will attend please ring as soon as you can, but by the 1st of December at the lastest.

Both Public Houses will be open on New Year's Eve.

Update

The Wakes was again a most successful event. £1,639 was made "on the day" with Mig's quiz raising £229 and Granville and Maureen's Fish Race and coffee evening £248. After marquee hire and other expenses the total raised was an outstanding £1,909.73p.

Other successful fund raising events also took place over the summer. "Music and poetry for a summer evening" raised £172.55p and was a relaxing and enjoyable occasion. Not quite so relaxing but very enjoyable the sponsored walk along Offa's Dyke raised £140. All these events were for church restoration funds.

Church

Wednesday 17th November Chapel Lawn, 6.30pm Service, 7.00pm Supper, 8.00pm An open meeting with Bishop John Saxbee, all in Chapel Lawn Village Hall.

Saturday 27th November Concert in Everest Hall with Newtown Male Voice Choir 7.30pm.

Monday 29th November Everest Hall. Church Poultry Whist Drive 8.00pm.

Saturday 11th December Christmas Fayre, 6.30pm and Auction 7.00pm.

Friday 17th December at 7.30pm Carol service with Knighton Town Silver Band in aid of the Samaritans.

Friday 24th December at 3.00pm Crib Service. 11.30pm Midnight Eucharist.

Saturday 1st January 2000 Millennium Service and bell ringing 12.00 noon.

Sunday 16th January 11.00am Christingle Service.

Harvest Festival. A "full house" enjoyed a very lively address given by the Rev Nick Read Agricultural Chaplain for the Diocese. It was lovely to see so many people tucking into a delicious supper afterwards. A profit of £193.70 was made.

Parish Survey (Llanfair)

The results of the Parish survey for Llanfair will be delivered with "The News". The returns as you will see were excellent and a great many opinions were expressed. It's interesting to see how many points of view there are and hopefully the results will help some parish developments in future.

WI

At the Annual Meeting very satisfactory reports were given of the Institute's activities over the past year. One highlight was winning the cup at Knighton Show with our exhibit "Heart of Wales".

Forthcoming events are:

Friday December 3rd Christmas decorations with Mary Roberts.

Saturday December 18th a Christmas Entertainment in Everest Hall at 7.30pm with festive refreshments.

Monday December 20th Carol Singing around the Parish for Cancer Research.

Thursday January 6th Christmas Dinner and party at the Castle Inn Knucklas.

Friday February 4th a talk on collecting old letters by Sadie Cole.

Youth Club

Extravaganza!

Saturday December 4th at 7.00pm an exciting new venture in the Everest Hall. A chance to socialise with cheese and wine, find those unusual Christmas gifts and at the same time support our local Youth Club. Stalls will include The Body Shop, Christmas decorations, unusual jewellery, pictures, silk craft and hats. There will also be a Christmas raffle. Tickets £3.50 or from any Youth Club parent, or you can pay at the door.

Book Group

We have now sent all the material from individual house holders in Llanfair and Lloyney to the printers. Several people have been asked to write about local clubs, societies and interests. If you are one of these people may we have your contribution as soon as possible please. If you have anything of interest you would like to contribute please give it to Jocelyn, Mary, Joan or Anne by the end of November.

Barry Swancott helps clear the churchyard. Summer 1999

James Thomas dressed for action in churchyard clearing

Millennium Committee

Patricia Appleton-Fox has been doing research into the history of the area up to the 18th century. She has taken a global view and then narrowed it down to Llanfair. A copy of her work is going out to Llanfair residents with this newsletter. It should prove quite interesting to local people and the children expecially will gain a great deal by seeing Llanfair in relation to other places.

Village Exhibition. Included in our village exhibition next August will be a display of old implements and artefacts belonging to local people. We must have lots of interesting things hidden away! If you have anything you would like to lend please contact Phillipa Boast soon so that your offer can be noted.

Parish Charities

It has been decided that each child in Llanfair Parish will be presented with a mug to commenmorate the Millennium. A mug of slightly different design will be available for local people to buy as a momento if they wish.

Parish Council

At the recent meeting on 19th October it was decided that the Parish Precept next year should be reduced by 11% as the District and County are almost bound to raise their charges it was felt that local residents would appreciate this gesture!

Lloyney

The 'Brighten Up Lloyney' Group are organising a raffle to raise funds for their Christmas party for both children and adults. Some of the proceeds will be used for the Chernobyl children. There are many outstanding prizes including a TV. Tickets are available from the Lloyney Inn and from members of the Group. The draw will take place on December 5th at the party which will follow a similar pattern to the successful event held last year.

The 'Brighten Up Lloyney' Group meets at the Lloyney Inn on the first Tuesday of every month at about 8.00pm. New memberes are always very welcome.

Village Hall Committee

Monday December 6th at 7.30pm the Annual General Meeting of the Village Hall Committee will take place when anyone who wishes to attend will be welcome.

The October Quiz made a profit of £68 and was enjoyed by all those who attended. Thanks were expressed to John Peregrine for setting enjoyable questions. The next Village Hall Quiz will be March 2000. The most recent Whist Drive attracted 7 tables and made a profit of £44.30 for Hall funds. Whist enthusiasts please note November 29th!

Bridge

The Chicago bridge evening on October 6th raised £500 for The Samaritans. Thanks to everyone who helped to make it a highly enjoyable and profitable evening.

The next edition will be in February 2000.
I wish you all 'A Happy New Year' – Anne.

Millennium celebrations

(Above) Kate Morgan sings at the Millennium Party

(Above left and left) During… and after

(Below left) Joseph and his mother Anne welcome the New Year

(Below right) John Gwilt, Jim Williams, Andrew Beavan, Joan Hobby, Andrew MacLauchlan, Ruth Davies, Mary Morgan

The Year 2000 in Llanfair Waterdine and Lloyney

To personalize your book put in your own photograph